LORD, DELIVER ME FROM CHURCH FOLKS

BRIAN GANGES

Lord, Deliver Me from Church Folks
Copyright © 2013 Brian Ganges

ISBN-13: 978-0-9850763-9-9

Publisher's Note
Printed and bound in the United States of America. All rights reserved. No part of this book may be reproduced or transmitted in any form or by any means, electronic or mechanical, including photocopying, recording, or by an information storage and retrieval system-except by a reviewer who may quote brief passages in a review to be printed in a magazine, newspaper, or on the Web-without permission in writing from the publisher.

Although the author and publisher have made every effort to ensure the accuracy and completeness of information contained in this book, we assume no responsibility for errors, inaccuracies, omissions, or any inconsistency herein.

Peace In The Storm Publishing, LLC.
P.O. Box 1152
Pocono Summit, PA 18346

Visit our Web site at
www.PeaceInTheStormPublishing.com

...making the word of God of no effect through your tradition, which you have handed down. And many such things you do.
— Mark 7:13

Stand fast therefore in the liberty wherewith Christ hath made us free, and be not entangled again with the yoke of bondage.
—Galatians 5:1

DISCLAIMER

Please be advised that the final few chapters of this book are noted with an asterisk. These chapters may contain information that some might consider to be of a mature nature.

PARENTAL DISCRETION IS ADVISED

From the Author

*L*ord, Deliver Me From Church Folks is the book that your pastor and unlearned Church folks don't want you to read. This book unveils many of the misconceptions, the errors and the cult-like grasp of bondage that are used to entangle the people of faith. For too long, many believers have followed the traditions of men, cultural biases, the desires of the locale, and other external prejudices instead of the Word of God. As a result, these actions have (in many ways) choked out the integrity of the power of the Scriptures in many people's lives. I desire to be a vessel for God to rescue those who have eyes to see and ears to hear what the Holy Spirit is saying to His people.

Enjoy!

And ye shall know the truth, and the truth shall make you free.

—John 8:32

TRIBUTES

A Tribute to God

Lord, it would take one hundred million eternities to cover one thousandth of how good You've been to my family and me. So all I can do is say:

THANK YOU, JESUS, FOR YOUR:

- *Goodness*
- *Mercy*
- *Kindness*
- *Forgiveness*
- *Patience*
- *Peace*
- *Covenant*
- *Understanding*
- *Love*
- *Truth*
- *Guidance*
- *Help*
- *Sound mind*
- *Comfort*
- *Protection*
- *Revelation*
- *Wisdom*

- *Knowledge*
- *Healing*
- *Presence*
- *Righteousness*
- *Victory*
- *Salvation*
- *Redemption*
- *Gifts and talents*
- *Strength*
- *Boldness*
- *Life*
- *Family and friends*
- *And for everything You have done, are doing, and will do!!!!*

A Tribute to My Dad

You have impacted me in ways that I cannot completely articulate. When your life has been touched intangibly and so significantly, how can you express your gratitude sufficiently? I have been blessed in my life with the opportunity to experience many things. One of which is having an Earthly father that was actually active in raising me and teaching me things that the streets or a mother could never properly do. Any fool can have sex with a woman and make a baby, but only a man will "man-up" and be responsible for his actions. Manhood is a mental growth or transformation, a conviction, a reality of whom God has made you rather than a physical maturity. Thank you for the lessons.

Some of the Lessons Learned

There are many valuable lessons that you taught me. Some were huge lessons, and some were simply details that mattered a lot. For example, by attending my scholastic sporting events, award ceremonies, PTA meetings, etc., you taught me about supporting and validating loved ones. You were actively involved in raising me. You taught me how to tie a tie, and how to shine my own shoes. You taught me how to break in a baseball glove. You instilled in me a good work ethic, a sense of accountability and personal responsibility, the importance of a good education, and a marketable skill. You taught me how to shave my face. You taught me to think for myself and to not follow the crowd. You taught me to get involved in and to give back to the community. You taught me to stay away from drugs and alcohol. You taught me to mind my own business, among other things.

Some Memorable Times

As a teenager, I remember you telling me that I wouldn't understand the things that you were telling me until I was in my mid-twenties and I had my own family. You were so right. You imparted so much in me, and it was always right, even though I didn't realize it at the time. But eventually, I came to understand the lessons you taught me. How blessed and fortunate I am/was.

I'll always remember when we went to the celebration of the March on Washington in the early '80s. I had a chance to go to a party with my friends or to go with you to this historic event. I went with you on that terribly hot day, where the refreshment vendors were in limited supply. But you did whatever you could to get me something to drink and eat and keep me as comfortable as possible, even when there wasn't enough for you. You did many more things, but that was something that stood out to me.

I learned from you not to give up on your responsibilities. This is a Biblical teaching, but it's always helpful to see someone that you admire, a touchable person, walking out solid principles for daily living. I followed your example to be actively involved with and responsible for my own child, your granddaughter. I learned from you about being a father because as it was so eloquently put in the immortal words of Fred G. Sanford, "It's much harder to be a father than it is to become one."

"The Tree" was the classic example of a seemingly meaningless conversation under an ordinary tree that forever will be branded on the pages of my heart; and it was such because it was an intimate time that we shared. The subject matter was irrelevant, but what was relevant was that my father was imparting intimacy into me: time alone with my Dad, just talking, eating, and hanging out. I believe moments like these led me later in life into a relationship with Christ. I longed for that intimacy that you provided me on occasions such as that, and I have come to know that there is nowhere else to find it other than in Him.

God uses fathers, like you, because Earthly fathers are a physical representation of Him here on the Earth. Fathers are, and should be, the embodiment of authority, leadership, protection and provision. I always felt and sensed this with you. I knew you were in charge, and I always looked to you for direction. I always felt safe when you were around, and all of my needs were always supplied. I only hope that I can take the torch and run further than you in this life. I am proud to carry your last name and I LOVE YOU VERY MUCH!

A Tribute to My Mom

How can I list all of the things that you've done for me, and how can I tell you how much I love you? I can write a short list because there aren't enough pages in a book to describe how much you mean to me. We've become closer in my adult years; but I always knew that you were special to me. I could tell you these things personally, and I will do that, but I wanted the world to know how important you have been to me for the last four decades.

- You always loved me unconditionally from childhood to adulthood. Thank you!
- You guided the affairs of the house with discretion, and you disciplined and instructed me properly. Thank you!
- You were always the quiet, behind-the-scenes strength and support that God gave me. Thank you!
- You made sure that our needs were met when your own needs may have been lacking. Thank you!
- You worked an extra job to provide a better tomorrow for us. Thank you!
- You did all that you could to provide a safe and clean environment for us. Thank you!
- You sacrificed for your family and you weren't recognized. Thank you!
- You didn't abort me. Thank you!

- You get less pay for the same job that a man does, but you always supported me. Thank you!
- You have a servant's heart. Thank you!
- You are not materialistic. Thank you!
- You're a good example before your family, friends and community. Thank you!
- Despite your busy schedule, you always made time for me. Thank you!
- You conduct yourself like a lady and you dress modestly. Thank you!
- You're an independent and confident woman. Thank you!
- You know your worth. Thank you!
- You don't associate with negative, busybody women. Thank you!
- You lead by example. Thank you!
- You're a pretty cool ol' gal. Thank you!
- The world knocks you down, but you rise up again. Thank you!
- The world said that you couldn't make it, but you proved them wrong. Thank you!
- You are real and not a phony. Thank you!
- We have had great times of openness, honesty and reflection. Thank you!
- I always felt comforted and nurtured by you. Thank you!
- You helped me achieve my dreams when you may not have achieved all of your dreams. Thank you!

- I always know that you are just a phone call away. Thank you!

- For all of the lives you've touched directly and indirectly, Thank you!

- I'll always remember my sophomore year in college and I was sick with the flu. I was nineteen years old, and all I wanted to do was sleep and call you to comfort me. That was better than any medicine. Thank you!

- I'll always remember when you took me to the doctor to get the pain in my arm checked out. When the doctor touched it, I cried in pain. Although you weren't in physical pain, you cried with me because I was in pain. Thank you!

Peace and Love to you, Mom! You will always be my girl! Thank you and I love you more than you know!

"We might as well be frank and face the truth. While we have hundreds of superior men in the pulpits, North and South, East and West, the majority of our religious leaders have preached too much Heaven and too little practical Christian living. In many, the spirit of greed, like the horse-leach, is ever crying, 'Give me, give me, give me.' Does the absorbing task of supplying their personal needs bind leaders to the moral, social and spiritual needs of our people?"

— Nannie Burroughs, corresponding secretary of the Woman's Convention of the National Baptist Convention, U.S.A.

"If there is a decay of conscience, the pulpit is responsible for it. If the public press lacks moral discernment, the pulpit is responsible for it. If the church is degenerate and worldly, the pulpit is responsible for it. If the world loses its interest in Christianity, the pulpit is responsible for it. If Satan rules in our halls of legislation, the pulpit is responsible for it. If our politics become so corrupt that the very foundations of our government are ready to fall away, the pulpit is responsible for it."

— Charles Finney, 19th Century Revivalist

Introduction

Dear Friends,

I would like to personally thank you for taking the time to read "Lord, Deliver Me From Church Folks." I take no credit for the concept of the book; I give all of the credit for the inspiration to God. However, I would like to take a brief moment to tell you a little bit about the book.

For years, I have been reading the New Testament and I have always been amazed at how ignorantly and religiously (as opposed to righteously) the Pharisees and the Sadducees behaved. These supposed "people of God" were ceremonially correct; but they had very little, if any, spiritual connection with God. They knew the words of the Book, but they didn't know the Author of the Book.

Jesus' arrival on the Earth meant that the religious "apple cart" was about to be overturned; and the religious establishment wasn't about to take a back seat to a young kid that was born in an animal's feeding box. Sadly enough, the Pharisees and the Sadducees didn't discern Jesus; they merely saw Him in the flesh. They gave lip service to being God's representatives, and *their actions* confirmed that they had no heart-felt devotion to God.

Unfortunately, that same lip service and outward devotion to God exists in many of today's Church folks. Even worse, many of these Church people, although ignorant, are well-meaning and well-intentioned people. But well-meaning and well-intentioned doesn't always equate to the truth, or being right. Think about some of the Church folks that you know. No one, including me, is perfect, but we should all take a proverbial step back and ask ourselves if we are doing all that we know to do to be more like Christ on a daily basis. Everyone falls short, and we should be honest with ourselves about that. This doesn't mean that we have to advertise our sins to our friends and families, or lay prostrate in sackcloth and ashes to prove how real we are. But, if we recognize our limitations, we can strengthen our own individual walks, as well as others, and in turn, be able to help those who desire help in their walk. Then we can all be the salt and light that Christ commanded us to be.

We have a terrible divide in the twenty-first century Body of Christ. We have wolves in sheep's clothing, and we also have sheep in wolves' clothing. So we have people who look like believers in our midst, and we also have believers who are deceived and look like the enemy. It's a horrible situation for the Church, but we must use discernment and the wisdom of God in order to fix the mess that has been made.

Additionally, believers are divided by: doctrines, Bible versions, literal vs. allegorical interpretations, opinions, myths, misconceptions, and a host of other issues. How can we bring healing to the nations when the Body of Christ is in such shambles? Sadly, there are many people who profess Christ but can't discern truth outside of the Ten Commandments.

So, I decided to write this book, not because I am a "perfect follower of Christ," but because at one point in my life I believed every fallacy, myth, false teaching, and tradition that I address in this book. I also wrote this book because we need to address some issues that many saints are afraid to confront. It's time for Christ's followers to grow up, to deal with our insecurities, to be salt and light, and to press forward in the good fight of faith. The more we argue with one another, and ninny over this Church or that mode of worship music, or which Christian's flaws are worse, etc., we will continually fall victim to the enemy's "divide and conquer" plan.

How can we provide the answers that the world needs if our belief systems are not founded upon the truth? Where is the demarcation line and distinction that separates the world from the Church? Didn't Paul say that the Body of Christ is the "ground and the pillar" of the truth? Aren't we supposed to be salt and light?

"Lord, Deliver Me From Church Folks" helps you to separate the hot from the cold, the spiritual from the carnal, and the righteous from the unrighteous. If you haven't read my first book, "Piecing the Puzzle

Together," I encourage you to do so, because you are about to hook onto the second book in this series of teachings.

No matter where you are in your faith, you will be challenged. The Word will force you to look at it and yourself; and then you will be left to make a decision to read the information and study it to verify if it is truth, or you can simply disregard what you have read. Either way, the beauty of God's Word is that He gives us the answer to the test, but He also gives each individual the option to choose the way in which he/she wants to travel.

Thank you for investing your time and energy into this book. I don't take it, or you, for granted, and I'm honored that you have decided to join me.

So sit back and enjoy the message as I speak from my heart to yours.

Yours in Christ,

Preface

Dear Friends,

I consider "Lord, Deliver Me From Church Folks" to be a safe place. It is a safe place in which and around which practical, and sometimes tough and/or controversial topics can be discussed.

For too long, the "truth bearers" have been void of any substantive input regarding so many of today's pressing issues. In many of today's Churches, it is common for topics like homosexuality, suicide, tattoos and piercings, tithing, politics and religion, interracial dating/marriage, masturbation, gambling, obeying your pastor, speaking in tongues, pornography, racism among believers, and a host of other issues to be swept under the proverbial rug. I uncover all of these topics and more in this book, and I do so because I use to belong to Churches that taught a lot of erroneous doctrines. I am willing to articulate what so many people have thought, but might have been ashamed to mention publicly.

Unfortunately, many ministries are regurgitating the flawed teachings that they learned from the preacher who taught them; and they passed these teachings along to the next generation like a family heirloom. That is the epitome of unsound teaching. What "Lord, Deliver Me From Church Folks" does is it allows the reader to get in line with the Biblical way of thinking. For example, if you have a button-down shirt, you have to place the first button from the top down into the first hole from the top down. Then you have to put the second button from the top down into the second hole from the top down. When this is done, the other buttons and holes will be in line and you can button your shirt correctly.

I've decided to write this book with some creativity. As Paul wrote the epistles as letters to various believers throughout Europe and Asia Minor, I, too, am writing letters to God's people on a myriad of topics.

I don't provide answers to everything, but I sure get the conversation started. I do provide some solutions, but like I said, "Lord, Deliver Me From Church Folks" is a safe place for you to have discussions with others, or you can just meditate about some of these topics in your alone time with God. Every letter won't be relevant to you, but if one of these letters helps to set you free, then "Lord, Deliver Me From Church Folks" did its job.

I appreciate you, and get ready to read the book that your pastor doesn't want you to read.

Yours in Christ,

Contents

Section One: The Letters of Conduct

An Open Letter to Believers in Christ Everywhere 37
Used for the Sake of the Call 43
Holiness: Separation from Sin, not from Sinners 46
When the Messenger is Attacked 53
Christians Don't Sin 56
Christians and Foul Language 57
Religious vs. Righteous 59
A Relationship with the Word 61
Prophe-lie 64
Proverbs 31 Woman 66
Obey Them Who Have the Rule Over You 68
Forgive and Forget 71
God's Grandchildren 73
Say Your Grace/Bless Your Food 75
Rejoicing at the Calamities of Others 76
Balance vs. Priorities 78
The Desires of Your Heart 80
Agape Love 84
How We Should Treat One Another 87
Control vs. Empowerment 92

Relationship vs. Fellowship 95

SECTION TWO: THE LETTERS OF DOCTRINE

The Armor Bearer 99
Matthew 18, Part 1 (Binding and Loosing) 103
Matthew 18, Part 2 (Christ in Our Midst) 107
Authority in the Name of Jesus Christ 109
The Clergy vs. the Lay People 116
Why We Must Study: The Attitude of the Bereans 119
The Who, What, Where, Why, and How of Seed Sowing 124
Heaven is Closed 127
The Lord's Supper is a Church Snack 129
Read/Follow the Bible 131
Tithing 135
Operating in Spiritual Gifts and Spiritual Maturity 141
Baptizing/Christening Babies 143
Why Good Things Happen to Bad People, Why Bad Things
    Happen to Good People 144
The Great Commission to All 147
It's Testing Time 149
Talents/Gifts/Abilities 153
Fear God 155
Love is an Action Word that Protects the Truth 157
We are All God's Children: The Ecumenical Lie 161

The "When the Praises Go Up, the Blessings Come
 Down" and the "Praise Confuses the Enemy" Lies 164
Sinners Saved by Grace 167
Who Is the Anti-Christ? 168
Once Saved, Always Saved 170
Israel: God's Chosen People 173
Rapture Ready 183
Faith Is Action, Faith In Action 185
Women are the Weaker Vessel 193
Spiritual Discernment 195
Turn the Other Cheek 200
Acts 2:38 203
Receiving Eternal Life 205
You Must be Born Again (The First Baptism) 207
Water Baptism (The Second Baptism) 210
Being Filled with the Spirit (The Third Baptism) 212
New Convert Zeal vs. Walking by Faith 218
How to Pray Scripturally 220
Fine Tune Your Faith by Pursuing God's Word 225
We have the Complete Victory 228
How the Mind Works 231
Listen to and Follow Your Heart 235

SECTION THREE: THE LETTERS OF SOCIAL ISSUES

Temptation and Sin 243
Right with God, Wrong on the Issues of the Day 249
Tattoos and Piercings 252
Racism in America and in Church Folks 254
Where are the Men(tors)? 260
Suicide 268
Legislating Morality 272
The Causes of Poverty 274
Christian Left (Liberal) vs. Christian Right (Conservative) 279
What Does Liberty Look Like? 290
The Emperor has No Clothes 292
White Racists and Black Pacifists in the Church 295
Thoughts to Consider 300
The Lesbian, Gay, Bi-Sexual, and Transgender
    Agenda: The Religious/Political Football 303
Gambling 308
Why are Churches so Segregated? 310
Where is Jehovah Jireh (God our Provider)? 313
Drinking and Smoking for Christians 319
Thou Shalt Not Kill 322
Do We Support the Gift of Life? 324
Race, Hype, and Misguided Allegiance vs. Truth 326
Protection 332
Excellence and Achievement have Nothing to Do with Color ... 337
Is Going to the Movies Sinful? 339

Secular Music 341
Divorce and Re-Marriage to Another 345
Sex, Sex and More Sex 348
Sexless Marriage 352
The Pornography/Masturbation Question 354
Interracial Dating/Marriage 357
Using Contraception is a Sin 360
Should Christians Date? 362
Conclusion 368

SECTION ONE: THE LETTERS OF CONDUCT

AN OPEN LETTER TO BELIEVERS IN CHRIST EVERYWHERE

Greetings Family!

Grace be to each and every one of you and peace from God the Father, and from our Lord Jesus Christ. For those of you who don't know me, my name is Brian Ganges. I'm just a regular guy who loves the Lord, liberty, my family and friends, and my fellow man.

The reason for this letter is very simple. I wish to express some concerns that I have regarding the state of the modern-day assembly of God (believers in Christ). Obviously, I am not the leader of the faith. I'm not a pastor of a church building, but I have been a member of the Body of Christ for over twenty years. In that time, I have seen the good, the bad, and the ugly in the family of God; and I believe what I have to say can help us to be better individually and corporately.

First, let me just say that I love you guys with the love of God, and we are all one in Christ Jesus. We are a spiritual family; and a family should be able to address serious matters when situations arise. My motives are pure, and I pray that everyone has the heart to receive the spirit and the intent of what I have to say, rather than making this a personal matter.

I know that some leaders become intimidated or dismissive if they are approached, questioned, or challenged—even in a non-threatening manner—by someone who isn't "on their level." I am a brother in the Lord, so I am on every believer in Christ's "level." I come in humility, and not as a disciplinarian, or a hater. This isn't about titles, but rather about family; and I deserve the same respect that I am offering. So please allow me to be open and honest with you, sibling-to-sibling.

This message isn't for everyone, but I still need to say it for those who need to hear it.

Second, I am very concerned about the soundness and Biblical accuracy of many doctrines that are being taught in many ministries. As a result of these teachings, I have found the spiritual discernment and the sound understanding of the Scriptures among many Christians to be very low. I see many ministries that are focused more on the ministry personality, rather than the anointed message of holiness, faith, love, forgiveness, hope, truth, evangelism, redemption, and the personhood of Jesus Christ. Many seeker-friendly ministries stress the importance of comfort, convenience, the (financial) bottom line, the latest "spiritual" cliché, product sales, tolerance, church attendance, and the cutting edge of Christian marketing. The Scriptures teach us that the Holy Spirit points us to Jesus, but a lot of these religious tactics do quite the opposite.

Notice that I am not calling anyone out by name, nor am I accusing anyone of purposefully and/or intentionally deceiving people. I'm not calling anyone a false prophet, anti-Christ, an agent of satan, and I am not denying anyone's salvation in Christ. I try to look for the best in people; and even in this hard message, I'm trying to find some way to give ministries the benefit of the doubt. It's hard to do with all of the unscriptural practices and teachings that are permeating the Church as a whole. But I don't want to pretend that everything is fine in the Church, because it's not. The Church has a lot of problems that we need to fix immediately. The world has enough (actual) false prophets and hireling teachers deceiving people. We don't need deception, error, or a lack of insight to be funneled through the people of God, too. So please, let's get focused and ministry-minded for the sake of lost souls who need to be set free, and for the believers who need to be perfected in the Gospel message.

Who is to blame for this failure? The Church and (more specifically) the Church leadership are to blame, of course. Didn't James 3:1 state that the teachers of the Word of God would have the greater condemnation? Yes, because the leaders have been entrusted with a greater accountability/responsibility to perfect the saints and to edify them. To whom much is given, much is required. Correct? Didn't Christ commission His body of believers to be salt and light? Isn't Christ the (spiritual) Head and His believers are the (spiritual) Body of Christ? Of course, and the reason why the world is deteriorating morally is because the Church (led by the preachers) has stopped being salt and light.

Many Christians have stopped living/teaching sound Biblical principles, and have become commercialized conduits full of catchy religious phrases, long and powerless prayers, and gimmicks to attract more people (and their money) into their building. I'm not against prosperity, but ministry must be the main motive and priority for why ministries do what they do. *What is your ministry motive? What are your ministerial priorities?*

Third, I liken the state of the modern-day Church to the time when Jesus was rejected in the Nazarene synagogue.

Now He did not do many mighty works there because of their unbelief.

— Matthew 13:58

That is where the 21st century Church is right now. Many ministries aren't preaching the Word. The Word contains faith, and if no Word (faith) is being preached, then the people will have little to no faith. Faith comes by hearing the Word of God; and without faith it is impossible to please Him. So the result of not preaching the Word is a state of unbelief in the Church, the inability to please God, and a lack of the demonstration and the power of God.

We need the anointed Gospel (the good news) and the manifestation of the Spirit of God. We need the anointing that destroys the yoke of bondage in people's lives. Where is that power? I see a lot of yokes, but I don't see those yokes being destroyed by the anointing; rather, I see a lot of yokes destroying the people of God and our society. I see mega-ministries on TV, and I see Facebook posts and pages with thousands of "likes" with some of the most unscriptural status updates, schedules for the latest conferences, breakthrough seminars, and prayer meetings. But where are the results and the works of the salt and the light in action?

Fourth, I believe the time to make a quality decision is upon us. The people of God have to decide whether or not they will side with the Lord and His Word. It's easy to say, "I'm on the Lord's side." But unfortunately, some Christians and ministries have been known to support, to defend, to encourage, and to enable doctrines and issues that are contrary to the Word of God. This is inexcusable and an affront to Heaven. Many in the Church also sit quietly on the sidelines and say nothing as the principles of truth sometimes get trampled in our society.

Christians CANNOT promote the wrong things; nor can they **NOT** stand up **AGAINST** the wrong things, because saying **NOTHING** makes one an accomplice in the wrongdoing that is being committed. I understand that having a 501(c) (3) tax exemption status limits an organization's legal ability to speak out on certain issues. But it's time to sound the alarm and be on the right side of issues and doctrine. God forbid if a ministry chose a tax exemption status over the ability to preach the uncompromised Word of God.

Is the Church leadership 100% responsible for this failure in the Church? Is the coach who gets fired because the team is playing poorly 100% responsible? No, but if an organization is going to be corrected and re-focused, it must be done through the leadership. God is the ultimate leader, but since He has entrusted His preachers to guide/oversee the fellowship of the saints, the pressure falls on the leadership.

Fifth, we need to build complete people: spirit, soul, and body. Society is nothing more than a bunch of communities; communities are nothing more than a bunch of families; and families are nothing more than a bunch of individuals. When we build individuals, we build families. When we build families, we build communities. When we build communities, we build a society. Look at our society: the crime rate, divorce rate, illegitimacy rate, illiteracy rate, murder rate, government corruption rate, the abortion rate, and the complete moral breakdown of society. We have Churches on every street corner in some neighborhoods. My question is: are the ministries of today building people? Or are they building churches, ministries, or an Earthly name and legacy?

Preachers are supposed to reproduce the Christ in them in the people. But many times, the people take on the characteristics of their Earthly leaders. Are preachers feeding people the unadulterated Word of God, or are people getting fed the religion and the personality of the preacher? A plant will only grow according to the quality of the water, air, sunlight and nutrients it is given. The same is true for the people of God. If people are fed a superficial (spiritual meal) message, then the congregation will grow according to the quality of that type of meal. A milk Gospel will produce baby Christians. A religious Gospel will produce weak, religious Christians. A sound Gospel will produce sound Christians. *Can you understand that*? Certainly, individuals have a responsibility for their own development, growth and maturation, but those who are called to perfect the saints are called with a holy calling to care for God's people. *What are ministries feeding the people of God?*

I don't want to belabor this matter and seem as though I am sending condemnation to my brothers and sisters. I come only as a messenger with optimistic expectations for the advancement of God's Kingdom. Whether or not you, me, or anyone else cooperates with God is irrelevant. God's plan will go forth. It would be in everyone's best interests to obey God and to follow His Will. I know many Christians who have questions and have wondered about some of the same things that I addressed. But many of them may have been too afraid to say anything to a preacher. Fortunately, I am willing to speak the hard truth, and I am not here to protect my reputation; nor am I here to score brownie points with preachers in hopes of one day speaking at their Churches. I just want people to get helped and blessed by the Word of God, because this is about the eternal souls of humanity.

Again, I bid peace and love to everyone. There are no hard feelings on my part, and my conscience is clear. The message has been delivered. I didn't judge, sentence, harass, or attempt to strip anyone of their salvation. I hope that everyone reads this message objectively and introspectively, and takes these thoughts to God in prayer. If this message resonates with you, then please make the necessary adjustments. If not, thank God and encourage everyone to email, fax, copy, post, or share this message with every Christian, whether they are in leadership or not. We have work to do! I'm praying for the leadership and the entire Church family.

Let's continue to press towards the mark of the high calling of God in Christ Jesus, because we can and must do better.

Yours in Christ,

USED FOR THE SAKE OF THE CALL

Dear Friends,

Many of us want to be used by God for His purpose because we know that His purposes are good.

> *For I know the thoughts that I think toward you, saith the Lord, thoughts of peace, and not of evil, to give you an expected end.*
> —Jeremiah 29:11-14

But do we really want to be used? Many times we fail to realize that being used isn't always a pretty thing. Sometimes we will be ridiculed for our beliefs, and sometimes we will be harassed, attacked, and even harmed. Sometimes people will misinterpret our intentions. But do you really want to get used in this life for the purpose that God intended?

Sometimes people can't get past their emotions, and they allow themselves to be governed by the dictates of their mind. But we have to remember that we have to be focused spirit, soul, and body. The most important aspect of this is the mind, because if your mind is focused on the task at hand, it won't matter what goes on around you, positive or negative. People may not always agree with you, and they might not understand you or they may not like the way you do things; but if you know the plan, the vision, and the direction in which you're going, then continue on the path to success.

Jackie Robinson

It is very well-documented that before Major League Baseball was integrated, there were many good baseball players in the Negro leagues. We are all familiar with Jackie Robinson, his great play, his many accomplishments, and his wonderful smile. But some people may not know that Jackie Robinson was *chosen* to break the color barrier in major leagues back in the '40s. Yes, he was chosen. Jackie Robinson wasn't the only player that was capable of playing in the major leagues. But he was *chosen* to play because he had the type of temperament and attitude that could withstand the ridicule, the insults, and the racism of that day.

There was one player in particular, whom some baseball historians say was better than Jackie Robinson. His name was Josh Gibson. I wasn't alive to see Josh Gibson play, but stories suggest that he was a much better player than Jackie Robinson. That doesn't take away from Jackie Robinson's talent and career, but those are the claims that were made. According to many sources, Josh Gibson's attitude, short fuse, and either his unwillingness or inability to deal with the ignorance of racism during those times, caused him to lose out on a great opportunity. Josh was a vessel, but he wasn't ready to be used for the task, at hand.

Uncle Tom/Josiah Henson

I'm sure everyone has heard of Uncle Tom. Uncle Tom was a fictional character in Harriet Beecher Stowe's nineteenth-century classic, "Uncle Tom's Cabin." The main character, Uncle Tom, was based upon the life of a slave, named Josiah Henson. Henson was a Christian man, and he was a vessel whom God used to free and to educate many slaves. Since Henson and Tom were both slaves, they had limited freedoms, but they found favor in the eyes of God and their masters. Both men were entrusted to handle money, to manage the slaves, and to take care of other matters for their masters. They were elevated to places of trust and responsibility because of the favor of God, and their attitudes.

I know that many folks in the black community ridicule Uncle Tom; and today, the term "Uncle Tom" is used as a disrespectful term towards another black person; it's synonymous with being a sellout. But the next time someone uses the term, "Uncle Tom" in a negative manner, ask them if they have ever read the book or if they have ever researched the "Real Uncle Tom," Josiah Henson. Most people have never heard of the man who was the inspiration for the character. When you get a moment, read the book or research the life of Josiah Henson. But the neighborhood lingo will teach you that an "Uncle Tom" is a sellout, or a black person who kisses up to the white man. In slavery times, you had to do what you had to do. You had to play within the rules of the game of the time. If Henson or Uncle Tom would have been too vocal, encouraged an uprising, or would've stood up in a 1960's type civil rights manner, they would've been killed immediately; and they would have never been able to fulfill their missions. But, they both had another agenda, and they were able to set many slaves free. Neither Uncle Tom, nor Josiah Henson was perfect, but they used their positions with an end in mind for good.

Likewise, you have to make yourself available for God's plan. So allow God to use you for His glory, wherever you are and in whatever you do.

Yours in Christ,

Holiness: Separation from Sin, not from Sinners

Dear Friends,

Often times, Christians don't have enough balance. Many Christians are too spiritual, and many are too worldly. These extremes cause huge problems in our individual walks with God, because unbeknownst to many of us, they cause people who might be watching and/or emulating our lives to stumble.

We must understand our role in this world as representatives of a Holy God. Some Christians are afraid of that "Holy" designation because with it comes a lot of responsibility and discipline. The word "holiness" comes from the Greek word "hosiótēs," which means to look to the application of what God defines as sanctioned. Simply put, holiness is a separation from worldliness, and a separation to God for His use.

Additionally, the believers in the Lord Jesus Christ are whom the Bible refers to as the "Church." The Church is not the building where people go to worship God and hear the Word preached. The word, "Church" in the New Testament is translated from the Greek word "ekklesia." It comes from two words: "ek" meaning "out" and "kaleo" meaning to "call." Hence, the Church is more accurately defined as the "called out" because we have been called out from the kingdom of darkness and we have been translated into the Kingdom of His Son (Jesus).

> *Giving thanks unto the Father, which hath made us meet to be partakers of the inheritance of the saints in light: who hath delivered us from the power of darkness, and hath translated us into the kingdom of his dear Son.*
>
> — Colossians 1:12-13

In other words, we have been made accountable to a new set of laws of another spiritual Kingdom: a new way of doing things. We have been called to separate ourselves from a worldly lifestyle, not from worldly associations. Remember, we still live in a secular world, and everyone on planet Earth isn't a born-again believer in Christ.

Christ taught us:

Let your light so shine before men, that they may see your good works, and glorify your Father, which is Heaven.
— Matthew 5:16

If the "called out" ones only shine during the Church services and in segregated settings away from secular people, how are we letting Christ shine through us?

In the times of Jesus, the word "ekklesia" was a political term defined as an assembly of the people convened at the public place of council for the purpose of deliberating (thoughtful evaluation of all relevant factors). So God meant for His people to be involved in the relevant issues of the day. But if the people of God are not committed to the concepts of holiness and what it means to be His people, then we are not fulfilling our mission to be salt (a preserving agent for truth).

Wrong Associations and Relationships

Do not be unequally yoked with unbelievers. For what partnership has righteousness with lawlessness? Or what fellowship has light with darkness? What accord has Christ with Belial? Or what portion does a believer share with an unbeliever? What agreement has the temple of the living God with idols? For we are the temple of the living God; as God said, I will make dwelling among them and walk among them, and I will be their God, and they shall be my people. Therefore, go

out from their midst, and be separate from them, says the Lord, and touch no unclean thing; then I will welcome you, and I will be a father to you, and you shall be sons and daughters to me, says the Lord Almighty.
—2 Corinthians 6:14-18

What did Paul tell the Corinthians, in context, in the above-mentioned verse? What insight can we gain from those Scriptures? Paul taught about attempts to mix righteousness and unrighteousness: compromise that affects the integrity of the Word. So he gave the Corinthians an example of principle and a practical application. The principle: don't mix righteousness and unrighteousness. The application: idolatry.

Many times, Christians use this Scripture to advocate not having friendships or associations with people who aren't Christians. That is not a clearly contextual interpretation of what Paul was illustrating.

If a believer in Corinth had an idolatrous (unbelieving) friend or relative, this Scripture wouldn't forbid the relationship; it would forbid the Christian from participating with the unbeliever in idolatry. If the unbeliever asked, "Would you help me sacrifice an animal and eat the meat with me before my gods?" The Scripturally correct answer would be "No." The key to understanding this is "fellowship" or "participation" with the unbeliever being in the wrong. Association, in and of itself, with unbelievers, is not forbidden. Only partaking in sinful acts is forbidden.

How did Jesus handle this issue with association?

And it came to pass, as Jesus sat at meat in the house, behold, many publicans and sinners came and sat down with Him and His disciples. And when the Pharisees saw it, they said unto His disciples, Why eateth your Master with publicans and sinners? But when Jesus heard that, He said unto them, they that are whole need not a physician, but they that are sick. But go ye and learn what that meaneth, I will have mercy, and not

sacrifice: for I am not come to call the righteous, but sinners to repentance.
— Matthew 9:10-13

He sat, ate and associated with unbelievers, but He didn't sin with them. He associated with them in order to let His light shine. But He was never unequally yoked in a covenant with them or their sin, and there was no attempt to combine righteousness and unrighteousness.

There is another Biblical example illustrating that not all association or relationship with unbelievers is automatically sinful. Paul taught the Corinthians:

But to the rest speak I, not the Lord: If any brother hath a wife that believeth not, and she be pleased to dwell with him, let him not put her away. And the woman, who hath a husband, that believeth not, and if he were pleased to dwell with her, let her not leave him.
— 1 Corinthians 7:12, 13

Paul didn't instruct believers (regarding marriages between a believer and an unbeliever) to separate from the sinner. No, he instructed the believer to stay in the relationship.

For the unbelieving husband is sanctified by the wife, and the unbelieving wife is sanctified by the husband: else were your children unclean; but now are they holy. But if the unbelieving depart, let him depart. A brother or a sister is not under bondage in such cases: but God hath called us to peace.
—1 Corinthians 7:14-15

But let's be clear, God does not advocate sinners and saints marrying one another. But if two sinners get married, and later one of them becomes a believer, salvation in Jesus Christ is not a license to divorce an unbelieving spouse. It might be difficult for a believer to live a Christian life with an unsaved partner. But the Scripture is clear that the believer should remain with their spouse with the full knowledge that the believer is a part of a new spiritual kingdom, and that they cannot be unequally yoked in sin. Now, I will say that you can't live in bondage and in dangerous situations. God did give us common sense. If your spouse is evil and putting the family and you in a harmful situation, then you have the right and the obligation to keep yourself safe.

Here are some Scriptures admonishing us to live a life of separation from the world's way of doing things and separation to God's way of doing things:

Pursue peace with all people, and holiness, without which no one will see the Lord.
—Hebrews 12:14

I have given them (believers) Thy Word; and the world hath hated them, because they are not of the world, even as I am not of the world.
—John 17:14

Love not the world, neither the things that are in the world. If any man love the world, the love of the Father is not in him. For all that is in the world, the lust of the flesh, and the lust of the eyes, and the pride of life, is not of the Father, but is of the world. And the world passeth away, and the lust thereof: but he that doeth the will of God abideth forever.
—1 John 2:15-17

...know ye not that the friendship of the world is enmity with God? Whosoever therefore will be a friend of the world is the enemy of God.
—James 4:4

Enter ye in at the strait gate: for wide is the gate, and broad is the way, that leadeth to destruction, and many there be which go in there at.

—Matthew 7:13

Can two walk together, except they be agreed?

—Amos 3:3

But you are a chosen generation, a royal priesthood, a holy nation, His own special people, that you may proclaim the praises of Him who called you out of darkness into His marvelous light; who once were not a people but are now the people of God, who had not obtained mercy but now have obtained mercy.

—1 Peter 2:9-10

Therefore, whoever hears these sayings of Mine, and does them, I will liken him to a wise man who built his house on the rock: and the rain descended, the floods came, and the winds blew and beat on that house; and it did not fall, for it was founded on the rock. But everyone who hears these sayings of Mine, and does not do them, will be like a foolish man who built his house on the sand: and the rain descended, the floods came, and the winds blew and beat on that house; and it fell. And great was its fall. And so it was, when Jesus had ended these sayings, that the people were astonished at His teaching, for He taught them as one having authority, and not as the scribes.

—Matthew 7:24-29

(Jesus said:) Do not think that I came to bring peace on earth. I did not come to bring peace but a sword. For I have come to set a man against his father, a daughter against her mother,

and a daughter-in-law against her mother-in-law; and a man's enemies will be those of his own household. He who loves father or mother more than Me is not worthy of Me. And he who loves son or daughter more than Me is not worthy of Me. And he who does not take his cross and follow after Me is not worthy of Me. He who finds his life will lose it, and he who loses his life for My sake will find it.
—Matthew 10:34-39

Don't be afraid of holiness or intimidated by it. We can live normal lives in a secular world and can still please God. The problem is that many Christians live life on defense, instead of just living life. You can't live in fear that you will sin and displease God. Live life according to the Word that you know, and if you fall, get up and walk in His Word again. Don't allow religion to keep you alienated from the people who need to see your light shine. Go shine!

Grace and peace to you all.

Yours in Christ,

WHEN THE MESSENGER IS ATTACKED

Dear Friends,

This letter is for every faithful believer in Christ who has been falsely accused and/or attacked by the secular world and/or Church folks. It's a cruel and harsh world, and sometimes our worst enemies can be those who are closest to us.

And a man's foes shall be they of his own household.
—Matthew 10:36

Other times, fellow citizens and, of course, Church folks can be the biggest enemies of all. For thousands of years, the biggest enemies of the Gospel message have been religious leaders. Many times, because of fear and ignorance, they resist any move of God that is not under their control. Paul admitted that his greatest opponents were the religious Jews who followed him, caused trouble, and even tried to have him killed. Paul said he was:

...in perils of my own countrymen.
—2 Corinthians 11:26

Satan used the unbelieving Jews to be Paul's thorn in the flesh. He said they were sent to constantly "buffet him," (2 Corinthians 12:7).

This letter should serve as an encouragement to you if you are (as the saying goes) taking one for the team. If you are doing and saying the right things, and you are taking heat for it, then you should hold your head high and rejoice.

Jesus said:

No servant is greater than his master. If they persecuted Me, they will persecute you also.

—John 15:20

The disciple is not above his master, nor the servant above his lord. It is enough for the disciple that he be as his master, and the servant as his lord. If they have called the master of the house Beelzebub, how much more shall they call them of his household?

—Matthew 10:24-25

Look at how Jesus was misrepresented and falsely accused for doing the right thing. Again, I say, be encouraged, because you are in good company. Regarding Jesus, He was accused of being a deceiver:

And there was much murmuring among the people concerning Him: for some said, He is a good man: others said, Nay; but He deceiveth the people.

—John 7:12

He was accused of being a blasphemer:

Jesus saith unto him, Thou hast said: nevertheless I say unto you, Here after shall ye see the Son of man sitting on the right hand of power, and coming in the clouds of Heaven. Then the high priest rent his clothes, saying, He hath spoken blasphemy; what further need have we of witnesses? Behold, now ye have heard His blasphemy.

—Matthew 26:64-65

He was accused of being demon possessed and insane:

And many of them said, "He has a demon and is mad. Why do you listen to Him?"

—John 10:20

So just remember, saints of God, it isn't as bad as you think it is on the battlefield for the Lord. We will get knocked down and talked about; that is to be expected. Just know that when you are persecuted for righteousness' sake, then you have a reason to rejoice. Just don't give them a reason to accurately accuse you of wrongdoing.

Also, remember that the naysayers are generally cowards. They use us as scapegoats and they attack us because they are too cowardly to call God all of the names that they call us. We are only representatives, so when we are received, they are receiving Christ and God. But to these secular folks and carnal Church folks, we are the straw men that they create in God's stead; and when they attack us, they are actually attacking God.

Verily, verily, I say unto you, He that receiveth whomsoever I send, receiveth Me; and he that receiveth Me receiveth Him that sent Me.
—John 13:20

It is a pathetic spectacle, but this is how some people encourage themselves in their delusional world of error. So don't take the attacks personally. Instead, I say, rejoice!

Stay strong and stay encouraged.

Yours in Christ,

Christians Don't Sin

Dear Friends,

I had a conversation with a couple of friends a few weeks ago, and the subject came up about how Christians live sinless lives. Personally, I don't know any Christians who live sinless lives, including me. We endeavor to live holy lives before God, but to say that we don't sin is a lie. Maybe everyone doesn't fornicate, murder or steal; but I know a lot of Christians who gossip, speak evil of people, lie, don't walk in faith, are busybodies, etc. So your sin might not be one of the "bigger sins," but sin is sin.

We can say that we don't practice, nor do we purpose in our hearts to sin willfully. But we can't truthfully say that we don't sin. Even God knew that we would miss the mark from time to time, and He built into the covenant a way to make things right when we do go astray.

> *If we say that we have no sin, we deceive ourselves, and the truth is not in us. If we confess our sins, he is faithful and just to forgive us our sins, and to cleanse us from all unrighteousness. If we say that we have not sinned, we make Him a liar, and His word is not in us.*
> —1 John 1:8-10

Don't be religious and pretend that you don't mess up, maybe even on multiple occasions for the same issue. Just be real and acknowledge your shortcomings. Pray for one another, bear one another's burdens, confess your sins one to another, and help one another overcome in Christ. I'm so thankful to God for the progress that you folks are making.

I will see you soon.

Yours in Christ,

CHRISTIANS AND FOUL LANGUAGE

Dear Friends,

I would like to address you all once again with something that the Lord has placed upon my heart. I know some of you might get annoyed with me writing to you, every so often, with a new teaching, revelation, or insight; but the Word of God is so rich and it is such a spiritual anchor for all of us.

I would like to teach you about the words that we speak. I know that most of us have used foul language in the past, but I don't believe that it is appropriate for us to use as believers. Now, please don't get all bent out of shape without listening to what I have to say and the context in which I am saying it.

Christians are representatives and ambassadors of Christ. Our job is to speak the oracles of God and to walk accordingly. It's pretty hard to justify our witness for Christ when we have the potty mouth.

Let your speech be always with grace, seasoned with salt, that ye may know how ye ought to answer every man.
— Colossians 4:6

But the tongue can no man tame; it is an unruly evil, full of deadly poison. Therewith bless we God, even the Father; and therewith curse we men, which are made after the similitude of God. Out of the same mouth proceedeth blessing and cursing. My brethren, these things ought not so to be. Doth a fountain send forth at the same place sweet water and bitter? Can the fig tree, my brethren, bear olive berries? Either a vine, figs? So can no fountain both yield salt water and fresh.
—James 3:8-12

Let the words of my mouth, and the meditation of my heart, be acceptable in thy sight, O LORD, my strength, and my redeemer.

—Psalm 19:14

Let no corrupt communication proceed out of your mouth, but that which is good to the use of edifying, that it may minister grace unto the hearers.

— Ephesians 4:29

If using profanity is your weakness, don't worry. If you yield to God, ask Him to help you speak that which is pleasing to Him, repent, and meditate on the above-referenced Scriptures, your vocabulary will change. But you must make a conscious effort to initiate the change; then He will change you from the inside out.

Yours in Christ,

Religious vs. Righteous

Dear Friends,

Are you a religious (ceremonial) person, or are you a righteous (in right-standing with God) person? When dealing with God and a lifestyle that is pleasing to Him, there are two words that people generally associate with His people: righteous and religious.

The religious person is typically the type who is more concerned with impressing people rather than pleasing God. Jesus spoke of the religious people of His day:

> *Beware of the scribes, which love to go in long clothing, and love salutations in the marketplaces, And the chief seats in the synagogues, and the uppermost rooms at feasts: Which devour widows' houses, and for a pretense make long prayers: these shall receive greater damnation.*
> —Luke 12:38-40

The extent of their goodness was external. They were the Temple officials who knew the Law, but they had no heart for God.

> *And the Lord said unto him, now, do ye Pharisees make clean the outside of the cup and the platter; but your inward part is full of ravening and wickedness. Ye fools, did not he that made that which is without make that which is within also? But rather give alms of such things as ye have; and, behold, all things are clean unto you. But woe unto you, Pharisees! For ye tithe mint and rue and all manner of herbs, and pass over judgment and the love of God: these ought ye to have done, and not to leave the other undone. Woe unto you, Pharisees! For ye love the uppermost seats in the synagogues, and greetings in the markets. Woe unto you, scribes and Pharisees, hypocrites! For ye are as graves which appear not, and the men that walk over them are not aware of them.*
> —Luke 11:39-44

Today, religious people have a similar hubris about them, but their mannerisms are a bit different.

Having a zeal for God, but not according to knowledge.
—Romans 10:2

They pray loud and long, but they never get any results.

Having a form of godliness, but denying the power thereof: from such turn away.
—2 Timothy. 3:5

Religious people can shout "Hallelujah," they can dance, and they know all of the famous Church clichés. But the substantive proof of a God empowered life is not evident. You wouldn't dare ask these people to pray for you or ask for Godly counsel; nor would you want to accidentally step on their shoes, so as to avoid being cursed out in Church.

The solution is to walk in righteousness (in right standing with God). That might sound religious, but it's true.

But if we walk in the light, as He is in the light, we have fellowship one with another, and the blood of Jesus Christ, his Son, cleanseth us from all sin.
—1 John 1:7

Just walk in the Word that has been revealed to you and as you seek more, and as God sees that you are ready for more, He will reveal more to you. Grow in grace and walk it out.

Yours in Christ,

A Relationship with the Word

Dear Friends,

I write this letter as a reminder to you that we must have a relationship with the Word.

> *These were more noble than those in Thessalonica, in that they received the word with all readiness of mind, and searched the scriptures daily, whether those things were so.*
> —Acts 17:11

The Berean believers are a good example to follow, in terms of having a heart to scrutinize and to receive the Scriptures. They didn't take the preacher's word for anything, and they didn't shout "Amen" after every sentence. They understood that the Word of God was alive, and not just a book to read in order to feel pious.

> *For the Word that God speaks is alive and full of power (making it active, operative, energizing, and effective); it is sharper than any two-edged sword, penetrating to the dividing line of the breath of life (soul) and (the immortal) spirit, and of joints and marrow (of the deepest parts of our nature), exposing and sifting and analyzing and judging the very thoughts and purposes of the heart.*
> —Hebrews 4:12 (Amplified)

The Word is spiritual; and in order for you to digest it, you must do so spiritually.

> *Thy word have I hid in mine heart, that I might not sin against thee.*
> —Psalm 119:11

Since the spirit is the very essence of a human being, when you begin to incorporate the Word of God into your heart through reading and meditation, you become one with that Word. Think of how a husband and wife become one; they are actually two distinct people, but the covenant relationship and the intimacy they share unifies them. That is how your commitment to the Word should be: you should be one with the Word. What does that mean? It means that your connection to the Word should be so strong that when you speak, it should be as though God is speaking; and that means the same results should be expected and seen.

And the seventy returned again with joy, saying, Lord, even the devils are subject unto us through Thy name.
—Luke 10:17

How can you strengthen your relationship with the Word of God?
First, realize that the Word of God is, in fact, God's inspired Word, and be a diligent student of His Word.

All scripture is given by inspiration of God, and is profitable for doctrine, for reproof, for correction, for instruction in righteousness: That the man of God may be perfect, thoroughly furnished unto all good works.
—2 Timothy 3:16-17

Second, hear the spoken Word and let it get down into your heart.

So faith comes by hearing (what is told), and what is heard comes by the preaching (of the message that came from the lips) of Christ (the Messiah Himself).
—Romans 10:17

Third, be confident in the power of the Word of God, whether it's Jesus, or the written Word of God spoken from a heart of faith.

For this purpose the Son of God was manifested, that he might destroy the works of the devil.
—1 John 3:8(b)

Don't let anyone or anything come between your relationship with the Word of God and you. Your victory is assured in it, and your failure is assured if you are separated from it.

Yours in Christ,

PROPHE-LIE

Dear Friends,

Has someone ever tried to prophesy over you or had a Word from the Lord for you? I have had people with genuine words of the Lord for me, and I've had Church folks give me "words and prophesies" from the Lord, too. Now, don't get me wrong, I do believe that God can send a messenger into your life to confirm, to exhort, or to edify you; that is Scriptural. But what isn't Scriptural is when people try to speak things into your life that God never said.

Here's a good rule of thumb to remember: if some "spiritual" person wants to give you a Word from the Lord or prophesy into your life, then you are obligated to test that word and/or prophesy. If he/she tells you something that the Lord has never told you, then he/she is lying. If it's a generic blessing, the quoting of the Scripture (in context), or encouragement from the word, then receive it and agree with it.

God doesn't direct your life through other people. He directs your life through His Word, and through the Holy Spirit who resides in your spirit. It's really quite simple, and there's nothing spooky about it. Don't be intimidated by titles, positions, or how spiritual a person might sound. There are a lot of flaky people in the Church whose motives aren't always pure. I have seen a lot of unsuspecting Christians get swept away, by "more mature" Christians who gave them "a word/prophesy/vision" from the Lord. These weren't confirmations. They were just deceived people spreading their deception to unsuspecting people.

It is quite possible that they were Christians, maybe they were just deceived Christians. So don't jump to conclusions and call them demons, but definitely expose their error. Hopefully, your bold actions/ words will convict them and act as a deterrent to speaking loosely in the name of God in the future.

Yours in Christ,

Proverbs 31 Woman

Dear Friends,

Too often, I hear some Christian women claiming that they are, or aspire to be, like the woman described in Proverbs 31. I applaud the desire to want to emulate a positive role model, but I think that women need to remember that the woman in Proverbs 31 was a very dedicated woman. It's easy to get caught up in the "Churchy" Proverbs 31 confessions and claims of what you would like to manifest in your life. But this woman didn't just wake up one morning as the woman described in the chapter. She was probably trained that way, and very diligent in becoming a better woman for God, her family and herself. Hence, I would venture to say that becoming a Proverbs 31 woman should be more than just a confession of your mouth; it is work in progress.

Look at some of the things this woman mastered in her life:

- A Proverbs 31 woman is charitable with a servant's heart. Proverbs 31: 12, 15, and 20.

- A Proverbs 31 woman is NOT materialistic, nor is she wasteful. She spends her money wisely and her finances are in order. Proverbs 31: 14, 16, and 18.

- A Proverbs 31 woman is committed to her marriage, she is an asset to her husband, and she shows him respect. Proverbs 31: 11-12, 23 and 28.

- A Proverbs 31 woman is a woman of faith and she seeks God's Will for her life and follows His ways. Proverbs 31: 26, 29 – 31.

- A Proverbs 31 woman teaches her children according to the Word of God. Proverbs 31: 26 and 28.

- A Proverbs 31 woman is a wise woman and a good manager of her time. Proverbs 31: 13, 19, and 27.

- A Proverbs 31 woman is a wonderful homemaker. Her home is neat and loving, and she is hospitable and warm to all of her guests. Proverbs 31: 15, 20–22, and 27.

- A Proverbs 31 woman cares for her family and her own natural wellbeing. She is not only a beautiful person on the inside, but she also maintains her physical attractiveness. Proverbs 31:10, 14, 15, 17, 21, 22, 24, and 25.

- A Proverbs 31 woman is a diligent worker in everything. Proverbs 31: 13, 16, 24, 31.

This is a woman after God's heart and He dedicated an entire chapter to her. She is what every woman should strive to emulate, because her heart desires more of God.

Yours in Christ,

Obey Them Who Have the Rule Over You

Dear Friends,

The title of this letter comes from a Scripture:

> *Obey them that have the rule over you, and submit yourselves: for they watch for your souls, as they that must give account, that they may do it with joy, and not with grief: for that is unprofitable for you.*
>
> —Hebrews 13:17

This Scripture is used by a lot of preachers, and most of the time the Scripture is taken out of context. It is usually taught to mean that the congregation should obey whatever the pastor and the leadership tells them, because to disobey them is to disobey God. The preachers also manipulate the people by adding that they (the preachers) have to give an account to God on the people's behalf.

If you research the original Greek text of this verse, the word for "obey" is the Greek word "peitho," which means to yield to persuasion. The word "obey" is a mistranslation by the King James translators. It is not an error in the Word of God, because the original text shows us what was stated. Therefore, "Obey them that have the rule over you, and submit yourselves" is more accurately translated, "Allow yourself to be persuaded by those who are more mature in Christ than you." This is an exhortation to listen to/yield yourself to the instructions of those who are trying to help you in the faith. This is not a command to mindlessly follow your Church leaders.

In the situations in which we are required to obey, we are only required to obey laws, rules, and commands that don't oppose God's Word.

> *And when they had brought them, they set them before the council. And the high priest asked them, saying, "Did we not strictly command you not to teach in this name? And look, you have filled Jerusalem with your doctrine, and intend to bring this Man's blood on us!" But Peter and the other apostles answered and said: We ought to obey God rather than men.*
> —Acts 5:25-27

> *Be ye followers of me, even as I also am of Christ.*
> —1 Corinthians 11:1

What do we do if the laws of the land are contrary to the Word of God? There is a very simple answer to this, but it will take courage and integrity to implement.

I've had some discussions recently regarding some historical events. Some of our greatest heroes were those who broke the law of the land, in order to be catalysts for positive change. The question is: Were these people wrong for what they did, since they broke the law of the land for a moral cause?

1. Slavery was legal in America. But was Harriett Tubman wrong for freeing the slaves via the Underground Railroad?
2. God is a God of love and compassion. Was Jesus wrong for whipping the moneychangers and throwing them out of the Temple?
3. God's people are supposed to obey civil authority. Were the three Hebrew boys in the Book of Daniel wrong for disobeying the King's command to worship the idol?
4. It was against the law to speak out against the king. Was John the Baptist wrong for publicly declaring that Herod shouldn't be involved in immoral sexual acts?
5. It was once illegal for an African-American person to sit in the front seat of a public bus. Was Rosa Parks wrong for refusing to move to the back of the bus?

6. It was against the law for anyone to disobey the laws of the British king. Were the Colonists wrong for fighting back against the British Crown in order to win their independence?
7. The Law forbad anyone to be healed on the Sabbath. Was Jesus wrong for healing on the Sabbath?
8. The Nazis were exterminating millions of Jewish people. Should the German people have obeyed the Nazis and turned in the Jewish people to the Nazi regime?
9. Were the Jews wrong for not telling King Herod where the baby Jesus lived?
10. Finding answers in science is a good thing. But should we let the Government do whatever it wants? Were the Willowbrook State School and the Tuskegee experiments moral?
11. If unjust laws exist, should we exercise or surrender our right to protest/petition our government for a redress of our grievances?

There will be some natural consequences to bear for not obeying man's laws. But where man demands obedience, we must make sure that we are not simultaneously working against God by disobeying His moral laws. If man's way is against God's way, we must resist and believe that God will honor us for standing on the integrity of His Word.

Yours in Christ,

FORGIVE AND FORGET

Dear Friends,

I know that we are often reminded to forgive those who have sinned against us. In fact, Jesus was very explicit in his teachings about forgiveness in the Sermon on the Mount.

> *For if ye forgive men their trespasses, your Heavenly Father will also forgive you: but if ye forgive not men their trespasses, neither will your Father forgive your trespasses.*
> —Matthew 6:14-15

His example of forgiveness on the cross was even more powerful. So, it behooves us to follow what He taught us about forgiveness in word and deed.

Have you ever heard of people going a step further than forgiveness? Some people say that you have to forget the wrongdoing committed in order to completely forgive. That is not true, because forgiveness and forgetting have nothing to do with one another. Forgiveness is pardoning someone for a wrongdoing, and not requiring them to suffer any punishment for the wrongdoing. Forgetting is simply a loss of memory. You can forgive without forgetting or remembering the past. The question is: will the past control your present and your future? If the answer is "yes," then you haven't truly forgiven in a Biblical manner.

When people say forgive and forget, they are simply adding to the Scriptures. You can forgive a "friend" or "family" member who stole from you, but you don't have to forget that you were robbed. As a result of the robbery, you might not press charges against the perpetrator or hold a grudge against him/her, but you still might be reluctant to let him/her in your house again. What does forgetting have to do with forgiving?

Try telling a rape or domestic violence victim to forget about the horrible incident. It's hard enough to forgive the perpetrator of the crime, but to add "forget" to the equation would be next to impossible. Yes, with God all things are possible, but there is no requirement, commandment, or mandate from God to forget the past. If the past isn't a stumbling block, why not learn from the past? If the past still is a haunting experience, then only God can heal that wound.

Religion says: "Forgive and forget." The Word of God says:

For if you forgive people their trespasses (their reckless and willful sins, leaving them, letting them go, and giving up resentment), your Heavenly Father will also forgive you. But if you do not forgive others their trespasses (their reckless and willful sins, leaving them, letting them go, and giving up resentment), neither will your Father forgive you your trespasses.
—Matthew 6:14-15 (Amplified)

The Word never teaches us to forget. Forgive, but don't forget to learn from the past so that we can change the present and the future.

Yours in Christ,

GOD'S GRANDCHILDREN

Dear Friends,

I hope that you are all doing well today, and I also hope and pray that this letter is a blessing to you.

Many times, when I witness my faith to people, I hear a common set of responses to the question, *"If you died today, where would you spend eternity?"* People generally tell me that they believe they will be in Heaven. Then I ask them, *"What evidence do you have that you will be in Heaven?"* Typically, I get answers like, "I'm a good person," "I don't hurt people and I try to do the right thing," "I pray," "I love God," "I go to Church," "I read the Bible," "I got baptized," and a host of other answers.

But there are two answers that have always stood out to me: "My parents took me to Church" or "My parents are saved." What does going to Church or someone else's salvation have anything to do with your salvation?

So then each of us shall give account of himself to God.
—Romans 14:12

And there is no creature hidden from His sight, but all things are naked and open to the eyes of Him to whom we must give account.
—Hebrews 4:13

So the excuse that infers that "I'm covered (spiritually) because my parents have, or some other relative of authority in my life, has a relationship with God" is not valid.

> *But as many as received Him, to them gave He power to become the sons of God, even to them that believe on His name.*
>
> —John 1:12

What does this mean? It means that we are all God's creation, but we **ARE NOT** all God's children. One must become a child of God through the gift of salvation provided by Jesus Christ; but no one can piggyback into a walk with God on the coat tails of someone else.

> *I assure you, most solemnly I tell you, that unless a person is born again (anew, from above), he cannot ever see (know, be acquainted with, and experience) the kingdom of God.*
>
> —John 3:3

Everyone must be spiritually born again by confessing the Lordship of Jesus Christ, and believing in His death, burial and bodily resurrection as payment for their sins. Salvation is immediately granted, the person is no longer a sinner, and he/she is instantly a Christian (a new, spiritual creature in Christ Jesus). That is how simple it is to receive the assurance of your eternal destiny in God. At that point, you are a child of God, because God has no grandchildren.

Stay encouraged, and may the peace of God be with you all.

Yours in Christ,

Say Your Grace/Bless Your Food

Dear Friends,

We were told as children to "say grace over our food" or to "bless our food." Many of us didn't know what that meant, but we did what we were told. In the epistle to Timothy, Paul wrote:

> *Now the Spirit speaketh expressly, that in the latter times some shall depart from the faith, giving heed to seducing spirits, and doctrines of devils; Speaking lies in hypocrisy; having their conscience seared with a hot iron; Forbidding to marry, and commanding to abstain from meats, which God hath created to be received with thanksgiving of them which believe and know the truth. For every creature of God is good, and nothing to be refused, if it be received with thanksgiving: For it is sanctified by the Word of God and prayer.*
> —1 Timothy 4:1-4

Paul taught the Church to receive our food (that is sanctified by the Word of God and prayer) with thanksgiving. There are a lot of things that we do and say out of tradition, but they have no roots in Scripture.

In regards to blessing your food, the word "bless" in the New Testament is the Greek word "eulogeo." This is where we get the word "eulogy" and it literally means to say good or positive things. Does it make sense to say positive things over your food? Should we tell the Lord that this sandwich is going to taste great and it will nourish my body? Or should we just thank the Lord for the food as the Scripture teaches us?

I choose to follow what the Scriptures teach.

Yours in Christ,

Rejoicing at the Calamity of Others

Dear Friends,

Have you ever been happy to see the bad guy "get it" in the end of a movie? Did you ever say, "That's what you get," or "you deserved it" when someone received recompense for something they did wrong? I have done that before, and I even got a sense of satisfaction from seeing evil repaid. I knew that was the wrong sentiment, but my flesh got the best of me at that time.

The beauty of the Scriptures is that we can learn from our mistakes, and we can also receive instruction on the proper way of doing things. Simply put, if someone does the wrong thing, we are not supposed to rejoice at their misfortune.

> *Rejoice not when thine enemy falleth, and let not thine heart be glad when he stumbleth: Lest the Lord see it, and it displease him, and he turn away his wrath from him. Fret not thyself because of evil men, neither be thou envious at the wicked: For there shall be no reward to the evil man; the candle of the wicked shall be put out.*
>
> — Proverbs 24:17-20

The love message and lifestyle doesn't wish to repay evil for evil or rejoice when evil reaps what it has sown. Our lifestyle should always stand for what is right. People will reap what they have sown. But our job is to obey the Scriptures so that God can intervene and work on the person who needs to repent.

If we concentrated more on Jesus' words regarding praying for our enemies and doing good to them who hate us, then I believe that God would have an open door to move on our faith. As a result, we could see more Damascus road experiences, and if not that extreme, then at least people would consider the Lord as the jailer did in Acts 16.

We never know how our faith will affect those around us, because we live in such an interconnected world. Your faith and obedience doesn't just help you, and we will never know all of the people that it does affect. Just know that obedience to His Word is His Will for us.

Yours in Christ,

Balance vs. Priorities

Dear Friends,

Our mission, and one of our main reasons for living, is to be in right relationship with God, so that we can spread the good news of His Kingdom. This mission does not exclude us from having fun and partaking in the lighter side of life. We simply have to learn two words: balance and priority.

Balance

Balance connotes an equal distribution of weight, so that everything is on an even plane and can run smoothly. If you don't balance the tires on your car, the car will shake, and you will not have a smooth ride. If we use the same analogy for a lack of balance in our lives, we will also have a shaky life that won't run smoothly.

You can't work for twenty-four hours per day. You can't read the Bible for twenty-four hours per day. You can't associate with your friends and family for twenty-four hours per day. You can't sleep for twenty-four hours per day. But you can do all of those things if you balance your time, because doing so would put everything into perspective.

Priority

Priority means that which requires special attention, or something that is done first. When you get up in the morning, whatever is the first thing you do, that is a priority. Whether it's getting something to eat, going to the bathroom, praying, getting a cup of coffee, or watching television, that is a priority. No one can tell you if your priority is right or wrong. God and you have to make that determination.

Once you make an assessment of the things that are priorities in your life, you can further assess and determine whether or not they are, in fact, real priorities. This is where you find out what is really important to you. Once you list your priorities, you can devise a plan and a balanced attack to get everything done on a daily, weekly and monthly basis. But you must differentiate the difference between balance and priority. Although they are different, they work hand-in-hand.

Stay encouraged, brethren until I see you all again.

Yours in Christ,

The Desires of Your Heart

Dear Friends,

Before you read any portion of this letter, I would like for you to please follow my instructions.

Please list ANY three things that you would ask for if you were granted three wishes. I will explain why shortly. You don't have to be a Christian to partake in this semi-interactive exercise. But remember that I am asking each of you to answer a subjective question; everyone won't respond in the same manner, and there are no wrong answers.

Often times, we are told to **NOT** judge a book by its cover, because although the cover might not be so attractive, the information contained within the pages of the book might be invaluable. But no matter how often that message is communicated, and no matter how many times we listen to Dr. King's "I Have a Dream" speech (which admonishes us to judge not by the skin color, but by the content of one's character), we knowingly or unknowingly judge people and things based upon exterior qualities. But I tend to listen to what is on the inside of a person. I'm not referring to a person's heartbeat; I am referring to listening to what comes out of a person's heart (spirit) based upon the words that come out of their mouth. The Scriptures teach us:

For out of the abundance of the heart his mouth speaks.
—Luke 6:45

This letter will reveal what is in your heart (spirit), and your three wishes will reveal what is important to you, and why. We all have dreams, desires, and goals. They vary from person to person, but we all have them. Where a stable job and a nice place to live might be important to a husband and father of three kids, an Elmo doll and an Oreo cookie might be important to a two year old. Neither of these desires is wrong, but the mentality, age, and the situation of these two people causes a big difference in what is important to each of them.

For those of you who don't know this, God is not a slot machine. You can't give God some money, yank on His arm, and expect for Him to dump on you; nor is He your fairy God Father who grants wishes to you when you get into a bind. But for the sake of this letter, let's pretend that you have now been granted **ANY** three wishes. If you followed the above-mentioned instructions, you should already have chosen three wishes. So, now it is my turn to name my wishes. Then, I will give my reasons for these choices with some additional analysis.

First, I would choose the unlimited wisdom of God. People might frown upon this wish and say, "Ah man, that's stupid, but of course you'd say that so that you would appear all holy and spiritual." No, that is not correct. I'd seriously ask for the unlimited wisdom of God because with this unlimited resource, I could navigate through any situation with ease. I would know exactly what to do in any given situation, and there would be no mistakes. Wisdom, in short, is the direction to use the information that you have. Some people have information, but no direction. So, not only could I help myself, but I would also be able to help others in a tremendous way.

Second, I would choose the unlimited discernment of God. This wish would enable me to know the intent of a particular thing and the motives of everyone. Sometimes, people's motives are good, but their actions might not quite match their motives, at least not initially. I remember an episode of the Andy Griffith Show where Andy wanted his son, Opie, to donate some money to the orphanage so that they could buy the needy children some clothing. Opie decided to give three cents out of the two dollars that he had in his piggy bank. Andy was disappointed in Opie and he asked Opie to give more to help the less fortunate. Opie refused and said that he was going to buy something for his girlfriend. After a while, it was revealed that Opie's girlfriend didn't have a coat and Opie planned to buy her a coat because she was less fortunate. Sure, Opie could have just informed his father that he was saving his money to buy his less fortunate girlfriend a coat, and I'm sure Andy would've understood completely. But the point is that sometimes, you have to let things play out for a while before you understand what some people are doing and why. Many times, if you don't know people's motives, you don't know if they are friend or foe. Andy made it seem as though Opie didn't want to help the unfortunate, but that wasn't the case.

In short, I would use the discernment of God to reveal the situation and people's motives to me. Conversely, there are times when a "supposed" friend has an ulterior motive, but you defend and/or support this person because they seem like a friend. Discernment cuts out all of the guesswork and waiting; and immediately I would know what to expect.

Third, I would wish for the ability to transfer these gifts to whomever I please. I wouldn't transfer these gifts to everyone, because some people don't want to see reality. As crazy as it sounds, some people prefer delusion, and they are so full of pride that if you showed them truth, they might prefer their erroneous beliefs in order to appease their egos. The perfect example is Lucifer. He lived in the very presence of Almighty God, and his pride wouldn't allow him to remain a servant to Greatness. Lucifer wanted to be the Greatness. That's sad, because his pride cost him eternity; and there are also many people whose lives are based upon the bad decisions that they have made. Pride and deception keep many of them on that path.

So, those are my three wishes. These are not my "religious brownie points with God" answers. You might have chosen something similar, and maybe not. But look at your answers and ask yourself why you chose your answers. Maybe you chose the ability to fly. Okay if so, why? Is wealth your choice? Why? Maybe you want fame. If so, why? Maybe your choices would be different in a few years, maybe not. But an exercise like this is a good self-examination to locate what is on your mind.

Why is it important? The Scriptures tell us why.

Delight yourself also in the Lord, and He will give you the desires and secret petitions of your heart.
—Psalm 37:4

As long as your desires are God's Will, He will honor you and He will give you those things that are in your heart.

For all the promises of God in him are yea, and in him Amen, unto the glory of God by us.
—2 Corinthians 1:20

He won't hurt your boss because he fired you. God won't strike a negligent driver down with lightning because he cut you off on the highway. But if you have a genuine heart for God and your motives are pure, then He will give you the desires of your heart. Do you want a spouse? Marriage is a good thing that God created. But are you chasing the spouse, or are you delighting yourself in the Lord so that He can give you the desire of your heart (as opposed to your flesh)? There's a big difference between the two. Are you lonely, or are you just ready to have sex legally in the eyes of God? Or do you want to be a team player and start a family that brings glory to God? Do you want to own your own home? Were you a good steward over the apartments that you rented? Were you trustworthy? Did you take care of someone else's property? The Scriptures teach us:

And if ye have not been faithful in that which is another man's, who shall give you that which is your own?
—Luke 16:12

Think about the connection between delighting yourself in the Lord and receiving the desires of your heart. Once your heart is aligned with His heart, your prayer life will change for the better, and you will see more consistent results.

Yours in Christ,

[signature]

AGAPE LOVE

Dear Friends,

Love is a word that has become so cliché in the Body of Christ as well as in secular circles. People say that they love to play basketball, they love to eat spaghetti, or that they love a particular person. But what does this term "love" actually mean? There are different types of love.

> *Above all things have intense and unfailing love for one another, for love covers a multitude of sins (forgives and disregards the offenses of others).*
> —1 Peter 4:**8** (Amplified)

> *Love endures long and is patient and kind; love never is envious nor boils over with jealousy, is not boastful or vainglorious, does not display itself haughtily. It is not conceited (arrogant and inflated with pride); it is not rude (unmannerly) and does not act unbecomingly. Love (God's love in us) does not insist on its own rights or its own way, for it is not self-seeking; it is not touchy or fretful or resentful; it takes no account of the evil done to it (it pays no attention to a suffered wrong). It does not rejoice at injustice and unrighteousness, but rejoices when right and truth prevail. Love bears up under anything and everything that comes; is ever ready to believe the best of every person, its hopes are fadeless under all circumstances, and it endures everything (without weakening). Love never fails (never fades out or becomes obsolete or comes to an end).*
> —1 Corinthians 13:4-**8** (Amplified)

The Scriptures mention love. But how can you really know "love" and recognize it? Does it mean that you should just accept any ill treatment or disrespect? Does it mean whatever happens in life, just take the good with the bad and you will get your wonderful reward in Heaven one day? No, it does not. In Jesus' day, there were a few words that were all translated as love.

- **Agape**: the unconditional love that God expresses.
- **Stergos**: the love that is demonstrated for family members.
- **Phileo**: the affection of friendship (same sex or not).
- **Eros**: the erotic, lustful and self-gratifying sexual appetite.

Of these four words, "agape" is the main type of love that is mentioned in the New Testament. "Eros" is never mentioned, not even in reference to sex in marriage; that is because (agape) sex is supposed to be an act of giving of yourself to your spouse to please him/her. Although, both parties are to benefit from the joining together, the act isn't a self-seeking, self-satisfying type of sexual encounter. If both parties are focused on pleasing the other person, then no one will be disappointed.

Agape love has no strings attached; and it isn't concerned with money, status, health, beauty, geographical location, height, weight, or anything else. It is only concerned about the welfare of others, with no motive or expectation of payment in return. Agape love forgives and loves unconditionally; and gives selflessly, not selfishly.

Have you ever told someone that you loved him or her, but you didn't treat him or her according to "agape" love? You acted ugly and paid someone back because you were treated unfairly. You got an attitude because you did the right thing and you were disrespected in return. If any of these is true, then you were not walking in love. If you have said, "I'll tolerate you until I am tired of you," "I will forgive you if you apologize and buy me a present," "I'll be nice, if you are nice to me," "don't do me wrong and I won't have an attitude." That is not the love that God demonstrates towards us, nor is it the manner in which He expects us to conduct ourselves.

Does agape love sound like the love that we see people expressing towards one another today? No, but once you grasp this concept and see that agape is what Jesus illustrated on the cross, and understand that we've been commanded to implement it, then and only then will you begin to change your sphere of influence, and you will begin to experience the love that God intended for us all to share.

> *A new commandment I give to you, that you love one another; as I have loved you, that you also love one another. By this all will know that you are My disciples, if you have love for one another."*
>
> —John 13:34-35

Yours in Christ,

How We Should Treat One Another

Dear Friends,

This letter is very practical, because it simply cites the Scriptures that relate to how we are to treat one another.

> *A new commandment I give unto you, that ye love one another; as I have loved you, that ye also love one another.*
> —John 13:35

> *This is my commandment, that ye love one another, as I have loved you.*
> — John 15:12

> *These things I command you, that ye love one another.*
> —John 15:17

> *Be kindly affectioned one to another with brotherly love; in honor preferring one another.*
> —Romans 12:10

> *Owe no man anything, but to love one another: for he that loveth another hath fulfilled the law.*
> —Romans 13:8

> *Wherefore receive ye one another, as Christ also received us to the glory of God.*
> —Romans 15:7

And I myself also am persuaded of you, my brethren, that ye also are full of goodness, filled with all knowledge, able also to admonish one another.
—Romans 15:14

Salute one another with a holy kiss. The churches of Christ salute you.
—Romans 16:16

For our comely parts have no need: but God hath tempered the body together, having given more abundant honor to that part which lacked. That there should be no schism in the body; but that the members should have the same care one for another. And whether one member suffer, all the members suffer with it; or one member be honored, all the members rejoice with it.
—1 Corinthians 12:24-26

Greet one another with a holy kiss.
—1 Corinthians 16:20 and
2 Corinthians 13:12

For, brethren, ye have been called unto liberty; only use not liberty for an occasion to the flesh, but by love serve one another.
—Galatians 5:13

With all lowliness and meekness, with long-suffering, forbearing one another in love.
—Ephesians 4:2

And be ye kind one to another, tenderhearted, forgiving one another, even as God for Christ's sake hath forgiven you.
—Ephesians 4:32

Submitting yourselves one to another in the fear of God.
—Ephesians 5:21

Put on therefore, as the elect of God, holy and beloved, bowels of mercies, kindness, humbleness of mind, meekness, longsuffering; forbearing one another, and forgiving one another, if any man have a quarrel against any: even as Christ forgave you, so also do ye. And above all these things put on charity, which is the bond of perfectness.
—Colossians 3:12-14

Let the word of Christ dwell in you richly in all wisdom; teaching and admonishing one another in psalms and hymns and spiritual songs, singing with grace in your hearts to the Lord.
—Colossians 3:16

But as touching brotherly love ye need not that I write unto you: for ye yourselves are taught of God to love one another.
—1 Thessalonians 4:9

Wherefore comfort one another with these words.
—1 Thessalonians 4:18

Wherefore comfort yourselves together, and edify one another, even as also ye do.
—1 Thessalonians 5:11

But exhort one another daily, while it is called today; lest any of you be hardened through the deceitfulness of sin.
—Hebrews 3:13

And let us consider one another to provoke unto love and to good works.
—Hebrews 10:24

Not forsaking the assembling of ourselves together, as the manner of some is; but exhorting one another: and so much the more, as ye see the day approaching.
—Hebrews 10:25

Confess your faults one to another, and pray one for another, that ye may be healed. The effectual fervent prayer of a righteous man availeth much.
—James 5:16

Seeing ye have purified your souls in obeying the truth through the Spirit unto unfeigned love of the brethren, see that ye love one another with a pure heart fervently.
—1 Peter 1:22

Use hospitality one to another without grudging. As every man hath received the gift, even so minister the same one to another, as good stewards of the manifold grace of God.
—1 Peter 4:9-10

Likewise, ye younger, submit yourselves unto the elder. Yea, all of you be subject one to another, and be clothed with humility: for God resisteth the proud, and giveth grace to the humble.
—1 Peter 5:5

Greet ye one another with a kiss of charity. Peace be with you all that are in Christ Jesus. Amen.
—1 John 5:14

But if we walk in the light, as he is in the light, we have fellowship one with another, and the blood of Jesus Christ his Son cleanseth us from all sin.
—1 John 1:7

For this is the message that ye heard from the beginning, that we should love one another.
—1 John 3:11

And this is his commandment that we should believe on the name of his Son Jesus Christ, and love one another, as he gave us commandment.
—1 John 3:23

Beloved, let us love one another: for love is of God; and every one that loveth is born of God, and knoweth God.
—1 John 4:7

Beloved, if God so loved us, we ought also to love one another.
—1 John 4:11

No man hath seen God at any time. If we love one another, God dwelleth in us, and his love is perfected in us.
—1 John 4:12

And now I beseech thee, lady, not as though I wrote a new commandment unto thee, but that which we had from the beginning, that we love one another.
—2 John 1:5

The Word of God has spoken. Amen!

Yours in Christ,

Control vs. Empowerment

Dear Friends,

Although we are born again believers in Jesus Christ, we must also remember that we are fallible human beings. We have the Spirit of God living on the inside of us, but we also have the ability and the free-will to do the wrong thing. This is a reality with which we must contend until our last day on Earth.

I want you to think about two categories: control and empowerment. Are you a person of control, or are you a person of empowerment? Is your favorite preacher a person of control or of empowerment? Does your favorite politician promote an agenda of control or empowerment?

I am asking these rhetorical questions because while many of us would never want to be controlling, many of us are controlling. It's human nature to want to be in control, and to a degree and in context, control can be a good thing. Likewise, empowerment also has its pros and cons.

Control

Generally, when someone mentions control it has a negative connotation associated with it. Some people are labeled as "control freaks" or controlling, and they seek to diminish the power of an individual or a large number of people in order to accumulate power into the hands of one person or a small number of people. But not all control is bad. Corporations employ a "Controller" or "Comptroller" which is a senior accounting position; speed limit signs control the speed and traffic on the roads; and airport runways have air traffic controllers who maintain order for arriving and departing flights.

However, I know of many situations where people thrive on the dependency of others. To them, it is very empowering and rewarding to be relevant in the lives of people who aren't empowered. They are seen as advocates for the less fortunate. We should advocate for those who don't have a voice, but we must examine the hearts, motives and actions of these so-called advocates. Sometimes, these "advocates" are two wolves advocating for one sheep to be on the dinner table.

Have you ever been to a church service, but no one had their Bible open to follow along with the sermon? Those people were dependent upon the preacher to feed them the Word of God. That is not empowerment; that is opening a door to be controlled, because you can't agree with something that you can't prove or verify. Yet, all of the people in attendance will shout "Amen" during various parts of the sermon.

Some politicians love dependency, as well. Many times, it means more votes and more funding to care for the unfortunate folks in our communities. Again, I'm all for helping out those who are less fortunate, but we need to discern whether the politician's goal is to control or to empower the people. This is what must be reconciled in the minds of individuals, and only the Spirit of God can reveal people's hearts. But we can also see patterns of behavior that are clear signals of people's intentions. We should never be naïve when reality is giving us the answers we seek.

Empowerment

People who are willing to work themselves out of a job are people of empowerment. They are the people who wish to make individuals independent, responsible, and accountable for their own actions. A doctor who is willing to help people to get off of medicines and to rid themselves of ailing conditions is a person of empowerment. Some doctors would be satisfied with treating symptoms year after year, but that is not empowering the patients to be free from the doctor's care.

A business owner who seeks to help others start their own successful businesses and generate abundant profits for themselves and their employees is a person of empowerment. I know some insecure business owners who are afraid of more competition in the marketplace, but people who have that drive to be entrepreneurs cannot be stopped.

A parent who insists upon driving their adult son/daughter to and from school, work, and various places is not empowering that son/daughter with independence. Instead of sharing the car or helping the son/daughter to get a license and a car, this parent keeps the child in a crippling state of dependence. Again, empowerment is about helping others to be independent and productive.

A school that teaches students to think for themselves, to ask questions, and to engage in critical thinking about the world around them is empowering their students. Teaching self-sufficiency through an agrarian lifestyle is a form of empowerment.

> *"Give a man a fish and you feed him for a day. Teach a man how to fish and you feed him for a lifetime."*
> —Chinese Proverb

When people are informed about non-aggressive forms of self-defense, such as karate or ethical use of legal weapons, then they are empowered to defend themselves, and they won't feel helpless or defenseless if an unfortunate situation arises. Many times, you only have seconds to act when the police are minutes away.

My goal is to never need to instruct or correct you again. My goal is to have each and every one of you to instruct and correct others who are in your sphere of influence. I can only tell and teach you how to fly; but I can't fly for you. So jump off the cliff, spread your wings and do what you have been taught.

Yours in Christ,

Relationship vs. Fellowship

Dear Friends,

The Bible teaches us about relationship and fellowship. Sometimes it seems as though the two words are used interchangeably, but there is a difference between the words relationship and fellowship.

Relationship explains how we are connected. I'm related to John because his grandmother's brother was my grandfather. So John is my second cousin. That is how we are related. Fellowship alludes to spending quality time together. You don't have to be related in order to fellowship with one another. But you do have to have a connection in order to fellowship. Aunts, uncles, grandparents, nephews, brothers, sisters, parents, and nieces are all relationships; but not everyone who is related necessarily fellowships with one another.

This goes for family members as well as with our relationship with God. Every human being is related to God solely in a Creator/creation relationship. Every believer in Christ is related to God in a Creator/creation and in a Father/child relationship. But that doesn't necessarily mean that every believer fellowships with the Father.

Fellowship is:

1. the intimate part of the relationship.
2. where you learn the Father's heart.
3. when you can share your deepest and darkest secrets with God.
4. where God can make you whole.
5. when you begin to clearly hear His voice.
6. not a time, place or a set period of time. It is a mutual arrangement made exclusively for each other.
7. an exchange.

You're already related to God. Now move into fellowship with Him by committing more quality time to Him. When you commit more time to your kids or your spouse or your job, it usually produces good results for you. How much more will the results work in your favor if you are sowing more time into the things of God?

Yours in Christ,

SECTION TWO:
THE LETTERS OF DOCTRINE

The Armor Bearer

Dear Friends,

The "armor bearer" teaching has put many unsuspecting believers into spiritual bondage to the church leadership. Some believers have been sold on the assumption that, in order to enter their ministry calling, they must faithfully serve someone else's ministry. Others are fed a steady diet of "submission to authority" without ever questioning the teaching or the teacher's integrity. This "armor bearer" teaching is modeled after the Old Testament military model where only the royalty, the nobles, and the wealthy could afford true weapons of war. The balance of the army was everyday working men, who assembled as a temporary force, and not as a standing army. These men did not own weapons or armor of their own, except for what they could salvage from dead soldiers of previous battles.

The wealthy had servants (or armor bearers) whose job it was to maintain, to repair and to carry their armor and weapons, and to aid their masters. There were few standardized armies, and Israel was no exception, particularly during the early reign of King Saul. Only the kings and nobles had custom-made armor built to only fit them. When David went up to face Goliath, King Saul put his own armor on him, but it was too big for David. So David resorted to using the weapons to which he was already accustomed.

Under the Roman Empire, there was more of a standardized army with standardized weapons and armor. In this model, everyone from the privates to the generals had a basic armor and standardized weapons. They were uniform, and they fought as a unit, not as a mass of individual soldiers. There were no armor bearers in this army, because every soldier was an armor wearer, who was responsible for the maintenance and repair of his issued gear. Paul gave us the analogy of armor and the Christian life in Scripture.

> *Finally, my brethren, be strong in the Lord, and in the power of his might. Put on the whole armour of God that ye may be able to stand against the wiles of the devil. For we wrestle not against flesh and blood, but against principalities, against powers, against the rulers of the darkness of this world, against spiritual wickedness in high places. Wherefore take unto you the whole armour of God that ye may be able to withstand in the evil day, and having done all, to stand. Stand therefore, having your loins girt about with truth, and having on the breastplate of righteousness; and your feet shod with the preparation of the gospel of peace; above all, taking the shield of faith, wherewith ye shall be able to quench all the fiery darts of the wicked. And take the helmet of salvation, and the sword of the Spirit, which is the word of God: praying always with all prayer and supplication in the Spirit, and watching thereunto with all perseverance and supplication for all saints.*
>
> —Ephesians 6:10-18

In the Old Testament, the Holy Spirit came upon the king, priest and prophet for a specific duty, and for a specific period of time. Under that covenant, to disrespect one of those three direct representatives of God was to disrespect God Himself. Similarly (in secular Government), if an ambassador left a country to travel to another land, that ambassador represented and spoke on behalf of the leader who sent him/her. The king, priest and prophet were God's Old Testament ambassadors.

Touch not mine anointed, and do my prophets no harm.
—Psalm 105:15

That Scripture was contextually fitting for the Old Testament. Unfortunately, the previous verse has been abused and misinterpreted by people who support that idea that preachers are on a higher level with God than the ordinary folks who aren't preachers. But today, every believer in Christ is an anointed ambassador for Christ.

Now then we are ambassadors for Christ, as though God did beseech you by us: we pray you in Christ's stead, be ye reconciled to God.
—2 Corinthians 5:20

The Holy Spirit has been poured out upon ALL FLESH: young and old, Jew and Gentile, male and female, bond or free, noble or common. He has not only been poured out upon us, but now, he dwells in us; that is one thing that sets the New Covenant apart from the Old Covenant. No longer does He anoint a chosen few, but He anoints all who believe.

But you have an anointing from the Holy One, and you know all things...but the anointing which you have received from Him abides in you, and you do not need that anyone teach you; but as the same anointing teaches you concerning all things, and is true, and is not a lie, and just as it has taught you, you will abide in Him.
—1 John 2:20 and 27

So know your place in the New Testament. You are an armor wearer, not someone's armor bearer.

Yours in Christ,

Matthew 18, Part 1
(Binding and Loosing)

Dear Friends,

There are a few portions of Matthew 18 that are misunderstood by many in the Body of Christ. I have heard many Church folks say (during a prayer) in deliverance services, conferences, and in prayer lines, "I bind you, demon, in the name of Jesus Christ" and "I loose angels to go on assignment to bring money/favor in Jesus' name." Honestly, I use to pray like that, and I don't wish to confuse casting out devils (a Scriptural function of New Testament believers), and binding the enemy (an out-of-context doctrine), because they are totally different. I never saw an example of Jesus, Peter, Paul, nor any other New Testament believer ever "bind" or "loose" a demon, money, or a person. But the influence of the Evangelical, Pentecostal, and Charismatic movements have convinced millions of believers (without the proper perspective and context) to believe doctrines that aren't in the Bible.

Jesus did mention "binding" and "loosing" to His disciples. But what was the context of what Jesus meant? Here is what Jesus said:

> *Verily, I say unto you, whatsoever ye shall bind on Earth shall be bound in Heaven: and whatsoever ye shall loose on Earth shall be loosed in Heaven.*
> —Matthew 18:18

In the entirety of this account, Jesus spoke of binding and loosing in the context of forgiving and dealing with someone who has sinned against you, even if they will not admit to it. But the terms "bind" and "loose" have a totally separate meaning. In essence, He was teaching about Church discipline, and so many Christians have twisted Matthew 18:15-20 like pretzels in so many ways, that I had to write two letters to try to correct the erroneous doctrines.

Jewish history teaches us that "binding" and "loosing" were common terms used by rabbis, and the disciples knew exactly what Jesus was explaining to them when He used these terms. "Binding" and "loosing" are words that simply meant "forbidding" and "permitting," respectively. These terms were used in reference to things, such as rules and regulations; not people. In fact, the very wording that Jesus used, "whatever," not "whoever" confirms that the passage refers to things (in this case beliefs and actions), not to people. Binding (forbidding) and loosing (permitting) were necessary because the Law of Moses could not contain all the regulations necessary to govern every unique situation and circumstance in society. So, the religious leaders were required to bind (forbid) and loose (permit) activities among the children of Israel that were not specifically mentioned in the Law of Moses. The same thing was true in Jesus' day, and that is the reference in Matthew 18:18. We also have to remember that the epistles weren't written until twenty or so years after Jesus ascended to the Father. The early believers didn't have a Bible to reference; so they had to determine through careful study, deliberate discussions, a great deal of prayer, and the leading of the Holy Spirit, what the truth of the matter really was in a given situation.

Today, we are still binding (forbidding) and loosing (permitting) things. Just like in the Old Testament, today's church, or religious groups have standards, an unwritten code of ethics, rules/regulations, and/or likes and dislikes that are not specifically noted in God's Word. But we can draw insight from the Scriptures and our hearts, and bind (forbid) and loose (permit) things according to that insight. This is why Christians truly need to be sensitive to the leading of the Holy Spirit, because many people can get into spiritual bondage "in the name of holiness." For example, a group or Church can bind (forbid) the deacons from congregating at the large oak tree on the Church grounds because they smoke cigarettes and leave the cigarette butts on the ground. A Church could also bind (forbid) lewd and revealing attire to be worn during Church services. Conversely, the Church can loose (permit) things for convenience's sake, so long as nothing immoral becomes of it.

Another translation of Matthew 18:18 will certainly give this subject a clearer understanding of what Christ said:

Truly, I tell you, whatever you forbid and declare to be improper and unlawful on Earth must be what is already forbidden in Heaven, and whatever you permit and declare proper and lawful on earth must be what is already permitted in Heaven.
—Matthew 18:18 (Amplified)

The body of Christ is to teach that it is God who first binds and/or looses, and then we follow His leading and do the same thing on Earth. It's part of having the keys to the kingdom!

Binding the Strong Man

There is another account in Scripture where Jesus used the word "bind" regarding demons.

But if I cast out devils by the Spirit of God, then the kingdom of God is come unto you. Or else how can one enter into a strong man's house, and spoil his goods, except he first bind the strong man? And then he will spoil his house.
—Matthew 12:28, 29

In verse 29, Jesus uses a metaphor to illustrate what He actually came to the Earth to do: to spoil the strong man's house or to destroy his demonic influence over people's lives. Luke's account of the same story eliminates the word "bind."

When a strong man armed keepeth his palace, his goods are in peace: but when a stronger than he shall come upon him, and overcome him, he taketh from him all his armor wherein he trusted, and divideth his spoils.
—Luke 11:21-22

In short, Jesus taught that satan was a strong man, his house was this world's system, and his "goods" were the people who were in spiritual bondage to the will of the enemy. Then Jesus said that a Stronger One, referring to Himself, overcame him.

> *These things I have spoken unto you, that in me ye might have peace. In the world ye shall have tribulation: but be of good cheer; I have overcome the world.*
> —John 16:33

The word "bind" **WAS NOT** the key to the account in Matthew 12. If the word "bind" was the focus, then both Gospel writers would have included the word "bind." But they both included the fact that a strong man's house was destroyed by a Stronger Man—Jesus; and his house **WAS NOT** destroyed because people screamed at satan and bound him in Jesus' name. What Jesus did on the cross and His resurrection were sufficient, and they were what bound him.

> *Since then the children share in flesh and blood, He Himself likewise also partook of the same, that through death He might render powerless him who had the power of death, that is the devil; and might deliver those who through fear of death were subject to slavery all their lives.*
> —Hebrews 2:14-15

I encourage that you all study the matter for yourselves. If you were taught that binding and loosing demons was the context of that account, then I pray that your spiritual eyes have been opened to the truth and the proper context of the Scriptures.

Blessings to all of you.

Yours in Christ,

Matthew 18, Part 2
(Christ in Our Midst)

Dear Friends,

Have you ever heard or read the following Scripture?

Again, I say to you that if two of you agree on Earth concerning anything that they ask, it will be done for them by My Father in Heaven. For where two or three are gathered together in My name, I am there in the midst of them.
—Matthew 18:19-20

Often times, believers will use this Scripture in a prayer to "invoke the presence" of God for a particular meeting, event or situation, as if God isn't omniscient (everywhere at the same time and on the inside of us). People will also use this Scripture as a model for what constitutes a church gathering—two or three people. Well, obviously both of those popular interpretations are wrong or else I wouldn't be writing to you. So let's get some perspective and context, so that we can preserve the integrity of the Word of God.

What is Christ actually teaching us in these Scriptures? He is actually giving us a guideline for discipline in the church. Let's look at the preceding verses to make it clearer.

"Moreover, if thy brother shall trespass against thee, go and tell him his fault between him and thee alone: if he shall hear thee, thou hast gained thy brother. But if he will not hear thee, then take with thee one or two more, that in the mouth of <u>two or three</u> witnesses every word may be established. And if he shall neglect to hear them, tell it unto the church; but if he neglects to hear the church, let him be unto thee as an heathen man and a publican."
—Matthew 18:15-17

In verse 16, I underlined the words "two or three." I did that because the "two or three" who are gathered together in verse 20 are the same ones who are confronting a trespassing brother in verse 16. These Scriptures have to do with confronting a matter privately, and dealing with it publicly, when necessary. There were no Bibles they could have used for a reference or guide. The early disciples had to be in tune with the Lord and follow the leading of the Holy Spirit who lived on the inside of them. Christ was letting His disciples know that He is with them as they confront a brother/sister in sin. At times, it is a difficult task to discipline or to confront a grown man or woman and deal with matters of such serious nature. But we must do it in order to preserve the standard of truth among the Body of Christ. If someone commits an act that needs to be addressed:

1. Confront the accused. Hopefully, there is repentance and reconciliation. If not...

2. Take two or three witnesses with you and repeat Step #1. If that doesn't work...

3. Take the matter before the Body of believers; and if that doesn't work...

4. Kick the unrepentant out of the fellowship.

Now this isn't a prescription for dealing with petty little squabbles. This is for more serious things like causing division, adultery, fornication, stealing, cheating, etc., and it is a well-illustrated account that describes what a church can/must do regarding unrepentant members of the fellowship. Christ encourages His followers by saying He is with them when they have to make the hard decisions.

Stay encouraged and continue to study the Scriptures.

Yours in Christ,

Authority in the Name of Jesus Christ

Dear Friends,

Too often, we see examples of manipulation by Christian leadership against people's individual free will. Unfortunately, these acts of manipulation are a usurpation of God's authority. When we think of authority, we tend to think of someone who is in charge, and how disobeying the instructions of an authority figure will bring consequences.

We must first realize that Jesus has all authority, and He delegated His authority to us so that we can exercise it over the power of the enemy, not over one another.

> *And Jesus came and spoke to them, saying, "All authority has been given to Me in Heaven and on Earth."*
> —Matthew 28:18

> *Behold, I give you the authority to trample on serpents and scorpions, and over all the power of the enemy, and nothing shall by any means hurt you.*
> —Luke 10:19 NKJV

That word "authority" comes from the Greek word "exousia," which means conferred power, or the approval to operate in a designated jurisdiction. Simply put, authority refers to the delegated power God gives to all of His children, which allows them to act to the extent they are guided by Him and/or His revealed Word. Notice that God gave His followers authority over the enemy's power (ability, might, or strength). That is important to understand because authority trumps power.

If a police officer stands on the highway and commands the driver of an eighteen-wheeler to pullover, the driver is obligated to pullover based upon the authority vested in the police officer. Obviously, the eighteen-wheeler is more powerful than a person standing in the middle of the road. The truck driver could run over the cop and kill him/her. If that happened, the authority delegated to that cop to maintain law and order would hunt that truck driver down, and any power/resources at the authority's disposal would be used to bring that driver to justice. That is why authority trumps power, because if you violate the first line of authority, the second line will step in. If the second line fails, the third line will step in, and if justice isn't served, the authority will continue all the way back to the source of the authority: God. That is why those in authority and those in subjection to authority need to understand and to honor authority in its proper context.

How Authority is Meted Out

How is authority to be carried out? We view parents, police officers, politicians, judges, employers, teachers, and others as authority figures in our lives. All authority comes from God, but there is a secular manner in which authority is used, and there is also a spiritual manner in which the body of believers should use it.

Jesus said:

> Ye know that they which are accounted to rule over the Gentiles exercise lordship over them; and their great ones exercise authority upon them. But so shall it not be among you: but whosoever will be great among you, shall be your minister (servant): And whosoever of you will be the chiefest, shall be servant of all. For even the Son of man came not to be ministered unto, but to minister, and to give his life a ransom for many.
>
> —Mark 10:42-45

Jesus taught us the difference between the secular model for leadership and the Kingdom of God model for leadership. The former is a top-down, command-and-control hierarchical structure, very much like we see in the military or corporate America: ruler vs. servant. The latter is a relational model where Christ is the Head, and everyone in the Body of Christ (preachers and the congregation) is equal to one another in God's eyes. As the old Baptist preachers use to say, "There are no big "I's" and no little "U's" in Christ."

Look at what else Jesus said about leadership:

> *But be not ye called Rabbi: for one is your Master, even Christ; and all ye are brethren. And call no man your father upon the Earth: for one is your Father, which is in Heaven. Neither be ye called masters: for one is your Master, even Christ. But he that is greatest among you shall be your servant. And whosoever shall exalt himself shall be abased; and he that shall humble himself shall be exalted.*
> —Matthew 23:8-12

Basically, Christ taught His followers that no one is the teacher or leader of any other person; only Christ is the leader and teacher of the saints, and the believers in Christ are simply spiritual siblings to one another. In the family of God, there can only be one leader: Christ. But if God uses a person to be a teacher and example to the saints, they should do so as a humble servant, not as a person who seeks to be served.

Mother Church or Denominational Authority

There are a lot of people who believe that our Christian lives need to have a person or a group of people to whom we should be accountable. Ultimately, we are accountable to God, but I do agree with having accountability among the brethren, just as long as it is willing, mutual, and within the context of Scripture.

Many times, people use the Acts 15 model of the Jerusalem Council to justify having an Earthly, centralized body to whom we should give account. But upon a clearer examination of the Scriptures, we find this not to be an accurate assessment of the Jerusalem Council's role.

In Acts 15, there were some people from the Jerusalem church who brought an erroneous teaching to the church at Antioch. Paul and Barnabas decided to visit the Jerusalem church to settle the matter.

Why is this important and how do we put this situation into context? The erroneous teaching originated in Jerusalem and that is why they dealt with the situation at Jerusalem with the local council. If the teaching came from Antioch or Ephesus they would've dealt with it there. It just so happened that the apostles were in Jerusalem, and since the apostles were there, the assumption is that the protocol is to have a person or group to whom we should submit.

There is no scriptural evidence that supports submission to a mother church or to a denominational authority. There is no hierarchy in the Godhead, and neither is there one in the church. There are different functions in the Godhead as there are different functions in the body of Christ. But as the Father, Son and Holy Ghost are one, so are Christians all one in Him.

Submission/Subjection/Obedience

Many times, the word "submit" appears in the New Testament, but the true picture of the word's true meaning isn't always clear. The word "submit" connotes a "do what you are told," slave/owner relationship. But that is not an accurate depiction of the message the Scriptures are trying to convey. The word "submit" in the New Testament is the Greek word "hupotasso," which more accurately should be translated as "subjection." Subjection is defined as one person voluntarily yielding himself/herself to another person. So this word has nothing to do with control or the threat of consequence; it is a willing, trusting, loving, and mutually agreed upon relationship. Further, the Bible teaches us to subject ourselves to one another.

> *Be subject to one another out of reverence for Christ (the Messiah, the Anointed One).*
> —Ephesians 5:21 (Amplified)

Like I said earlier, all of God's people possess God's authority, and that authority should never be misused to control others.

> *Neither as being lords over God's heritage, but being examples to the flock.*
> —1 Peter 5:3

To make it even clearer, when a person is in subjection to another, that is an act of humility, but that doesn't equate to obedience. Obedience is an action, but subjection is a matter of the heart. When the two work in tandem one with another, it is a beautiful thing. When husbands and wives are in subjection to one another, and various Christian relationships are in mutual subjection, we can expect to see the blessings of God flow.

Often times, we see obedience that isn't from the heart. We see people giving orders and someone obeying in order to avoid reprimand. That is neither obedience, nor subjection; and it definitely is not from the heart. The apostles were subject to the official authority of the religious leaders, yet they disobeyed the demands of the high priest for them to stop teaching in the name of Jesus. Peter's and the other apostle's actions and responses were in disobedience to the man-made law, but they were in obedience to the highest authority: God.

But Peter and the other apostles answered and said: "We ought to obey God rather than men."
—Acts 5:29

The key ingredient is context, and as long as no one has any ulterior motives or shady agendas, the authority of God can't be usurped and used to harm anyone. But we must understand our roles and functions in the Kingdom of God. We are a body fitly joined together in the Spirit of God, and our job is to work together in love and unity to see the work of God continue.

What's in a Name?

Many times, we hear about doing a certain thing (like prayer) "in the name of Jesus." People baptize new converts "in the name of Jesus." Then again, other folks baptize new converts "in the name of the Father, Son, and the Holy Ghost," and this causes a huge controversy between certain denominations. Some churches argue and fight about a little misunderstanding, and it causes division where there should be none. What did Jesus say about doing things in His name?

Jesus said (in regards to all believers):

And these signs shall follow them that believe; <u>In my name</u> shall they cast out devils; they shall speak with new tongues;

They shall take up serpents; and if they drink any deadly thing, it shall not hurt them; they shall lay hands on the sick, and they shall recover.
—Mark 16:17-18

For where two or three are gathered together <u>in my name</u>, there am I in the midst of them.
—Matthew 18:20

Go ye therefore, and teach all nations, baptizing them <u>in the name</u> of the Father, and of the Son, and of the Holy Ghost.
—Matthew 28:19.

And in that day ye shall ask me nothing. Verily, verily, I say unto you, Whatsoever ye shall ask the Father <u>in my name</u>, he will give it you.
—John 16:23

The misunderstanding is the word "name" that is underlined in these four passages. The word "name" does not mean a person's name, like Robert or Janice. That word "name" comes from the Greek word "onoma," which means everything the name covers, everything the thought or feeling of which is aroused in the mind by mentioning, hearing, or remembering the name. In other words, one's rank, authority, and interests are included in the "name" mentioned. So in the Scriptures above, the word "name" can be replaced with the phrase "full authority that exists (in the person being named)" and the meaning is made clearer.

So when we pray or do anything in Jesus' name, we are doing it on His behalf as if He was here doing the deed Himself. He gave us the Heavenly power of attorney to act in His stead.

Remember, the "name" is the authority, not the person. There are a lot of people in the world named "Jesus." But they are not the Messiah and there is no authority or anointing vested in them, and consider this:

1. Only Jesus Christ was predicted centuries in advance through many prophetic words.

2. The Bible was written by over thirty-five different people, on three continents, over a period of fifteen hundred years, in three different languages, and the central theme of each book is Jesus (a man the Old Testament authors never met).

3. The angel of the Lord appeared to the shepherds in the field and announced Jesus' birth. A multitude of the Heavenly host was with the angel praising God in celebration of Jesus (Luke 2:8-20). This is a very unique circumstance; as you know, angels don't routinely manifest themselves and sing because a woman gives birth.

4. God spoke audibly from Heaven concerning Jesus. On at least three different occasions, God confirmed Jesus to the inhabitants of the Earth (Matthew 3:17; Luke 9:35; John 12:28). Have you ever heard an audible voice speaking from Heaven? Most times, it's hard to clearly understand what someone might be saying to you from across the street, let alone from Heaven.

Jesus is no ordinary guy, and His name/authority speaks for itself.

Yours in Christ,

The Clergy vs. the Lay People

Dear Friends,

Why do so many people differentiate between the laypeople (laity or the congregation) and the preachers (the clergy)? Aren't we all one in Christ? Every time Paul wrote a letter, he always addressed the entire body of believers. He never wrote a letter to the evangelists or the prophets; he addressed all believers of the particular assembly.

For example, he wrote:

Paul, an apostle, (not of men, neither by man, but by Jesus Christ, and God the Father, who raised him from the dead) And all the brethren which are with me, unto the churches of Galatia: Grace be to you and peace from God the Father, and from our Lord Jesus Christ.

—Galatians 1:2-3

Paul called to be an apostle of Jesus Christ through the will of God, and Sosthenes our brother, unto the church of God which is at Corinth, to them that are sanctified in Christ Jesus, called to be saints, with all that in every place call upon the name of Jesus Christ our Lord, both their's and our's: Grace be unto you, and peace, from God our Father, and from the Lord Jesus Christ.

—1 Corinthians 1:1-3

Paul, and Silvanus, and Timotheus, unto the church of the Thessalonians which is in God the Father and in the Lord Jesus Christ: Grace be unto you, and peace, from God our

Father, and the Lord Jesus Christ. We give thanks to God always for you all, making mention of you in our prayers.
—1 Thessalonians 1:1-2

Paul, a servant of Jesus Christ, called to be an apostle, separated unto the gospel of God...to all that be in Rome, beloved of God, called to be saints: Grace to you and peace from God our Father, and the Lord Jesus Christ.
—Romans 1:1, 7

Paul and Timothy, bond servants of Christ Jesus (the Messiah), to all the saints (God's consecrated people) in Christ Jesus who are at Philippi, with the bishops (overseers) and deacons (assistants).
—Philippians 1:1

I believe this is important to make clear, because this false designation between clergy and laypeople is another example of how a hierarchical class system is formed among the body of believers and it causes harmful division among us.

The word "laity" comes from the Greek word "laos." This word means "the people." When it is used in the New Testament, it is referring to all believers in Christ. For example:

*But ye are a chosen generation, a royal priesthood, an holy nation, a peculiar people (**laos**); that ye should shew forth the praises of him who hath called you out of darkness into his marvelous light; Which in time past were not a people (**laos**), but are now the people (**laos**) of God: which had not obtained mercy, but now have obtained mercy.*
—1 Peter 2:9-10

The word "clergy" comes from the Greek word "kleros." This word means "a portion or a 'lot'." Again, when this word is used it is referring to God's people, not church leadership.

> *The elders which are among you I exhort, who am also an elder, and a witness of the sufferings of Christ, and also a partaker of the glory that shall be revealed: feed the flock of God which is among you, taking the oversight thereof, not by constraint, but willingly; not for filthy lucre, but of a ready mind; neither as being lords over God's heritage (**kleros**), but being examples to the flock.*
> —1 Peter 5:1-3

So, God's people are "laos" and "kleros," but the way many view the words "laity" and "clergy" is in a ruling class vs. a subject class context; the pulpit vs. the pews. I don't see that illustrated in God's Word. What I do see is that we are all one in Christ Jesus as a corporate body of believers.

> *There is one body and one Spirit, just as you were called in one hope of your calling; one Lord, one faith, one baptism; one God and Father of all, who is above all, and through all, and in you all.*
> —Ephesians 4:4-6

Stop the class warfare and the division, because we are all one in Him.

Yours in Christ,

WHY WE MUST STUDY:
THE ATTITUDE OF THE BEREANS

Dear Friends,

Although the Word of God is infallible, some humans have taken the liberty to change certain words and meanings of God's Word. However, this change doesn't take away from the Spirit, the intent, the power, and the true context of God's Word. Hence, we must study the Scriptures.

In the early 1600's, King James VI (who later became King James I of England and Ireland) ruled Scotland, and in addition to being the monarch, he was also the head of the Anglican Church. He commissioned a team of scholars to translate the Textus Receptus edition of the Greek text in hopes of producing a unified and new translation of the Bible (known today as the King James Version). Although King James was not personally involved in the translation, he did set out the guidelines for the translation process. Hence, the influence of Anglicanism is apparent in the Scriptures with the use of many parochial terms, and the emphasis of a hierarchical authority structure over a local Christian church resting in a bishop.

If I may offer my opinion here, I recommend everyone use (in addition to the King James Bible) a Greek Interlinear Bible/website for your studies. Then you can do a full Scripture text analysis, view the Strong's concordance reference number for words, the actual Greek words, the transliteration, and the English equivalent of the original Greek text. You are assured a more accurate Bible study experience with these tools at your disposal.

Now look at a few Scriptures with those modifications that are more closely aligned with the original Greek text. Unfortunately, there are some (human) mistranslations in the King James Version of the Bible, as well as in other versions.

For example, the Greek word "proistemi" is usually translated "rule," but the word more accurately should be translated "lead, guard, manage, guide, direct, or oversee."

> *One who <u>rules</u> his own house well, having his children in submission with all reverence for if a man does not know how to <u>rule</u> his own house, how will he take care of the church of God?*
> —1 Timothy 3:4-5

> *He must be one who <u>manages</u> **(proistemi)** his own household well, keeping his children under control with all dignity (but if a man does not know how to <u>manage</u> **(proistemi)** his own household, how will he take care of the church of God?)*
> —1 Timothy 3:4-5 (NASB)

The Greek word "proistemi" does not connote dictatorial rule as many espouse. There is a huge difference between ruling people, and guiding or managing people.

The Greek word "praxis" is usually translated "office," but the word more accurately should be translated "function."

> *For as we have many members in one body, and all members have not the same <u>office</u>.*
> —Romans 12:4

> *For just as we have many members in one body and all the members do not have the same <u>function</u> **(praxis)**.*
> —Romans 12:4 (NASB)

In the body of Christ, we don't have official offices. We have functions/duties. Many of our leaders are so caught up in statuses, titles, and positions, rather than function and service. The modern-day apostles, prophets, evangelists, pastors, teachers, reverends, etc. are NOT official titles and offices like: President, Mayor, Judge, or Lieutenant. Have you ever wondered why no one in the New Testament is ever referred to as Apostle Paul, Apostle Peter, etc.? Readers, analysts, and commentators of the New Testament might refer to them as Apostle Peter or Apostle Paul, but they never referred to themselves in that manner.

Calling someone Elder Johnson, Pastor Williams, Apostle Jackson, Prophet Smith, Evangelist Jones, Deacon Davis, etc. (as many Christians erroneously do today) was unheard of in the first century. Paul stated that he was an apostle, but he was merely stating his function as an apostle (one sent on a mission). He wasn't just basking in the aura of a title or a position of status as people served him. The saints need to understand who we are and what we have in light of Scriptural context, because often times, we misrepresent God and His Kingdom to other Christians and to the secular world.

The Greek word "episkopos" is usually translated "bishop," but the word more accurately should be translated "overseer."

> *This is a true saying, if a man desire the <u>office of a bishop</u>, he desireth a good work.*
> —1 Timothy 3:1

> *The word is faithful: if any one aspires to <u>exercise oversight</u> (**episkopos**), he desires a good work.*
> —1 Timothy 3:1 (Darby Translation)

The phrase "office of a bishop" is more accurately translated "to exercise oversight." The actual word for "office" is only used twice in the New Testament. In Luke 1:8-9, the word "office" is the Greek word "hierateuó." It is used in reference to the Levitical priesthood. The other reference is in Hebrews 7:5 and it was used to describe the Priesthood of Christ. Offices were never given to Christians. Can you see how the King James translators were influenced by the official hierarchy verbiage of their day? Unfortunately, people are hanging their faith on these misconceptions and this erroneous view of Christian leadership.

The Greek word "diakonos" is usually translated "minister" or "deacon," but the word more accurately should be translated "servant."

> *Likewise must <u>the deacons</u> be grave, not double tongued, not given to much wine, not greedy of filthy lucre; And let these also first be proved; then let them use <u>the office of a deacon</u>, being found blameless...Let <u>the deacons</u> be the husbands of*

one wife, <u>ruling</u> their children and their own houses well. For they that have used <u>the office of a deacon</u> well purchase to themselves a good degree, and great boldness in the faith which is in Christ Jesus.

—1 Timothy 3:8, 12, 13

*Likewise <u>servants</u> (**diakonos**) must be grave, not double tongued, not given to much wine, not greedy of filthy lucre; And let these also first be proved; then let them <u>serve</u> (**diakoneó**), being found blameless...Let <u>the servants</u> (**diakonos**) be the husbands of one wife, <u>leading, guarding, managing, guiding, directing, or overseeing</u> (**proistemi**) their children and their own houses well. For they that have <u>served</u> (**diakoneó**) well purchase to themselves a good degree, and great boldness in the faith which is in Christ Jesus.*

—1 Timothy 3:8, 12, 13

Again, the Greek Interlinear words were inserted and the meaning of these verses is completely different. Go back to the Greek Interlinear text and see what was actually written. Offices, positions, titles and status are the secular world's way of leading and ruling. The believers in Christ function under God's direct authority. No preacher stands in proxy between God and another believer; and again, no preacher has any authority over another believer. I know this stretches the mind of many Christians because we have been conditioned to think that we must submit to "spiritual authority" in the form of a pastor or a church covering. If Jesus is your Lord, then you are under His Lordship, covering, anointing, covenant, etc. There is no addendum to the New Testament.

The Greek word "ekklesia" is usually translated "church," but the word more accurately should be translated "assembly."

And I say also unto thee, that thou art Peter, and upon this rock I will build my <u>church</u>; and the gates of hell shall not prevail against it.

—Matthew 16:18

*And I say unto thee that thou art Peter, and on this rock I will build my <u>assembly</u> (**ekklésia**), and hades' gates shall not prevail against it.*
—Matthew 16:18 (Darby Translation)

Allow your mind to get renewed with the Word of God. I encourage you to study this on your own; and may those who have eyes to see and ears to hear and to properly respond to what the Spirit of God is saying. Be free!

Yours in Christ,

The Who, What, Where, Why, and How of Seed Sowing

Dear Friends,

I'm sure that you have all heard of the Parable of the Sower; and if you haven't read it, then you need to read it, and gain understand of its message/principles. Jesus said it is the most important of all of His parables.

And He said to them, "Do you not understand this parable? How then will you understand all the parables?"
—Mark 4:13

And again He began to teach by the sea. And a great multitude was gathered to Him, so that He got into a boat and sat in it on the sea; and the whole multitude was on the land facing the sea. Then He taught them many things by parables, and said to them in His teaching: "Listen! Behold, a sower went out to sow. And it happened, as he sowed, that some seed fell by the wayside; and the birds of the air came and devoured it. Some fell on stony ground, where it did not have much Earth; and immediately it sprang up because it had no depth of Earth. But when the sun was up it was scorched, and because it had no root it withered away. And some seed fell among thorns; and the thorns grew up and choked it, and it yielded no crop. But other seed fell on good ground and yielded a crop that sprang up, increased and produced: some thirtyfold, some sixty and some a hundred." And He said to them, "He who has ears to hear, let him hear!"
—Mark 1:1-9

Some religious folks will use this lesson to mean that we need to scatter a bunch of seeds far and wide. Sow all of the seeds that you can! What seeds? Well, according to the Parable of the Sower:

The sower sows the word.
— Mark 4:14

What does it mean to sow the Word? It can mean to proclaim, to distribute, to announce, to teach through speaking, literature, media outlets, an act of kindness, or a host of other creative ways to get the Word out to people. Why is how we sow seeds important? It is important because although we should be about our Father's business and win the lost and the hurting to His Kingdom, we should also be good stewards over the assets (seeds, power and anointing) that God has entrusted to us. Additionally, if there is sowing of seeds, the reciprocal action is also set in motion: reaping a harvest.

Look at the Parable of the Sower, it teaches us that there are four types of soils: the wayside, stony ground, among thorns, and good ground. The wayside is the person who just squanders opportunities and time. The stony ground is the bitter or hard-hearted person who has been hurt in the past and won't open their heart to truth. The "among thorns" is the person who is caught up in personality, looking good, being cool, staying trendy, and so concerned with the natural aspects of life that they miss the big picture. The good ground is the person who has an open and pliable heart towards the truth. This person has a humble heart, and a hunger and a thirst for righteousness. This person produces good fruit.

Blessed are those who hunger and thirst for righteousness, for they shall be filled.
—Matthew 5:6

The seeds (the Word) only produced a harvest in good ground. This is why we should monitor the time and resources that we give to certain people. Some people aren't interested in growing up, getting better, being successful, and being productive. Some people are just looking for a free ride, pity, an argument, or their next meal; and they will drain your resources, time, energy and your faith. Remember that the next time you are arguing with people who don't really want the Word of God.

Many do-gooders will say that I am teaching a lack of compassion, by not reaching out to people. Actually, I'm not saying that at all. I'm actually admonishing people to be *selective* and to treat your seeds like an investment. The Kingdom of God will grow based upon your spiritual business acumen. If you are a good, spiritual businessman or businesswoman, then the Kingdom will flourish. So, I'm not demonstrating a lack of compassion; I am displaying good stewardship and good time management skills. You have to discern people and their intentions before you invest into them. It took God a long time to get you to where you are today. Don't waste what God has invested in you.

> *Give not that which is holy unto the dogs, neither cast ye your pearls before swine, lest they trample them under their feet, and turn again and rend you.*
> —Matthew 7:6

Yours in Christ,

HEAVEN IS CLOSED

Dear Friends,

If you think about it, we live in a world of opposites: up and down, left and right, in and out, rich and poor, as well as old and young to name a few. But in this letter, I would like to address the word "closed." It is a relative term, which means that it has an opposite meaning. It alludes to an obstructed access of some sort. Is there some sort of correlation between Heaven and the word "closed?"

Heaven is closed; it does not have a door, a lock or a physical key. Heaven is a spiritual place. It is spiritually closed, and for that reason, Heaven must be accessed. Think about the ATM at your local bank; it is always in working condition, even if the bank is closed. But in order to get your money, you must first access it with your card and pin number. The ATM isn't going to eject money because you have money in the bank. It will only give you access to your funds if you access those funds on the bank's terms.

In Ezekiel 1:1, Matthew 3:16 and Acts 7:56, the Bible refers to people seeing Heaven being opened. Spiritually speaking, if Heaven opened, then it must have been closed. The relative term "opened" only makes sense if the opposite of that word was the previous state of being. So Heaven was closed, but then the Heavens were opened; something and/or someone accessed them. Remember the ATM? What happened, and what can we learn from these three instances that can give us some working Biblical insights and principles?

In Ezekiel 1:1, Ezekiel was being called and commissioned by the Lord for service. His obedience to the call of God caused Heaven to open and he saw visions of God. In Matthew 3:16, Jesus' obedience caused the Heavens to open and the Spirit of God descended like a dove and came upon Him. In Acts 7:56, Stephen's obedience in standing firm upon the Word of the Lord allowed him to see the Heavens opened and the son of God standing on the right hand of God.

To be clear, I don't know if these events happened on cloudy days, and the clouds rolled back. But the principle of the matter is the substantive portion of these Biblical excerpts. God responds to our obedience to His Word, and He also confirms His Word with signs following (Mark 16:20). If you are in a situation that requires God's intervention, then you need to look at the example of these three episodes and superimpose them over your particular situation. Obedience is the key! What did God speak to you: in His Word, through a spoken word, or through your spirit?

Remember this: you can always be sure that you are on the right side of God if you come to God on His terms. Be open to His Word and have an open heart to receive from God. What does God's Word say, in context, and how will you respond? God has a vested interest in your success and He wants you to succeed. You might ask, "What if I get tricked by the enemy?" "How will I know if God is leading me?" God knows your heart, and if you are sincere in your heart as opposed to your head, then God will honor you and make sure that you have the truth presented to you.

Look at these examples:

- In Acts 10, God connected a man (Cornelius) who meant well and whose heart was towards God with Peter who was able to instruct him in the way of truth.

- In Luke 11:9-13, Jesus taught that if a natural man will do whatever he could to provide for his children, how much more will our Heavenly Father give us the things that we need.

- In John 16:13, Jesus said that the Holy Spirit would guide us into all truth.

This was all done so that we could access what God has for us. What a mighty God we serve.

Yours in Christ,

The Lord's Supper is a Church Snack

Dear Friends,

Did you know that for many years after the Lord ascended to Heaven, the Lord's Supper was a full-fledged, down-to-Earth, joyous, non-religious communal meal? I know that you might not believe that if you go to a traditional institutionalized twenty-first century church. But the Scriptures and history teach that the early believers called the Lord's Supper "love feasts."

> *These are spots in your love feasts, while they feast with you without fear, serving only themselves. They are clouds without water, carried about by the winds; late autumn trees without fruit, twice dead, pulled up by the roots.*
> —Jude 1:12

The term "love feasts" doesn't sound like the traditional twenty-first century Lord's Supper experience. Without going into a long history lesson, the liberty of enjoying fellowship with the body over an informal meal was hijacked by religious tradition. It is now a very solemn and symbolic ceremony that is highlighted with confession of sins, condemnation, and a thimble full of grape juice (representing Christ's blood) and a tiny cracker (representing Christ's body).

The common focus of fellowship should be according to the Scriptures.

> *And they continued steadfastly in the apostles' doctrine and fellowship, in the breaking of bread, and in prayers.*
> —Acts 2:42

Eating with one another should be joyous, festive and a good time. A tiny piece of cracker, and sitting in a dimly lit sanctuary as everyone tries to remember what sins they committed during the week is not a joyous and festive love gathering. This was never the intention of the Lord's Supper, but it is my prayer and desire that you do your own research so that we all can return to the truth of what God intended for His people. The more we stay in religious acts of piety, the longer we continue in ignorance. If we line up with God's truth, the more revelation and a flow of God we will experience. He will confirm His Word with signs following.

Yours in Christ,

Read/Follow the Bible

Dear Friends,

Have you ever noticed that many Christians like to read the entire Bible in a year? Or some Christians boast about how many times they've read the Bible. It seems like a nice goal, but there is no Biblical mandate to read or to follow the Bible. We are taught that Jesus is the way, the truth and the life, and He commanded us to be followers of Him, not the Bible. He referenced the Law, He followed the Law, and He fulfilled the Law, but He never pointed us to the Law; He always pointed us to follow Him, because by following Him and relying upon His power, we can live above the Law.

Paul confirmed this:

> *Wherefore the law was our schoolmaster to bring us unto Christ, that we might be justified by faith. But after that faith is come, we are no longer under a schoolmaster. For ye are all the children of God by faith in Christ Jesus.*
> —Galatians 3:24-26

We can't go to the Law and find the true character and nature of God. We saw portions of His glory, character, and goodness revealed in the Old Testament, but the fullness of it came in Jesus Christ. There was an instance in the Beatitudes (The Sermon on the Mount) when Jesus referenced the Old Testament Law, but by His grace and truth He showed us a new way to follow God by following His (Jesus') teachings. Examples include:

> *You have heard that it was said to those of old, 'You shall not murder, and whoever murders will be in danger of the judgment.' But I say to you that whoever is angry with his brother without a cause shall be in danger of the judgment.*
> —Matthew 5:21-22 (New King James)

You have heard that it was said to those of old (in the Old Testament), 'You shall not commit adultery.' But I say to you (in the New Testament) that whoever looks at a woman to lust for her has already committed adultery with her in his heart.
—Matthew 5:27-28 (New King James)

Again you have heard that it was said to those of old, 'You shall not swear falsely, but shall perform your oaths to the Lord.' But I say to you, do not swear at all: neither by Heaven, for it is God's throne; nor by the earth, for it is His footstool; nor by Jerusalem, for it is the city of the great King. Nor shall you swear by your head, because you cannot make one hair white or black. But let your 'Yes' be 'Yes,' and your 'No,' 'No.' For whatever is more than these is from the evil one.
—Matthew 5:33-37 (New King James)

Christ taught His disciples the Old Testament, and then He taught His teaching. Christ also taught us that He came to do the Father's Will. So He didn't just come to randomly say and do things, this was God's plan.

And He that sent Me is with Me: the Father hath not left Me alone; for I do always those things that please Him.
—John 8:29

My meat is to do the Will of Him that sent Me, and to finish His work.
—John 4:34

If you had known Me, you would have known My Father also; and from now on you know Him and have seen Him." Philip said to Him, "Lord, show us the Father, and it is sufficient for us." Jesus said to him, "Have I been with you so long, and yet you have not known Me, Philip? He who has seen Me has seen the Father; so how can you say, 'Show us the Father'? Do you not believe that I am in the Father, and the Father in Me? The words that I speak to you I do not speak on My own authority;

but the Father who dwells in Me does the works. Believe Me that I am in the Father and the Father in Me, or else believe Me for the sake of the works themselves.
—John 14:7-11 (New King James)

Beware of those who point you to go directly to God without Jesus. Don't even let people point you to the Holy Spirit, because Jesus said that the Spirit of God would testify of Him.

But when the Comforter is come, whom I will send unto you from the Father, even the Spirit of truth, which proceedeth from the Father, he shall testify of Me.
—John 15:26

He shall glorify Me.
—John 16:14(a)

Don't follow your heritage, your preacher, a doctrine, your gender, your countrymen, me or anyone else. Follow Jesus, and people when they are following Jesus, and if they stop following Jesus, you have no obligation to follow them.

Be ye followers of me, even as I also am of Christ.
—1 Corinthians 11:1

For no other foundation can anyone lay than that which is (already) laid, which is Jesus Christ (the Messiah, the Anointed One).
—1 Corinthians 3:11 (Amplified)

...having been built on the foundation of the apostles and prophets, Jesus Christ Himself being the chief cornerstone.
—Ephesians 2:20

Religion, Our Path Away from Jesus

This reminder to follow Jesus is important because it demonstrates why religion is wrong. Most religious groups may accept some aspects of Jesus, but you can really tell who is following God or not by their acceptance or rejection of the personhood and Christhood of Jesus, and His statement that He is the only way to God (John 14:6). Groups that point to their organization and leadership, or attempt to go straight to God without Jesus are clearly in error.

Folks, keep your eyes on Jesus. He is our anchor, our help, and strong tower in time of need.

Yours in Christ,

TITHING

Dear Friends,

Lately, I've been getting a lot of letters and questions regarding tithing. The questions and concerns that people have regarding tithing have been more frequent, so I decided to address this issue as quickly and as thoroughly as possible. I don't want to make this an in depth study, but I just wanted to point out a few things and remind you about New Testament living, as opposed to Old Testament Law.

I don't want any of you to take anyone's word for any teaching, especially this teaching; and don't be so stubborn that you hold onto your own belief system without scrutinizing the Scriptures to verify what is right. So, I encourage you to emulate the study habits of the Berean Christians in the book of Acts. Paul taught them, but they always checked behind Paul's teachings with the Word of God to make sure that he was actually teaching God's Word to them.

All of the teachings that we need for modern-day Christian living are conveniently located in the New Testament. The person and the teachings of Jesus Christ are our spiritual foundation and the New Testament Epistles are the instructions the Church needs to build strong spiritual lives. We can learn principles from the Old Testament and we can learn some history there, as well, but we don't need to go back into the Old Testament Law to learn about prayer, salvation, giving, repentance, righteousness, covenant rights, baptism, judgment, etc. We live in the New Testament and that is where all of our teachings are located. We can learn from the Old Testament, but we must do so through Jesus Christ.

Question: Are we obligated or expected to tithe (ten percent) of our income to the Lord in the New Testament?

Please pay very close attention to the following points and research them for yourself:

- There were only two types of income that were accepted as the tithe in the Old Testament: agricultural production and animals. *"All the tithe of the land, whether of the seed of the land, or of the fruit of the tree, is the Lord's"* (Leviticus 27:30). This meant that a tenth of all agricultural produce of the land of Israel, whether herbs, seeds, fruits or vegetables, had to be tithed. The second type of income that was subject to the tithe was the increase of animals. *"All the tithe of the herd or flock, whatsoever passeth under the rod, the tenth shall be holy unto the Lord"* (Leviticus 27:32). However, if the tither couldn't or didn't want to bring the food, he could give money as a substitute, and he was penalized twenty percent. *"If a man will redeem ought of his tithe, he shall add unto it the fifth part thereof."* (Leviticus 27:31) The tithing law prohibited cattle ranchers from paying money at all. They were required to give the tenth animal, *"It shall not be redeemed"* (Leviticus 27:33).

- A large segment of people in Israel did not tithe. There were other workers besides farmers and ranchers, but they were never required to tithe. But in most of today's Churches, every believer is subject to the manipulation of tithing according to the dictates of the Church folks. Farmers and ranchers tithed, but their workers were never required to tithe off of their salaries. Fishermen, miners, lumberjacks, construction workers, carpenters, weavers, judges, military personnel, etc., were never required to tithe.

- Today, orthodox Jews (those who adhere to the traditional interpretation and application of the laws and ethics of the Torah) don't tithe because in the Old Testament, only the Levites (from the tribe of Levi) were able to receive the tithes. In 70 A.D., the Temple in Jerusalem and all of the lineal records were destroyed, so the Jews don't know who is an actual descendant of the tribe of Levi.

- There is not one New Testament example, teaching, instruction, or commandment to tithe.

- In regards to financial giving, the New Testament only teaches about alms giving (helping the poor) and (free will) offerings. We are to give freely from a willing and cheerful heart; not reluctantly, sorrowfully, or under compulsion. No one has the right to tell you what to give. If God touches your heart to give a specific amount, then follow your heart. But if that amount just happens to be ten percent of your salary for the week, it still isn't a tithe, because it isn't food and we don't live in Old Testament Israel.

- All New Testament references to the tithe are references to what was done in the Old Testament. The references Jesus made regarding the tithe were not about money, but food, i.e., mint, anise, cumin, rue and herbs, and these references were made before the Crucifixion (under the Law).

- Money (gold) is mentioned in Genesis 2, and it was used as a monetary medium of exchange since ancient times. Abraham, Solomon, Job and others were wealthy men, but we never see them or anyone else in the Scriptures tithe money. Why are Church folks requiring people to tithe?

- Many people claim that tithing is a principle that preceded the Law with Abram in Genesis 14 that just continues on forever. That is not true. Here is the context of that account: The kings of Sodom and Gomorrah, and their allies fought a battle against Chedorlaomer (the king of Elam) and his allies. Chedorlaomer and his allies won the battle, and they took all the food supply and other goods from Sodom. They also took, Abram's nephew, Lot (assumingly as a slave) and his possessions. When Abram heard what happened, he took 318 trained men and defeated the King of Elam. After the victory, Abram brought back all the goods, Lot and the people, and he met Melchizedek (King of Salem). They ate bread and wine and he blessed Abram. In appreciation to God for the victory, Abram gave ten percent of all the recovered spoils of the war (not his own money or possessions) to Melchizedek. The King of Sodom wanted to have his people returned to him, but he offered to give Abram all the goods of Sodom that were recovered. Abram refused, because he didn't want anyone to say that the King of Sodom made him rich. All of the spoils were returned to the King of Sodom and his allies, except for what the men ate and the tithe to Melchizedek. To use this sequence of events to justify tithing is very weak.

- The Lord Jesus Christ, not the tithe, is the covenant connector. When you become a Christian, you are spiritually and immediately made an heir of God and a joint-heir with Christ Jesus. Giving activates the principle of sowing and reaping in your life. But your connection to the covenant is only through your relationship with Jesus.

- There is no need to spiritualize the Law and incorporate it into the New Testament. You can't tithe money, your possessions, or your time; and you can't make tithing a New Testament practice. If sacrificing animals is not for today, then neither is tithing.

The issue is to clear up what kind of giving is Biblical. Tithing (under the Law) is not and has never been required during the New Testament. You can give any amount of money that you wish without condemnation according to what God lays upon your heart. If you wish to give a set amount of two, ten, thirty or fifty percent of your finances, possessions or time, just know that you are not tithing and giving above the tithe. You are merely offering your money, possessions and time, and you can expect for God to bless you according to what you have given in faith towards Him. Just make sure that your giving is the result of you following your spirit (heart). Don't follow the Law! Follow Jesus and the Spirit of God, because Jesus gave us the power to live above the Law.

Are you living under the (Old Testament) Law, or under (New Testament) grace? You can't live in both. Don't follow what other people are doing. You can follow their examples of faith, but allow God to lead you as you act on Biblical faith. You might see someone give five hundred dollars to a missionary work. Maybe their faith and obedience is at that level, but your faith is not quite at that level. If you have a heart to give, let the amount of the giving come from your heart. Don't let preachers scare you and manipulate you if you don't feel comfortable giving ten percent of your income. I've already shown you that ten percent is NOT a requirement. It's no one's business what you give. Your giving is between God and you. He's the only one who is going to bless you for your giving, so He is the only one who should direct your giving. Whatever amount of money you wish to give must be done with a willing, cheerful heart, and in faith.

Some people might ask, "Well, why are you making such a big deal about whether we call our monetary giving a tithe or an offering, alms or whatever? Aren't you just playing semantics?" No, I'm not playing semantics. Would you call a U.S. Dollar a Euro? No, you call it what it is. We are not tithing, so I'm letting you know that according to the Scriptures. When God gives instructions, He does so for a specific purpose. Too often, whether we are just ignorant of the facts or just being followers of dead traditions, God has to extend grace to us because we get into sin/error, or for whatever reason we are not aligned with His Word. He extends grace to us because He loves us, and He wants us to re-align ourselves with His Word. That re-alignment will bring a blessing into our lives.

Think about a little baby using the bathroom on himself/herself. In reality, using the bathroom on oneself is unacceptable, but that child has to learn and to understand how and when to use the bathroom. The parents extend grace to the child while he/she is taught the lessons of life. But a child that is seven-years-old shouldn't get the same consideration (unless there is a problem) because a normal seven-year-old who has been taught about bathroom etiquette knows better than to use the bathroom in his/hear pants. The same goes for God's children. Sometimes, we don't know the Word, so God extends us some grace and space so that we can grow and learn. That is a blessing. But when we learn the right way and do the right thing, God doesn't have to keep us on the spiritual training wheels any longer, and we can ride the bike ourselves; we don't have to wear spiritual pull-ups anymore; we don't have to eat mashed peas and carrots anymore. We are growing and maturing in Christ when we walk in His Word. When our children demonstrate more responsible behavior, we entrust them with more responsibilities, authority, blessings and favor. God treats us the same way. He can't release certain things to some of us, because although God is ready and willing, sometimes we aren't.

The Church needs to do things according to God's Word. Why else do we have our Bibles? We have them so that we can know God's Will. When we learn His Word and do it, He reveals His Word, we grow up, and we can receive more mature blessings and instructions. We are already blessed when we walk in God's grace even when we are learning God's ways. But how much more of a blessing is available to us if we walk in a more complete knowledge of His Word?

Again, I want you all to be clear that tithing is NOT a New Testament practice. I love each of you, and I want nothing but God's richest and most abundant blessings to be extended to you all. So, stay encouraged; love one another and walk in His way.

May the love of God, the grace of our Lord Jesus Christ, and the communion of the Holy Spirit be with you all until we meet again.

Yours in Christ,

OPERATING IN SPIRITUAL GIFTS AND SPIRITUAL MATURITY

Dear Friends,

I have seen many believers in Christ pose as such great spiritual beings because they flow in the gifts of the Spirit according to 1 Corinthians 12; and there is no doubt about it, because many of them do flow in those gifts. But what benefit is it to flow in spiritual gifts when your actions aren't a pure reflection of the manifested life of God.

> *Though I speak with the tongues of men and of angels, but have not love, I have become sounding brass or a clanging cymbal. And though I have the gift of prophecy, and understand all mysteries and all knowledge, and though I have all faith, so that I could remove mountains, but have not love, I am nothing. And though I bestow all my goods to feed the poor, and though I give my body to be burned, but have not love, it profits me nothing. Love suffers long and is kind; love does not envy; love does not parade itself, is not puffed up; does not behave rudely, does not seek its own, is not provoked, thinks no evil; does not rejoice in iniquity, but rejoices in the truth; bears all things, believes all things, hopes all things, endures all things. Love never fails. But whether there are prophecies, they will fail; whether there are tongues, they will cease; whether there is knowledge, it will vanish away. For we know in part and we prophesy in part. But when that which is perfect has come, then that which is in part will be done away. When I was a child, I spoke as a child, I understood as a child, I thought as a child; but when I became a man, I put away*

childish things. For now we see in a mirror, dimly, but then face to face. Now I know in part, but then I shall know just as I also am known. And now abide faith, hope, love, these three; but the greatest of these is love.
—1 Corinthians 13:1-13

Many people who seem to be spiritually gifted are not always as mature as they seem. For example, The Corinthian Church was the Church that was full of God's spiritual gifts (tongues, healings, miracles), yet in some ways they were very immoral. There was a specific incident that Paul addressed regarding Church members (a stepmother and a stepson) having an illicit affair (1 Corinthians 5). So, don't judge yourself by the standards of others who are "spiritual." Spiritual people have issues, too. Your standard is the Word of God, so keep your eyes on Jesus.

Work out your own soul's salvation with fear and trembling.
—Philippians 2:12(b)

Love is the revealing factor regarding one's maturity in Christ. Speaking in tongues, prophecy, and God using an individual to perform great healings and miracles are great things; but if there is no love and/or obvious growth in the Word, then all of the outward demonstrations of spiritual gifts are in vain.

Yours in Christ,

Baptizing/Christening Babies

Dear Friends,

The doctrine of water baptism has been hijacked by many religions, and sects of Christianity. The true, New Testament meaning of water baptism is illustrated by the example of Jesus Christ. He was baptized by John the Baptist as a symbolic gesture of fulfilling all righteousness. His example is ours to follow, so that we may symbolically identify with Christ's death, burial, and resurrection.

Simply put, water baptism is an outward expression of an inward conviction. There is no salvation, remission of sins, or right standing with God in water baptism. Baptizing babies is just another religious expression that has no sound Biblical foundation. Water baptism is only to be performed for those who have knowingly and willingly accepted Jesus Christ as their Lord and Savior. If water baptism is performed in any other capacity, you will simply be submerged into water as a dry sinner, and you will rise up as a wet sinner.

Babies are innocent, and they cannot be accountable for sin like you and me. Their hearts are pure and they are under God's grace for a period of time. Whenever they reach the level of maturity, comprehension, reason, and receive the conviction of the Lord, they will be accountable to accept the Lord and repent on their own.

But this letter is just another reminder to stay away from *religious traditions* that are vain, and have no ability to produce life, growth or spiritual benefit.

Yours in Christ,

Why Good Things Happen to Bad People, Why Bad Things Happen to Good People

Dear Friends,

I hate to see people struggle and endure hardships, especially good people. But many times, it seems as though many good people live good, decent lives, and struggle; meanwhile, many bad people live immoral lives and they continue to prosper and live life to the fullest. This is what I call a misconception of perception.

There are a few reasons why good things happen to bad people and why bad things happen to good people.

Bad Things Happen to Good People

Many times, Church folks want to quote Scriptures over every situation. I agree that we should speak words of faith that are in line with God's Word, but sometimes Church folks have a tendency to "over-spiritualize" life. If something goes wrong, some Church folks want to immediately blame the devil and claim that he is stealing, killing and destroying. Well, the enemy does those things, but sometimes we have to realize that every bad thing that happens isn't always the result of demonic activity.

Sometimes bad things happen to good people, because good people do bad things; not necessarily bad things meaning *evil things*, but bad things meaning not the right things. For example, if you don't drink enough water or exercise enough, that can cause some adverse conditions to your health. So, not drinking enough water and not exercising are not evil; rather, they are not the best health choices to make. Unfortunately, I know many Christians who wouldn't analyze the situation to try to narrow down the cause of the problem. They would simply see a bad circumstance and immediately point the finger at the devil or some sin that may or may not have been committed; and while Church folks are trying to cast out the devil, bind the devil, and quote Scriptures, your health is deteriorating.

Another reason why bad things happen to good people is because some people don't heed the warnings to stay away from bad things. Why does a basketball star like Len Bias (former University of Maryland star in the 1980's) die after his first time trying cocaine, yet others spend many of their most productive adult years using and overdosing on drugs? We've seen the many examples of people who fell upon hard times. A lot of heartache, trouble, and suffering of consequences could have been spared if a decision would have been made to do the right thing. When we get warnings, we should heed them. But we can't get the warnings, ignore them, and then get angry with God when we suffer the consequences for ignoring the warnings. It's like seeing the 55 mph speed limit sign, choosing to go 65 mph, and then getting angry at the police officer for giving you a ticket.

Another reason why bad things happen could be attributed to ignorance. We can suffer inconveniences, adversity, ailments, etc., by not knowing some tidbit of information that could help us. For example, most electrical devices are tagged with a large warning label not to use them near water for one obvious reason: mixing the two could result in electrocution and even death. The laws of science and life can be very unforgiving, and they don't take into consideration the possibility of a person's ignorance, so keep that in mind.

Good Things Happen to Bad People

Conversely, good things do happen to bad people, and it's not because God loves bad people more than He loves good people. God is love, and He loves all people equally. His mercy and grace are extended to people, because He wants everyone to turn to Him. Many times, born-again believers pray for drug users, prostitutes, and other high-risk offenders to be delivered from their destructive lifestyles, and God honors those prayers.

The effectual fervent prayer of a righteous man availeth much.
—James 5:16(b)

Sometimes, it seems as though some people can overdose on hard drugs, drive drunk, and escape all kinds of near-death experiences; yet they live to tell the story many times. If they don't immediately change their ways, some of them return to abuse their bodies. I do know that prayer works, but I also know that the enemy of our souls looks for avenues to destroy us; while God wants to bring deliverance. Either way, the decision to change belongs to the individual.

> *I call Heaven and Earth to record this day against you, that I have set before your life and death, blessing and cursing: therefore choose life, that both thou and thy seed may live: that thou mayest love the Lord thy God, and that thou mayest obey his voice, and that thou mayest cleave unto him: for he is thy life, and the length of thy days: that thou mayest dwell in the land which the Lord swore unto thy fathers, to Abraham, to Isaac, and to Jacob, to give them.*
> —Deuteronomy 30:19-20

In His Word are life, healing, prosperity, protection, blessing, and goodness. People who don't discern God's Will blame God when bad things happen, and that doesn't set faith in motion; it sets doubt and bitterness in motion, and that acts as a magnet on which the enemy can piggyback and do more of his destruction in the lives of people. As a result, the enemy remains insulated from guilt, and God is inadvertently characterized as the bad guy. This is precisely why God and situations must be discerned.

Yours in Christ,

The Great Commission to All

Dear Friends,

Traditionally, we have been taught that the Great Commission is the great clarion call to win the lost.

> *And Jesus came and spoke to them, saying, "All authority has been given to Me in Heaven and on Earth. Go therefore and make disciples of all the nations, baptizing them in the name of the Father and of the Son and of the Holy Spirit, teaching them to observe all things that I have commanded you; and lo, I am with you always, even to the end of the age."*
> —Matthew 28:18-20

Well, the Great Commission isn't just to reach the lost. Jesus said to teach ALL people to keep His teachings. This means that we also have to teach people who are already believers, yet unlearned in the Kingdom principles. Many times, people want to focus the Great Commission on soul winning. Catching new fish is great, but sometimes you have to clean and prepare the fish that you've already caught.

There are many families who are hurting, and some of them are having a tough time making the transition to successful Kingdom living. No one has clearly instructed them about how the Kingdom of God works. These people love God, but they haven't been properly trained in the Lord's timeless principles. How can we expect people to live a victorious life in Christ Jesus if we never help them and give them the tools to be successful?

Therefore, leaving the discussion of the elementary principles of Christ, let us go on to perfection, not laying again the foundation of repentance from dead works and of faith toward God, of the doctrine of baptisms, of laying on of hands, of resurrection of the dead, and of eternal judgment.

—Hebrews 6:1-2

So, let's be sensitive to the needs of those around us regarding ministry. We don't want sincere people to fall through the cracks. Perfecting the saints is as much a part of the mission, as winning the lost for Jesus Christ.

Yours in Christ,

It's Testing Time

Dear Friends,

We all go through trials, tribulations, and testing periods. They may only last for a day, a week, a month, or maybe even a year. No one likes to be inconvenienced with a test, but the reality is that if you are a living human being, you will be tested. So get ready for it. But can you ensure that you are not prolonging the testing period? It would be a shame to know that you could have possibly received your blessing sooner.

One thing you can do is understand that when you are in a situation, God already has a path mapped out to your victory. But He won't drag you along. You have to obey, be diligent, and pursue the victory; and your actions will have to speak louder than your Hallelujahs.

Here is a natural illustration: if you want to go from Dallas, Texas to Fort Worth, Texas, you have to go westbound. If you go eastbound from Dallas, you're going the wrong way. You can turn around and go west towards Fort Worth, but now your estimated time of arrival is going to be longer than originally anticipated. Do you understand that? This is how we prolong the suffering: we make the wrong choices during the test, and we have to do a U-turn, find the right road, and then continue traveling in the right direction.

That's how our life is when we go through trials, tribulations and testing periods. When we do the wrong things in the midst of the trials, we get lost and/or frustrated. When this happens we tend to get out-of-character, and we often make mistakes. This is how a three-day trial can become a two-month nightmare. The same thing happened to the children of Israel. They wandered in the wilderness for forty years and the Bible said it was actually an eleven-day journey to the Promised Land.

> *It is eleven days' journey from Horeb by way of Mount Seir to Kadesh Barnea.*
> —Deuteronomy 1:2

FOLLOW THE WONDER

Have you ever said or thought: "I wonder why...," "I wonder how...," "I wonder who...," "I wonder when...," "I wonder where...?" Asking questions, unresolved matters and dissenting views always cause new ideas and allow life's proverbial rocks to be unturned. When you are going through a test, it is very important to listen to the voice of God in your spirit.

God is omniscient, and He has all variables at His disposal in order to reach us. He can use people, things, circumstances, situations, and more to reveal the truth to us. We (humans) are finite creatures and, at times, we may not be able to discern the full scope of what is going on around us. But if we trust in His ability more than our own, we will experience more success in our lives.

> *The secret things belong to the LORD our God, but those things which are revealed belong to us and to our children forever, that we may do all the words of this law.*
> —Deuteronomy 29:29

> *Trust in the LORD with all thine heart; and lean not unto thine own understanding. In all thy ways acknowledge Him, and He shall direct thy paths.*
> —Proverbs 3:5-6

God wants to be a part of our lives, and He wants for us to be a part of His. But God is a gentleman and He will not impose His Will on us; however, He will make Himself known, sometimes demonstratively, and sometimes subtly. It's our responsibility to discern Him, and to respond to Him in a positive manner.

When God makes a subtle move towards someone, He is doing so for the sole purpose of getting a positive response from that person. This doesn't mean that God is expecting every non-believer to instantly accept Him. Like I said, God is a gentleman; He is also patient, gracious and merciful.

For example, if God wants to reveal Himself to a man who has an affinity for science; He may allow him to find a very unusual rock. After much research, the man has an open-ended conclusion about the rock's formation and composition. This finding will cause the man to do more research, which might lead him to further discoveries and more questions to be answered. As long as the man is open to truth, the truth will eventually be revealed to him.

Ask, and it will be given to you; seek, and you will find; knock, and it will be opened to you. For everyone who asks receives, and he who seeks finds, and to him who knocks it will be opened.
—Matthew 7:7-8

It's not up to God whether or not we discover the truth. The truth is already available to us, but our response to God's initial revelations, no matter how minute, will determine if we are given more truth.

And ye shall seek me, and find me, when ye shall search for me with all your heart.
—Jeremiah 29:13

Do you remember the analogy about going to Fort Worth from Dallas? You have to go west. If you are going east from Dallas, you can't get angry at God because you haven't arrived in Fort Worth. Again, there is a positive and a negative response to truth. A positive response will lead you to peeling a layer or two off of the proverbial onion and eventually seeing the ultimate prize. A wrong response to truth will lead to deception, because if something isn't true, it's false. But a wrong response can be corrected by going back to the place of error and making the correct response instead. Remember, stop driving east, turn around and go west and then you are headed in the right direction for Fort Worth.

One of the wonderful things about God is that He is impartial (Acts 10:34), and everyone has a fair opportunity to exercise their faith in order to discover the revelation of truth. As God gave every human a unique DNA and fingerprint, so also has He given every human a spiritual "light" that yearns to be fed.

> *He was not that Light, but was sent to bear witness of that Light. That was the true Light which gives light to every man coming into the world.*
> —John 1:9

People are looking for something to satisfy that passion for more, the desire for truth, that "light" that lights us all. People call it many things, but it all boils down to God reaching Himself out to humanity; and anyone who responds in a positive way will be rewarded.

> *Blessed are they which do hunger and thirst after righteousness: for they shall be filled.*
> —Matthew 5:6

You are guaranteed to pass the test of life if you follow the leading of the Teacher. The notes are given before the test, so He will prepare you for what is to come. God never blindsides us with a pop quiz without informing us of what He wants us to know. So know that if you are being tested, then you have been prepared to pass, and throughout the test He will never leave you nor forsake you.

Peace and love to all of you.

Yours in Christ,

Talents/Gifts/Abilities

Dear Friends,

God gives everyone at least one gift, talent, or ability. It might not be the gift, talent, or ability that all of the trendy people want, but what He gives you He expects for you to use it for His glory. When you discern your God-given gift, talent, or ability, then it is your responsibility to cultivate what God has given you through study, practice, prayer, etc. As you prepare yourself, God will begin to open doors of opportunity for you; and then it will be your responsibility to act upon those opportunities when they manifest.

Look at the Parable of the Talents in Matthew 15. An employer gave three of his workers (according to their abilities) a portion of his wealth to invest while he was gone. To one worker he gave ten talents, to another five talents, and to another one talent. When the employer returned to collect on his investment, he found that the workers with the ten and the five talents doubled his investment, and the employer was pleased with them. But the worker who had one talent did nothing productive with the wealth that was entrusted to him. If this story took place in 21st century America, the Government would have taken from the workers with ten and five talents, and they would have made all three of the workers equal with five talents a piece. That is not productive. But in this Bible story, the employer reprimanded the worker with the one talent because he was lazy and unproductive. So the employer took the one talent away from the worker, and he gave it to the most productive worker: the worker who had ten talents.

God doesn't give us excuses. He gives us talents/abilities/gifts/open doors of favor. Sure, things happen, but we are to never succumb to our circumstances; rather, we are supposed to yield to the Word and to the Spirit of God, and make sure that we are doing our part (in the natural) to be productive, efficient, and in right standing with God.

Remember this: our thinking determines the types of decisions that we make; and the decisions that we make determine the types of actions that we take; and the types of actions that we take determine the types of habits that we form; and those habits determine what type of life we will live.

How badly do you want to succeed? Will your pride allow you to work at a fast food restaurant, if necessary? It's not a glamorous job with a lot of great pay or benefits. But what if that is where you need to start? What if that is your stepping-stone in order to get you to the next step in the process?

> *A man's gift maketh room for him, and bringeth him before great men.*
> —Proverbs 18:16

Your gift, talent, or ability has to bring value to someone else. Otherwise, there is nothing of value to exchange. If no one else receives value from what you are offering, then why are you needed? See the value in what you are offering and what others need, and then you will see where you fit in this market of ideas, goods and services.

Finally don't forget to represent God in all that you do.

> *And whatsoever ye do in word or deed, do all in the name of the Lord Jesus, giving thanks to God and the Father by Him.*
> —Colossians 3:17

Success is in your hand, brethren. Use it for His glory.

Yours in Christ,

Fear God

Dear Friends,

Many times, the word "fear" carries a negative connotation referring to people who withdraw or hide from something or someone. The word "fear" is used in the Bible and it comes from the Greek word "phóbos." It is commonly used in a positive way in the Scriptures, and it more accurately describes reverential awe, honor and veneration for God.

And I saw another angel fly in the midst of Heaven, having the everlasting gospel to preach unto them that dwell on the Earth, and to every nation, and kindred, and tongue, and people, saying with a loud voice, fear God, and give glory to Him; for the hour of His judgment is come: and worship Him that made Heaven, and Earth, and the sea, and the fountains of waters.
—Revelation 14:6-7

We have to remember that God is love, and there is no reason to be afraid of God, because His intentions and plans for us are always good.

For I know the thoughts that I think toward you, says the Lord, thoughts of peace and not of evil, to give you a future and a hope.
—Jeremiah 29:11

Unfortunately, many Church folks (by the influence of the enemy) have made the Father out to be a bad guy. He is characterized as the old gray haired man who is looking down from Heaven waiting for us to make a mistake; and when we do, God is going to hit us with a large flyswatter or strike us down with lightning. It's these type of false accusations made against God that have been adopted by Church folks and the secular world, because they don't know Him intimately. These people know the pages of the Book, but they don't know the Author of the Book. They know His principles, but they don't know the Creator of those principles. God is good, and there is no reason to be fearful of a good Father.

> *Truly God is good to Israel, even to such as are of a clean heart.*
> —Psalm 73:1

Remember when Jesus was on the Earth? He was the embodiment, and the perfect representation of God. He said:

> *Jesus saith unto him, have I been so long time with you, and yet hast thou not known me, Philip? He that hath seen Me hath seen the Father; and how sayest thou then, show us the Father?*
> —John 14:9

Children are generally very leery of strangers, but innocent children were drawn to Jesus and He blessed them:

> *And they brought young children to him, that he should touch them: and his disciples rebuked those that brought them. But when Jesus saw it, he was much displeased, and said unto them, suffer the little children to come unto Me, and forbid them not: for of such is the kingdom of God. Verily I say unto you, whosoever shall not receive the kingdom of God as a little child, he shall not enter therein. And He took them up in His arms, put His hands upon them, and blessed them.*
> —Mark 10:13-16

So, let's be like the children and run to the Lord and let Him take us in His arms, because He has nothing but blessings for us.

Yours in Christ,

Love is an Action Word that Protects the Truth

Dear Friends,

There are many examples of love in action. I would like to briefly share them, because there still might be those who believe the myth that God strikes people down with lightning; or that God inflicts people with debilitating diseases in order to teach them a lesson. This unscriptural thinking is so far removed from love, and unfortunately, many Church folks believe it. But let's see what love will do according to the Scriptures.

Love is unstoppable, cannot fail or be defeated (1 Corinthians 13:8); and anyone who stands in the way of the agenda of love or tries to impede the progress of the agenda of love will be moved out of the way. Jesus said:

If you love me, keep my commandments.
—John 14:15

He didn't say this to be a mean dictator, but His commandments are for our protection and maintaining right standing with Him. There are times when God extends grace and mercy to us for a period of time, so that we can get back in line with His Will, but those who fall outside of His commandments and grace are subjected to another fate. Some might call that tough love.

Examples of Love in Action

First, satan was kicked out of Heaven. Jesus said:

And He said unto them, I beheld satan as lightning fall from Heaven.
—Luke 10:18

He didn't say that satan was asked to leave. He said that he fell like lightning. Anyone who has ever seen lightning knows that lightning appears and disappears in a flash. So satan was forcefully kicked out of Heaven, by love.

Second, Adam and Eve were kicked out of the Garden of Eden by God for their disobedience:

Therefore the LORD God sent him forth from the Garden of Eden, to till the ground from whence he was taken. So He drove out the man; and He placed at the east of the Garden of Eden Cherubims, and a flaming sword which turned every way, to keep the way of the tree of life.
—Genesis 3:23-24

Disobedience always costs us something, and in this instance Adam and Eve were banished from the Garden of Eden.

Third, Jesus cast the cattle buyers, dove sellers and the moneychangers out of the Temple.

The Passover of the Jews was soon approaching, and Jesus went up to Jerusalem. People were in the Temple selling oxen, sheep, and doves; and the moneychangers were doing business. When He had made a whip of cords, He drove them all out of the temple, with the sheep and the oxen, and poured out the changers' money and overturned the tables.
—John 2:13-16.

Jesus forcefully removed those who were using the Temple of Herod the Great (a sacred place to commune with God) as a cattle, sheep and dove bazaar.

Jewish pilgrims traveled from different countries to Jerusalem for the Passover. They had Greek, Roman or other currency, so the moneychangers converted their money (for a fee). But when Jesus arrived at the Temple, He realized a few things.

- The Temple was a scared place where God and His people communed.

- His people needed to be ritually clean (washed and bathed ceremonially) in order to pray. Imagine how cluttered and nasty the outer courts of the Temple must have been with cattle, sheep and doves all around the House of Prayer.

- In Mark's account of the story, this was the second time that Jesus had to cleanse the Temple. These moneychangers were interfering with the presence of God and His people, so Jesus cleansed the Temple of the problem.

Fourth, Jesus said that God forsook Him on the cross.

And at the ninth hour Jesus cried with a loud voice, saying, Eloi, Eloi, lama sabachthani? Which is, being interpreted, My God, my God, why hast thou forsaken Me?
—Mark 15:34

Did Jesus lie? What happened? Jesus became sin, and God was turning His back on sin.

For He hath made Him to be sin for us, who knew no sin; that we might be made the righteousness of God in Him.
—2 Corinthians 5:21

That is the nature of God to turn His back on sin, and what happened with Jesus crying out to God on the cross manifested the holiness of God to remain pure and separated from sin. God can't bless sin, but He does know each of our hearts, and He does extend grace and mercy accordingly. Thank God for it, because without it, we would be in trouble.

Other examples of love (that cannot be stopped) in action:

- Ananias and Sapphira dropped dead when they lied to the Holy Ghost. Acts 5:1-11.
- Paul smote Elymas the sorcerer with blindness because he tried to stop the preaching of the Gospel and the conversion of Sergius Paulus. Acts 13.
- Jesus said that if someone offends you, go to that person to reconcile. If that doesn't work, then take some witnesses. If that doesn't work, then take the offender before the Church, and then the last resort is to kick the unrepentant out. Matthew 18:15-17.
- Paul told the Roman Christians to *"Mark those who cause division and have no company with them."* Romans 16:17.

Remember, that God is love, and He cannot be destroyed or stopped. Further, love (God) will not kill you, because it is the enemy who comes to steal, to kill and to destroy (John 10:10). But if you go head-to-head against love (if grace and mercy aren't still protecting you), you will be removed from being a distraction.

For they have sown the wind, and they shall reap the whirlwind.
—Hosea 8:7(a)

Just remain on the right side of God/Love and you will be led in the right direction in all things.

Yours in Christ,

WE ARE ALL GOD'S CHILDREN: THE ECUMENICAL LIE

Dear Friends,

We have been seeing a huge move, by some, to unite everyone in the religious world. I'm all for unity, but I prefer to see unity in context with the Scriptures. Many people believe that we are all brothers and sisters, and God is everyone's Father. I believe that God Almighty created every human being and every race of people.

> *And (God) hath made of one blood all nations of men for to dwell on all the face of the Earth, and hath determined the times before appointed, and the bounds of their habitation.*
> —Acts 17:26

But everyone is not God's child. According to the Scriptures, one must accept Christ, and He will make you a child of God.

> *But as many as received him (Jesus), to them gave He power to become the sons of God, even to them that believe on His name.*
> —John 1:12

The Word of the Lord also teaches us:

> *While He was still talking to the multitudes, behold, His mother and brothers stood outside, seeking to speak with Him. Then one said to Him, "Look, Your mother and Your brothers are standing outside, seeking to speak with You." But He answered and said to the one who told Him, "Who is My mother and who are My brothers?" And He stretched out His*

hand toward His disciples and said, "Here are My mother and My brothers! For whoever does the will of My Father in Heaven is My brother and sister and mother.
—Matthew 12:46-50

According to Jesus, being God's child and Jesus' brother is an exclusive group, and He specifically mentions doing the Will of God as the prerequisite. Jesus is definitely speaking contrary to the ecumenical rhetoric that we are all God's children regardless of our different religious beliefs.

So the question is: who is correct? Is the ecumenical movement correct and is Jesus lying? Or is Jesus correct and is the ecumenical movement lying?

...let God be true but every man a liar.
—Romans 3:4

Cults

There is only the One True God: Jesus Christ; and then there are the other beliefs. Whether it's the Jehovah's Witnesses, Mormonism, Catholicism, Buddhism, Islam, or any other set of beliefs, if the Lord Jesus Christ and His Words are not the foundation and central theme of the belief, then it isn't of God. But we live in the Age of Tolerance, where absolute truths are despised, and sparing people's feelings is more important than telling the truth.

"Interfaith" conferences and meetings are being promoted and held by groups such as: "Interfaith Alliance" and "Human Rights First" all over the world. The ecumenical religious leaders want us to focus on our religious points of agreement. How can we do this if we all disagree on the pre-eminence of the central person of Jesus Christ and His doctrines?

Additionally, the fight to stamp out and discredit the purity of Christ and His true body of believers has been an ongoing thing that rears its ugly head from time to time. In 2007, Pope Benedict XVI approved a document stating that other Christian communities are either defective or not true churches, and that Catholicism provides the only true path to salvation. I remember when this story was reported, and hardly any of God's people were outraged and vocal. If a prominent Christian leader would have vocalized this same sentiment towards Catholicism, then the world would have been in an absolute uproar. But, the politically-correct police only work in one direction: to protect ecumenicalism.

Recently, Pope Francis was named "New World Pope" by Time Magazine; and he has made it clear that he is going to make ecumenical outreach a top priority. His belief that all religions are equally valid paths to the same destination is being taught in some Christian and non-Christian circles worldwide. This is error and the true people of God should never tolerate this for one minute. This "interfaith movement" is being promoted by many charitable foundations, and has international backing.

Don't be fooled by this charade. The Gospel message is so simple, so let's stay on the straight and narrow with Jesus Christ as our foundation.

The "When the Praises Go Up, the Blessings Come Down" and the "Praise Confuses the Enemy" Lies

Dear Friends,

I would like to share a Biblical account with you, and I also want to dispel a myth that some preachers are perpetuating in the Body of Christ regarding this particular misinterpretation.

Look at the following Biblical account:

And all Judah stood before the LORD, with their little ones, their wives, and their children. Then upon Jahaziel the son of Zechariah, the son of Benaiah, the son of Jeiel, the son of Mattaniah, a Levite of the sons of Asaph, came the Spirit of the LORD in the midst of the congregation; And he said, Hearken ye, all Judah, and ye inhabitants of Jerusalem, and thou king Jehoshaphat, Thus saith the LORD unto you, Be not afraid nor dismayed by reason of this great multitude; for the battle is not yours, but God's. Tomorrow go ye down against them: behold, they come up by the cliff of Ziz; and ye shall find them at the end of the brook, before the wilderness of Jeruel. Ye shall not need to fight in this battle: set yourselves, stand ye still, and see the salvation of the LORD with you, O Judah and Jerusalem: fear not, nor be dismayed; tomorrow go out against them: for the LORD will be with you. And Jehoshaphat bowed his head with his face to the ground: and all Judah and the inhabitants of Jerusalem fell before the LORD, worshipping the LORD. And the Levites, of the children of the Kohathites, and of the children of the Korhites, stood up to praise the

LORD God of Israel with a loud voice on high. And they rose early in the morning, and went forth into the wilderness of Tekoa: and as they went forth, Jehoshaphat stood and said, Hear me, O Judah, and ye inhabitants of Jerusalem; Believe in the LORD your God, so shall ye be established; believe his prophets, so shall ye prosper. And when he had consulted with the people, he appointed singers unto the LORD, and that should praise the beauty of holiness, as they went out before the army, and to say, Praise the LORD; for his mercy endureth forever. And when they began to sing and to praise, the LORD set ambushments against the children of Ammon, Moab, and mount Seir, which were come against Judah; and they were smitten. For the children of Ammon and Moab stood up against the inhabitants of mount Seir, utterly to slay and destroy them: and when they had made an end of the inhabitants of Seir, every one helped to destroy another.
—2 Chronicles 20:13-23

Some people believe, like the title of this letter, that praise confuses the enemy. That is completely erroneous and found nowhere in Scripture. But the claim that "praise confuses the enemy" or "when the praises go up the blessings come down" is falsely founded upon this Biblical account. Praise is not what won the victory for the children of Israel in this story. What happened? The Spirit of the Lord came upon Jahaziel and spoke through him to the children of Israel saying:

"Be not afraid nor dismayed by reason of this great multitude; for the battle is not yours, but God's. Tomorrow go ye down against them: behold, they come up by the cliff of Ziz; and ye shall find them at the end of the brook, before the wilderness of Jeruel. Ye shall not need to fight in this battle: set yourselves, stand ye still, and see the salvation of the LORD with you, O Judah and Jerusalem: fear not, nor be dismayed; tomorrow go out against them: for the LORD will be with you."
—2 Chronicles 20:15-17

When Jahaziel spoke these comforting words of deliverance from the Lord, then the people began to worship and praise the Lord. Their act of faith (in the midst of a physical battle against their enemies, they praised and worshiped God rather than picking up weapons) caused God to move on the children of Israel's behalf, and the enemies began to fight and to kill one another. In other words, they responded in faith to the spoken Word of the Lord, and God responded to their faith by sending the ambushments against the enemy. So praise is not the answer, but faith in and obedience to God's Word is the answer.

We have to be able to see these principles, so that we will know how to respond to God in particular situations. Praising God is a wonderful, spiritual experience. But it doesn't answer every problem. We don't want to be accused of being ignorant regarding the Scriptures, like Paul said regarding Israel:

They have a zeal for God, but not according to knowledge.
—Romans 10:2

So remember, let's follow the Word in context, and not what we think, how we feel, or what someone told us. Obedience to His Word is the only thing that assures us of the victory.

Yours in Christ,

Sinners Saved by Grace

Dear Friends,

I have heard so many Christians say to me over the years, "You know, Brian, we are just sinners saved by grace." When I hear that, it really bothers me, because it goes against everything the Scriptures teach us about our identity in Christ. How can you be a sinner and a believer in Christ Jesus at the same time? A believer can sin, but that doesn't mean that the believer is a sinner. You are either a sinner, or you are saved by grace. You can't be both; at least not at the same time. You can't be "A" and "Non-A" at the same time. It can't be raining and not raining at the same time. A sinner and saved person are "A" and "Non-A," respectively.

Don't sell yourself short and claim things about yourself that are not true. If you have accepted Jesus Christ as your Lord and Savior, then you are no longer a sinner.

> *Therefore if any man be in Christ, he is a new creature: old things are passed away; behold all things are become new.*
> —2 Corinthians 5:17

You might have even sinned since you accepted Christ, but that doesn't make you a sinner. You are a new creature according to the Scriptures. The word "new" comes from the Greek word "kainos" and the word "creature" comes from the Greek word "ktisis." Those two words together connote the idea of being a brand new creature who never existed before. So if the original text says that who you are now never existed before, then how can you now be a sinner and saved by grace? The simple answer and the good news is that you can't be both and you aren't both. You are simply saved by grace if Jesus is your Lord.

Stay encouraged and blessed.

Yours in Christ,

WHO IS THE ANTI-CHRIST?

Dear Friends,

I am amazed at how many Christians are so easily deceived about the end times. I think during the 2012 Presidential campaign, more unlearned Christians were afraid that President Obama was the anti-Christ, than at any other campaign that I can remember. In the 1980's, people were fearful that either Ronald Reagan or Gorbachev was the antichrist. Before that, people were speculating that JFK was going to resurrect from the dead and be the antichrist. More recently, Bill Gates was a popular candidate for being the antichrist, as well as George W. Bush and a few others.

The antichrist discussion isn't something to lose a lot of sleep over. But we can at least clear up the misconceptions about any politicians, or any other celebrity being the antichrist, because 1 John 2 says there were "many antichrists" and a "spirit of antichrist" already at work in the 1st century. An antichrist is also defined in the Bible as someone who denies that Jesus is the Christ. So an antichrist isn't just one person of whom we should be afraid.

The Bible also calls the antichrist:

- little horn; Daniel 7:8.
- beast; Revelation 13:1.
- man of sin...son of perdition; 2 Thessalonians 2:3.
- mystery of iniquity; 2 Thessalonians 2:7.
- wicked; 2 Thessalonians 2:8.

The "son of perdition" is the term that gives most people trouble, because it sounds as if it is only one person. But Jesus used the same term when referring to Judas Iscariot (John 17:12). The term is actually a principle (illustrating a supposed friend who is actually a deceiver) rather than a designation for one man to rule the world in the future.

John's epistles used the term antichrist, which alluded to those who were in the midst of the body of believers and later went out from them.

Little children, it is the last time: and as ye have heard that antichrist shall come, even now are there many antichrists; whereby we know that it is the last time. They went out from us, but they were not of us; for if they had been of us, they would no doubt have continued with us: but they went out, that they might be made manifest that they were not all of us.
—1 John 2:18-19

The antichrist had a deceptive nature, just like Judas. He was in the midst of the body of believers and turned evil. The books of Revelation and Daniel also call the antichrist a "beast." Daniel describes four beasts: a lion, a bear, a leopard, and a dragon-like beast with ten horns.
What are these beasts?

The fourth beast shall be the fourth kingdom upon the Earth.
—Daniel 7:23

So the antichrist is the beast, and the beast is a kingdom, not a man. This takes a little bit of cross-referencing to make the picture clearer. In 2 Thessalonians 2, "the man of sin," and the terms "the mystery of iniquity" and "wicked" can't be one man, because the mystery of iniquity was already manifest in the 1st century, and according to 2 Thessalonians 2:8, it would continue all the way until the visible return of Jesus Christ at the end of the age. How could that be one man? He would have to be over two thousand years old.

So, according to the Scriptures, the antichrist or the beast is a kingdom, not a person. So incorporate that Biblical principle into your end-time studies, and let's see where that leads you.

Yours in Christ,

Once Saved, Always Saved

Dear Friends,

Have you ever heard of the Once Saved, Always Saved (OSAS) doctrine? This is another one of the many false doctrines that causes a lot of division and confusion among the body of believers. Personally, I believe that this teaching says more than the proponents of the doctrine are admitting. The OSAS doctrine implies that no matter what you do and no matter how you live, God understands and He knows your heart; and you will always be in right standing with God. Although, God does know everyone's heart, He also knows that the unregenerate human heart/spirit is wicked.

> *And God saw that the wickedness of man was great in the earth, and that every imagination of the thoughts of his heart was only evil continually.*
> —Genesis 6:5

Once a person is spiritually born again, he/she is immediately and eternally saved. I believe this to be true, but you can't stop there. Stopping there confuses the doctrine, and it gives the illusion that all you have to do is say a simple prayer of repentance one time and you can live your life according to the way you see fit. I don't agree with that line of thinking, but the OSAS advocates espouse the acceptance of loose living rather than a separated life to God.

> *Follow peace with all men, and holiness, without which no man shall see the Lord.*
> —Hebrews 12:14

The common idea of the "Once, Saved Always Saved" proponents is that God is love (and He is), He knows my faults (and He does), and God will forgive me (and He will). But that is too open-ended and it leaves so much to be left to chance, misinterpretation, and heresy. These same people will claim freedom and liberty in Christ, and speak out against legalism (strict adherence, to law or prescription, especially to the letter rather than the spirit), and live their lives as if Jesus isn't their Lord and Savior. Now, I am in one hundred percent agreement with liberty in Christ and shunning legalism. But I also believe that obedience and holiness brings us closer to God and sin and rebellion takes us further away from God. Can sin eventually take you far enough from God so that you are lost forever? Many would say yes, but not for a believer. I totally disagree, because if you are willfully sinning and taking yourself further away from God, then I would question an individual's heart and salvation. Besides, we see the model on the cross what God will do to unrepentant sin. He forsakes and separates Himself from sin.

If you are a Christian, you have to be honest with yourself, and realize that your born-again experience does not exempt you from the ability to sin. You have the nature of God residing on the inside of you.

Whereby are given unto us exceeding great and precious promises: that by these ye might be partakers of the divine nature, having escaped the corruption that is in the world through lust.
—2 Peter 1:4

But any human being can be tempted and drawn away of their own lusts and enticed.

Let no man say when he is tempted, I am tempted of God: for God cannot be tempted with evil, neither tempteth he any man: but every man is tempted, when he is drawn away of his own lust, and enticed. Then when lust hath conceived, it bringeth forth sin: and sin, when it is finished, bringeth forth death.
—James 1:13-15

This is why God gave us the ability to make things right with Him through repentance, even after we get saved, because He knew that we have the ability to fail, as well as the ability to be contrite.

If we say that we have no sin, we deceive ourselves, and the truth is not in us. If we confess our sins, He is faithful and just to forgive us our sins and to cleanse us from all unrighteousness. If we say that we have not sinned, we make Him a liar, and His word is not in us.
—1 John 1:8-10

Anyone and anything, but God, can be lost. Just like you can lose the keys to your car, your rights and privileges by going to jail, your money, the trust of a loved one, you can also lose your salvation. Remember, you are still a free will, sovereign being with a choice. You can willingly blaspheme against the Holy Ghost, you can renounce Christ, or you choose a religion that worships a head of lettuce. Do you really believe that anyone who knowingly and willingly does any of those things will remain in right standing with God? I wonder what Judas Iscariot would say about this.

...but woe to that man by whom the Son of Man is betrayed! It would have been better for that man if he had not been born.
—Mark 14:21

What Jesus said doesn't sound like a blessing for Judas, and while no one was born again prior to the crucifixion of Christ, satan's fate and Judas' life were proof that anyone can fall from God's eternal grace. So let's not pretend that God didn't teach us about holiness, the straight and narrow, and judgment. God loves every one of us, but He wants us to come to Him and live for Him on His terms, not on our terms.

Yours in Christ,

Israel: God's Chosen People

Dear Friends,

I have had a lot of long and exhaustive discussions with Christians regarding the labeling of God's people. I know many Christians who wave Israeli flags and come to the nation of Israel's defense in almost every geo-political situation. They quote Scriptures about Israel:

> *Pray for the peace of Jerusalem: they shall prosper that love thee.*
> —Psalm 122:6

> *And I will bless them that bless thee (Abram), and curse him that curseth thee: and in thee shall all families of the Earth be blessed.*
> —Genesis 12:3

I am usually disheartened to have an intelligent conversation with Christians about this topic, because the discussions are rarely an interaction based upon the context of Scripture. Rather, they are primarily the basis of emotional pitches by some of today's most popular Evangelical preachers. People just parrot a few Scriptures (like the ones previously mentioned), but the well-meaning Christian who quotes their favorite preacher hasn't taken the time to be a student of the Scriptures to see if the context of what these preachers are saying is accurate.

Is the nation of Israel God's chosen people? According to the full context of the Scriptures, the answer is a resounding "NO!" I will explain my response with the Scriptures. Am I against the nation of Israel? Absolutely not! But I definitely am not an emotional Christian who listens to mainstream media personalities without verifying the information presented. Preachers are human and fallible just like me, so to repeat what they say without a true understanding and study of the Word on the subject is to knowingly do oneself a disservice. Again, the emotional people who engage in these types of discussions would say that I have made an anti-Semitic statement. The accusation would be ludicrous, and it has no credibility without Scriptural confirmation. So allow me to delve into the Scriptures to see if we can get to the bottom of this dilemma. Again, is the nation of Israel God's chosen people?

Abram, who later became Abraham, was the first of the three men named as the patriarchs of the Old Covenant with God. The three men were Abraham, his son Isaac, and Isaac's son Jacob. Hence, God was known as the God of Abraham, Isaac and Jacob.

Jacob's name was later changed to Israel after he wrestled with an angel. Israel means "Prince with God," and that is the first time the name "Israel" is mentioned in the Bible. A prince is a son of a king; remember that statement.

Jacob, or Israel, had twelve sons: Reuben, Simeon, Levi, Judah, Dan, Naphtali, Gad, Asher, Issachar, Zebulun, Joseph, and Benjamin; and these sons became the ancestors of twelve tribes. They went to Eygpt and were enslaved for many years, and then God sent them Moses as a deliverer.

And the Lord said to Moses, "When you go back to Egypt, see that you do all those wonders before Pharaoh which I have put in your hand. But I will harden his heart, so that he will not let the people go. Then you shall say to Pharaoh, "Thus says the Lord: Israel is My son, My firstborn. So I say to you, let My son go that he may serve Me. But if you refuse to let him go, indeed I will kill your son, your firstborn."
—Exodus 4:21-23

Wait a minute! I thought Israel was a person formerly known as Jacob who died many years prior to this incident. But in this account God told Moses to tell Pharaoh that the nation, whose name is Israel, is His Son. Again, remember that Israel means "Prince with God," so we can see that God has a special relationship with Israel (the man), and now Israel (the nation).

Now let's fast forward to the New Testament when Jesus was born and the evil King Herod wanted to kill all of the male children two years old and younger. So God warned Joseph to take Mary and Jesus to Egypt until further notice.

> *Now when they had departed, behold, an angel of the Lord appeared to Joseph in a dream, saying, "Arise, take the young Child and His mother, flee to Egypt, and stay there until I bring you word; for Herod will seek the young Child to destroy Him." When he arose, he took the young Child and His mother by night and departed for Egypt, and was there until the death of Herod, that it might be fulfilled which was spoken by the Lord through the prophet, saying, "Out of Egypt I called My Son."*
> —Matthew 2:13-15

Wait a minute! The Scripture clearly points to Moses and the children of Israel in Egypt. But the Gospel writer is attributing this as a prophetic word to be fulfilled in Jesus?

> *When Israel was a child, I loved him, and out of Egypt I called My son.*
> —Hosea 11:1

So, if we are following this correctly, "Israel" was a person formerly known as Jacob. Then, "Israel" was the nation of people who descended from Jacob's children who were enslaved in Egypt. Then, Matthew quoted Hosea who was speaking (in a historical context) about the children of Israel in Egypt; but the manifestation of the prophecy came to pass in Jesus. Again, let's remember that Israel means "Prince with God." Let's also remember that a prince is the son of a king.

So it looks as though this name "Israel" is more than just a name. It appears to be a covenant designation whose ultimate fulfillment was in Jesus Christ, the Son of God. But let's continue to look into the matter. What else can we learn about "Israel" from the Scriptures?

> *Now Joseph had a dream, and he told it to his brothers; and they hated him even more...Then he dreamed still another dream and told it to his brothers.*
> —Genesis 37:5, 9

> *Now the Midianites had sold him (Joseph) in Egypt to Potiphar, an officer of Pharaoh and captain of the guard.*
> —Genesis 37:36

Joseph had dreams and went to Egypt, and nearly two thousand years later we see another Joseph had dreams and went to Egypt.

> *Now when they had departed, behold, an angel of the Lord appeared to Joseph in a dream, saying, "Arise, take the young Child and His mother, flee to Egypt, and stay there until I bring you word; for Herod will seek the young Child to destroy Him."*
> —Matthew 2:13

Of Israel, God's Word says:

> *You have brought a vine out of Egypt.*
> —Psalm 80:8

Jesus says of Himself:

> *I am the true vine, and My Father is the vinedresser.*
> —John 15:1

Of Israel, Isaiah said:

> *But thou, Israel, art my servant, Jacob whom I have chosen, the seed of Abraham my friend.*
> —Isaiah 41:8

Matthew speaking of Jesus wrote:

> *Then the Pharisees went out, and held a council against Him, how they might destroy Him. But when Jesus knew it, He withdrew himself from thence: and great multitudes followed Him, and He healed them all; and charged them that they should not make Him known: that it might be fulfilled which was spoken by Esaias the prophet, saying, behold My servant, whom I have chosen; My beloved, in whom My soul is well*

pleased: I will put My Spirit upon Him, and He shall show judgment to the Gentiles.
—Matthew 12:14-18

Paul confirms the words of Isaiah:

Now to Abraham and His seed were the promises made. He saith not, and to seeds, as of many; but as of one, and to thy seed, which is Christ.
—Galatians 3:16

And if ye be Christ's, then are ye Abraham's seed, and heirs according to the promise.
—Galatians 3:29

So let's recap this new paradigm in 21st century Christianity. Jacob's name was changed to Israel, which means "Prince with God." Then his twelve sons went to Egypt, became slaves for many years, and God called that nation of people "Israel." Then the prophecies of the Old Testament prophets and the references made to the nation of "Israel" were fulfilled in Jesus. If these prophecies and references were fulfilled in Jesus, then that makes perfect sense, because Israel means "Prince with God" and Jesus is the Son of God, and a prince is a son of a king.

Sing praises to God, sing praises: sing praises unto our King, sing praises. For God is the King of all the Earth: sing ye praises with understanding.
—Psalm 47:6-7

So God is the King, and Jesus is the Prince or the Son of God; hence, He is the Israel of God (Prince of God). Christ is one with His Body of believers, and the Scriptures state:

For as many as are led by the Spirit of God, they are the sons of God. For ye have not received the spirit of bondage again to fear; but ye have received the Spirit of adoption, whereby

we cry, Abba, Father. The Spirit itself beareth witness with our spirit, that we are the children of God: and if children, then heirs; heirs of God, and joint-heirs with Christ; if so be that we suffer with Him, that we may be also glorified together.
Romans 8:14-17.

So if Jesus is the Son of God, then He is an heir of God, and so are His believers joint-heirs with Christ. We are one with God in Christ Jesus, and we (covenant believers in Jesus Christ) are the Israel of God, because of Christ. I know that goes against ninety-five percent of Church theology out there; but I defy anyone to challenge my conclusion and prove me wrong. The Scriptures are in harmony with my statement, but I will continue to make the case.

NATURAL ISRAEL AND SPIRITUAL ISRAEL

If you have read this far and you still believe that the children of Israel (the nation of people in the Middle East) are the chosen people of God, then you aren't following the principles and the parallels that are being presented. The "Israel" to which I am referring is a spiritual Israel of God in Christ Jesus. A native-born Israelite doesn't equate to one being a part of the spiritual Israel of God.

Then came to Him His mother and His brethren, and could not come at Him for the press. And it was told Him by certain which said, Thy mother and Thy brethren stand without, desiring to see Thee. And He answered and said unto them, My mother and My brethren are these which hear the word of God, and do it.
—Luke 8:19-21

Jesus is clear regarding those who are members of His spiritual family. He didn't mention that He was a Nazarene or a Bethlehemite. He never mentioned the land mass of Israel or the Temple of Jerusalem. He only mentioned that those who obey His Father are members of His spiritual family.

Look at another account with Jesus and a group of Jewish people:

And ye shall know the truth, and the truth shall make you free. They answered Him, We be Abraham's seed, and were

> *never in bondage to any man: how sayest Thou, Ye shall be made free? Jesus answered them, Verily, verily, I say unto you, Whosoever committeth sin is the servant of sin. And the servant abideth not in the house for ever: but the Son abideth ever. If the Son therefore shall make you free, ye shall be free indeed. I know that ye are Abraham's seed; but ye seek to kill me, because My Word hath no place in you. I speak that which I have seen with My Father: and ye do that which ye have seen with your father. They answered and said unto him, Abraham is our father. Jesus saith unto them, If ye were Abraham›s children, ye would do the works of Abraham. But now ye seek to kill me, a man that hath told you the truth, which I have heard of God: this did not Abraham. Ye do the deeds of your father. Then said they to Him, We be not born of fornication; we have one Father, even God. Jesus said unto them, If God were your Father, ye would love Me: for I proceeded forth and came from God; neither came I of Myself, but He sent Me. Why do ye not understand My speech? even because ye cannot hear My word. Ye are of your father the devil, and the lusts of your father ye will do. He was a murderer from the beginning, and abode not in the truth, because there is no truth in him. When he speaketh a lie, he speaketh of his own: for he is a liar, and the father of it.*
>
> —John 8:32-44

I wonder if the Evangelicals or any Jewish person will call Jesus an anti-Semite for saying that these Israelites were children of the devil. They claimed to be Abraham's seed, and in the natural, they were correct. But spiritually, Jesus pinned their connection to their spiritual father, satan (the father of lies).

> *For he is not a Jew, which is one outwardly; neither is that circumcision, which is outward in the flesh: but he is a Jew, which is one inwardly; and circumcision is that of the heart, in the spirit, and not in the letter; whose praise is not of men, but of God.*
>
> —Romans 2:28-29

Paul confirms what Jesus said about the natural lineage not being a determining factor of a person being a spiritual Jew or of God's spiritual Israel. God places a tremendous emphasis on the spiritual well-being of a person and a person's spiritual relationship with Him. Jesus said:

> *Jesus saith unto her, Woman, believe Me, the hour cometh, when ye shall neither in this mountain, nor yet at Jerusalem, worship the Father. Ye worship ye know not what: We know what We worship: for salvation is of the Jews. But the hour cometh, and now is, when the true worshippers shall worship the Father in spirit and in truth: for the Father seeketh such to worship Him. God is a Spirit: and they that worship Him must worship Him in spirit and in truth.*
> —John 4:21-24

Remember, Rahab and Ruth were both Gentile women, but their spiritual faith in the God of Heaven allowed them to be grafted into God's spiritual Israel. Additionally, Cornelius (Acts 10) was a devout Gentile whose well-meaning heart touched God to the point that He sent Peter to minister the Gospel message to him. God looks at the heart, not at the outside.

THE MYSTERY OF CHRIST

What is the Mystery of Christ? In a few of his letters, Paul makes a reference to this mystery.

> *Now to Him who is able to establish you according to my gospel and the preaching of Jesus Christ, <u>according to the revelation of the **mystery** kept secret since the world began but now made manifest, and by the prophetic Scriptures made known to all nations, according to the commandment of the everlasting God, for obedience to the faith</u>.*
> —Romans 16:25-26

*In Him we have redemption through His blood, the forgiveness of sins, according to the riches of His grace which He made to abound toward us in all wisdom and prudence, <u>having made known to us the **mystery** of His Will, according to His good pleasure which He purposed in Himself, that in the dispensation of the fullness of the times He might gather together in one all things in Christ, both which are in Heaven and which are on Earth—in Him</u>. In Him also we have obtained an inheritance, being predestined according to the purpose of Him who works all things according to the counsel of His will, that we who first trusted in Christ should be to the praise of His glory. In Him you also trusted, after you heard the word of truth, the gospel of your salvation; in whom also, having believed, you were sealed with the Holy Spirit of promise, who is the guarantee of our inheritance until the redemption of the purchased possession, to the praise of His glory.*
—Ephesians 1:7-14

Therefore remember that you, once Gentiles in the flesh—who are called Uncircumcision by what is called the Circumcision made in the flesh by hands— that at that time you were without Christ, being aliens from the commonwealth of Israel and strangers from the covenants of promise, having no hope and without God in the world. <u>But now in Christ Jesus you who once were far off have been brought near by the blood of Christ. For He Himself is our peace, who has made both (Jewish and Gentile believers in Christ) one, and has broken down the middle wall of separation, having abolished in His flesh the enmity, that is, the law of commandments contained in ordinances, so as to create in Himself one new man from the two</u>, thus making peace, and <u>that He might reconcile them both (Jewish and Gentile believers in Christ) to God in one body through the cross</u>, thereby putting to death the enmity. And He came and preached peace to you who were afar off and to those who were near. <u>For through Him we both (Jewish and Gentile believers in Christ) have access by one Spirit to the Father</u>. Now, therefore, you are no longer strangers and foreigners, but fellow citizens with the saints and members of the household of God, having been built on the foundation *of the apostles and prophets, Jesus Christ Himself being the chief cornerstone, in whom the whole building, being fitted together, grows into a holy temple in the Lord, in whom you also are being built together for a dwelling place of God in the Spirit.*

—Ephesians 2:11-22

*For this reason I, Paul, the prisoner of Christ Jesus for you Gentiles—if indeed you have heard of the dispensation of the grace of God which was given to me for you, how that <u>by revelation He made known to me the **mystery** (as I have briefly written already, by which, when you read, you may understand my knowledge in the mystery of Christ), which in other ages was not made known to the sons of men, as it has now been revealed by the Spirit to His holy apostles and prophets: that the Gentiles should be fellow heirs, of the same body, and partakers of His promise in Christ through the gospel</u>, of which I became a minister according to the gift of the grace of God given to me by the effective working of His power.*

—Ephesians 3:1-7

<u>*The **mystery** which has been hidden from ages and from generations, but now has been revealed to His saints.*</u> *To them God willed to make known what are the riches of the glory of this mystery among the Gentiles:* <u>*which is Christ in you, the hope of glory.*</u>

—Colossians 1:26-27

In short, these Scriptures pinpoint the main answer that is confusing so many people. Look at all of the underlined verses. <u>The mystery of Christ is that believing Jews and believing Gentiles are one spiritual body of believers in Christ Jesus, called Israel</u>. So people can stop looking to the land formerly called Canaan for the chosen people. Some of God's chosen people are there, because Messianic Jews have accepted Jesus Christ as the promised Messiah. But God's spiritual Israel is all over the world worshipping God in spirit and in truth.

God bless Israel!

Yours in Christ,

Rapture Ready

Dear Friends,

I don't want to offend anyone or give the impression that I don't care about the Word of God. But honestly, who cares when the catching away (the Rapture) of the saints will occur? We know that Jesus' return was referenced more than once in the Bible. But some Church folks can go to the extreme.

> *And when He had spoken these things, while they beheld, He was taken up; and a cloud received him out of their sight. And while they looked steadfastly toward Heaven as He went up, behold, two men stood by them in white apparel; which also said, Ye men of Galilee, why stand ye gazing up into Heaven? this same Jesus, which is taken up from you into Heaven, shall so come in like manner as ye have seen Him go into Heaven.*
> —Acts 1:9-11.

> *For the Lord Himself shall descend from Heaven with a shout, with the voice of the archangel, and with the trump of God: and the dead in Christ shall rise first: Then we which are alive and remain shall be caught up together with them in the clouds, to meet the Lord in the air: and so shall we ever be with the Lord. Wherefore comfort one another with these words. But of the times and the seasons, brethren, ye have no need that I write to you. For yourselves know that the day of the Lord so cometh like a thief in the night. For when they shall say, Peace and safety; then cometh sudden destruction upon them, as travail upon a woman with child; and they shall not escape. But you brethren are not in darkness, that that day should overtake you as a thief.*
> —1 Thessalonians 4:16-5:4

It will happen when it happens. I don't get excited about it or continue to think about it at length like a lot of people do. Personally, it's like the sunrise. It's going to happen eventually whether I'm conscious about it, eagerly anticipating its arrival, or not. I just continue to live life and the other things will take care of themselves.

So family, let's unpack our spiritual bags and be busy about our Father's business right here and now on the Earth. We have a lot of light that needs to shine, a lot of seeds that need to be sown, and a lot of salt that needs to preserve the right things in our society. Let's focus on that, and the Lord will be pleased. If He comes today, will you be ready? If He comes in a hundred years, will you be ready? If He comes sooner or later, will He find faith in the Earth? Will He find you working for the Kingdom? Let's focus on getting God's work done, and let's focus less on going to Heaven and leaving our Earthly missions undone.

I think many of us tend to forget that we are needed on Earth for a reason. Remember, this isn't about us, per se. It's about Him and His Kingdom. In that, we have a part to play for the greater good. Stay focused and encouraged.

Yours in Christ,

Faith is Action, Faith in Action

Dear Friends,

Are you one of those Christians who just confesses the Word, speaks the Word, and is always saying what God says regarding a situation? Are you a person of positive confession? Well, I do believe that we should speak in line with God's Word. In fact, that is what prayer is all about: wanting God's results to manifest in our lives according to His Will and Word.

What does the Word teach us about faith, action, and His Word?

What doth it profit, my brethren, though a man say he hath faith, and have not works? Can faith save him? If a brother or sister be naked, and destitute of daily food, And one of you say unto them, Depart in peace, be ye warmed and filled; notwithstanding ye give them not those things which are needful to the body; what doth it profit? Even so faith, if it hath not works, is dead, being alone. Yea, a man may say, Thou hast faith, and I have works: shew me thy faith without thy works, and I will shew thee my faith by my works. Thou believest that there is one God; thou doest well: the devils also believe, and tremble. But wilt thou know, O vain man, that faith without works is dead? Was not Abraham our father justified by works, when he had offered Isaac his son upon the altar? Seest thou how faith wrought with his works, and by works was faith made perfect? And the scripture was fulfilled which saith, Abraham believed God, and it was imputed unto him for righteousness: and he was called the Friend of God. Ye see then how that by works a man is justified, and not by faith only. Likewise also was not Rahab the harlot justified by

works, when she had received the messengers, and had sent them out another way? For as the body without the spirit is dead, so faith without works is dead also.
—James 2:14-26

First, you can't talk faith without having some corresponding action to confirm your confession. Don't be idle, you have to be working in faith and moving.

Why stand ye here all the day idle?
—Matthew 20:6

Second, faith believes and speaks in line with God's Word regardless of the circumstance.

We having the same spirit of faith, according as it is written, I believed, and therefore have I spoken; we also believe, and therefore speak.
—2 Corinthians 4:13

God gives life to the dead and calls those things which do not exist as though they did.
—Romans 4:17

While we look not at the things which are seen, but at the things which are not seen: for the things which are seen are temporal; but the things which are not seen are eternal.
—2 Corinthians 4:18

If thou faint in the day of adversity, thy strength (faith) is small.
—Proverbs 24:10

Third, faith remembers that God is always on the throne and working on your behalf. If you don't believe that God is there for you, then you might think that all hope is lost and you may decide to give up. Never take yourself out of the game of life.

Behold, He who keeps Israel shall neither slumber nor sleep.
—Psalms 121:4

Moses' Faith in Action

When Moses was leading the children of Israel out of Eygpt, he led them to the Red Sea. They were being chased by Pharaoh's army, and Moses assured them:

> *And Moses said to the people, "Do not be afraid. Stand still, and see the salvation of the Lord, which He will accomplish for you today. For the Egyptians whom you see today, you shall see again no more forever. The Lord will fight for you, and you shall hold your peace."*
> *—Exodus 14:13-14*

This was the first part of Moses' faith in action: he told the children of Israel that God will deliver and protect them.

> *And the Lord said to Moses, "Why do you cry to Me? Tell the children of Israel to go forward. But lift up your rod, and stretch out your hand over the sea and divide it. And the children of Israel shall go on dry ground through the midst of the sea.*
> *—Exodus 14:15-16*

This was God's instruction to Moses in response to His statement of faith regarding God protecting them from their enemy. As a result, God brought the manifestation.

> *Then Moses stretched out his hand over the sea; and the Lord caused the sea to go back by a strong east wind all that night, and made the sea into dry land, and the waters were divided.*
> *—Exodus 14:21*

All God needed was a faithful and obedient vessel. This is a good model for us to review and to superimpose over our own lives. We might not be leading a million people to the Promised Land, but we can use these principles of faith and obedience to gain victory in our own situations. When we obey the Word of the Lord, good things happen.

DAVID'S FAITH IN ACTION

This is a classic story of the decorated champion versus the undersized challenger. The mighty Philistine warrior, Goliath, challenged the children of Israel to send out a fighter. No one dared to challenge this giant, except a little boy named David.

> *But David said to Saul, "Your servant used to keep his father's sheep, and when a lion or a bear came and took a lamb out of the flock, I went out after it and struck it, and delivered the lamb from its mouth; and when it arose against me, I caught it by its beard, and struck and killed it. Your servant has killed both lion and bear; and this uncircumcised Philistine will be like one of them, seeing he has defied the armies of the living God." Moreover David said, "The Lord, who delivered me from the paw of the lion and from the paw of the bear, He will deliver me from the hand of this Philistine." And Saul said to David, "Go, and the Lord be with you!"*
>
> —1 Samuel 17:34-37

I believe that the faith of young David and Saul (for letting him fight) was the catalyst that brought victory to the children of Israel. David believed that if God delivered him and protected him before, that He would do it again.

> *We glory in tribulations also: knowing that tribulation worketh patience; and patience, experience; and experience, hope: and hope maketh not ashamed; because the love of God is shed abroad in our hearts by the Holy Ghost which is given unto us.*
>
> —Romans 5:3-5

Lord, Deliver Me From Church Folks

David drew faith from his past experiences to prepare his faith for the next battle with the seemingly impossible task of defeating the giant Philistine.

And the Philistine said to David, Come to me, and I will give thy flesh unto the fowls of the air, and to the beasts of the field. Then said David to the Philistine, Thou comest to me with a sword, and with a spear, and with a shield: but I come to thee in the name of the Lord of hosts, the God of the armies of Israel, whom thou hast defied. This day will the Lord deliver thee into mine hand; and I will smite thee, and take thine head from thee; and I will give the carcasses of the host of the Philistines this day unto the fowls of the air, and to the wild beasts of the earth; that all the earth may know that there is a God in Israel. And all this assembly shall know that the Lord saveth not with sword and spear: for the battle is the Lord's and he will give you into our hands. And it came to pass, when the Philistine arose, and came, and drew nigh to meet David, that David hastened, and ran toward the army to meet the Philistine. And David put his hand in his bag, and took thence a stone, and slang it, and smote the Philistine in his forehead, that the stone sunk into his forehead; and he fell upon his face to the earth. So David prevailed over the Philistine with a sling and with a stone, and smote the Philistine, and slew him; but there was no sword in the hand of David. Therefore David ran, and stood upon the Philistine, and took his sword, and drew it out of the sheath thereof, and slew him, and cut off his head therewith. And when the Philistines saw their champion was dead, they fled.

—1 Samuel 17:44-51

God is looking for obedient souls who will put their trust in God's Word. God is not impressed with degrees, wealth, status, and pedigrees. All he needs is for someone to have faith.

But without faith it is impossible to please him: for he that cometh to God must believe that he is, and that he is a rewarder of them that diligently seek him.

—Hebrews 11:6

SHADRACH, MESHACH, AND ABEDNEGO'S FAITH IN ACTION

The three Hebrew boys refused to bow before a pagan idol at King Nebuchadnezzar's command. They were believers in the God of Israel and they were willing to suffer punishment rather than forsake their God.

> *Nebuchadnezzar spoke, saying to them, "Is it true, Shadrach, Meshach, and Abed-Nego, that you do not serve my gods or worship the gold image which I have set up? Now if you are ready at the time you hear the sound of the horn, flute, harp, lyre, and psaltery, in symphony with all kinds of music, and you fall down and worship the image which I have made, good! But if you do not worship, you shall be cast immediately into the midst of a burning fiery furnace. And who is the god who will deliver you from my hands?"*
> —Daniel 3:14-15

Their spiritual and physical lives were in jeopardy. They had an immediate decision to make and they couldn't make the wrong choice.

> *Shadrach, Meshach, and Abed-Nego answered and said to the king, "O Nebuchadnezzar, we have no need to answer you in this matter. <u>If that is the case, our God whom we serve is able to deliver us from the burning fiery furnace, and He will deliver us from your hand, O king. But if not, let it be known to you</u>, O king, that we do not serve your gods, nor will we worship the gold image which you have set up."*
> —Daniel 3:16-18

Here is the faith of Shadrach, Meshach, and Abed-Nego, but many church folks misinterpret the context of their answer to the King. In the Daniel 3:16-18 Scriptures above, I have underlined the portions that have been confusing. Many Church folks interpret the verses to mean: <u>If that is the case</u> as "if you throw us in the fire" (which is the correct interpretation), and <u>But if not</u> as "if God doesn't deliver us out of the fire" (which is the incorrect interpretation). This incorrect interpretation leads people to believe that God might deliver the three Hebrew boys or He might not deliver them. It all just depends upon how God is feeling that day. This line of thinking carries on into some Church folks personal lives and they believe that God might or might not answer their prayers. He might or might not protect them, and He might or might not be with them, etc. That type of wavering thinking never produces positive results.

> *If any of you lack wisdom, let him ask of God, that giveth to all men liberally, and upbraideth not; and it shall be given him. But let him ask in faith, nothing wavering. For he that wavereth is like a wave of the sea driven with the wind and tossed. For let not that man think that he shall receive any thing of the Lord.*
> —James 1:5-7

So Daniel 3:16-18 should actually be interpreted:

> *"O Nebuchadnezzar, we have no need to answer you in this matter. If you do throw us in the furnace, our God whom we serve is able to deliver us from the burning fiery furnace, and He will deliver us from your hand, O king. But if you do not throw us in the furnace, let it be known to you, O king, that we do not serve your gods, nor will we worship the gold image which you have set up."*
> —Daniel 3:16-18

This is faith in action, because their words lined up with God being a deliverer and a protector. The King was true to his word and he threw the three Hebrew boys in the fire. But God protected them from all harm.

Allow these examples to serve as a model of how we should view God in our lives and how we should respond to a given situation in order to invoke His presence.

Yours in Christ,

WOMEN ARE THE WEAKER VESSEL

Dear Friends,

For thousands of years and in many cultures, women have been viewed as second-class citizens. Unfortunately, the Church has embraced this false view that is still keeping some women in bondage. Many people consider women to be weak according to the following Scripture:

> *Likewise, ye husbands, dwell with them according to knowledge, giving honor unto the wife, as unto the weaker vessel, and as being heirs together of the grace of life; that your prayers be not hindered.*
> —1 Peter 3:7

Well, to the unlearned who believe that women are weak, I will admit that I have a tremendous respect for women. Any person who can endure childbirth, monthly menstrual cycles, and a double-standard society, is a strong person. In the above-mentioned Scripture, Peter said that a man should give honor to his wife as if she was special, not weak. Treat her like you would treat a delicate and priceless piece of porcelain. This is how a woman of God should be honored, and Peter specifically used the word "honor" in the text. We don't honor weakness; we honor value, and women are illustrated in this verse as valuable, not as weaklings.

Additionally, whatever and whoever God makes is good.

> *So God created man in his own image, in the image of God created he him; male and female created he them. And God blessed them, and God said unto them, Be fruitful, and*

multiply, and replenish the earth, and subdue it: and have dominion over the fish of the sea, and over the fowl of the air, and over every living thing that moveth upon the earth. And God said, Behold, I have given you every herb bearing seed, which is upon the face of all the earth, and every tree, in the which is the fruit of a tree yielding seed; to you it shall be for meat. And to every beast of the earth, and to every fowl of the air, and to everything that creepeth upon the earth, wherein there is life, I have given every green herb for meat: and it was so. And God saw everything that he had made, and, behold, it was very good. And the evening and the morning were the sixth day.

—Genesis 1:27-31

If God created man in His image, and if God said that everything He created is good, and Eve came out of Adam (in God's image), then how are women weak? These are the questions that Church folks never reconcile. They hear a catchy phrase like, "women are the weaker vessel," and they mindlessly repeat it. It doesn't even have to be Scriptural. It just sounds Churchy, and Church folks parrot it.

Lord, Deliver Me From Church Folks!

Yours in Christ,

Spiritual Discernment

Dear Friends,

The human spirit is the part of the human existence that gets the least amount of attention, but it is the most important portion of the human existence. Why? It is because the Almighty Spirit Being (God) created the natural realm.

> *By faith we understand that the worlds were framed by the word of God, so that the things which are seen were not made of things which are visible.*
> —Hebrews 11:3

God also created the ability to discern His (Spirit) realm. Spiritual discernment is the ability to know information outside of the five basic natural senses (vision, touch, taste, smell, and hearing). It reveals the existence and/or source of the information, because everything that exists has a source.

When people say that the world happened by chance, that is an absurd statement. Just as a watch has a watchmaker, so does the Earth and humanity have a Creator. Agnostics and others argue that science created the worlds. Well, what is the origin of science? Science merely explains the creation process, and it confirms the existence of God. It doesn't eliminate God from the equation. Imagine a person walking up to a car and wondering how the car got there. Would it make sense to say that the car got there by chance or by science? Or imagine some spray-painted profanity on a building. Did that just happen to appear one evening? Or did someone put it there? Everything has a source whether it is good or bad.

Many people see the world through natural eyes, and there is nothing wrong with that. But when those natural eyes can only see the outer skin of the onion, and not the many layers beneath, then one will never be able to comprehend the underlying truth of a spiritual matter.

Here are a few Biblical examples of discernment:

When Jesus came into the region of Caesarea Philippi, He asked His disciples, saying, "Who do men say that I, the Son of Man, am?" So they said, "Some say John the Baptist, some Elijah, and others Jeremiah or one of the prophets." He said to them, "But who do you say that I am?" Simon Peter answered and said, "You are the Christ, the Son of the living God." Jesus answered and said to him, "Blessed are you, Simon Bar-Jonah, for flesh and blood has not revealed this to you, but My Father who is in Heaven."
—Matthew 16:13-17

This is a fine example of having knowledge that has never been taught on the Earth. Jesus confirmed that no human taught Peter the truth of Jesus' identity, but the information came straight from Heaven. This is important because the Bible teaches us that humans don't know everything (Deuteronomy 29:29), but God in His Sovereignty will reveal information, as He desires.

Now the king of Syria was making war against Israel; and he consulted with his servants, saying, "My camp will be in such and such a place." And the man of God sent to the king of Israel, saying, "Beware that you do not pass this place, for the Syrians are coming down there." Then the king of Israel sent someone to the place of which the man of God had told him. Thus he warned him, and he was watchful there, not just once or twice. Therefore the heart of the king of Syria was greatly troubled by this thing; and he called his servants and said to them, "Will you not show me which of us is for the king of Israel?" And one of his servants said, "None, my lord, O king; but

Elisha, the prophet who is in Israel, tells the king of Israel the words that you speak in your bedroom." So he said, "Go and see where he is, that I may send and get him." And it was told him, saying, Surely he is in Dothan." Therefore he sent horses and chariots and a great army there, and they came by night and surrounded the city. And when the servant of the man of God arose early and went out, there was an army, surrounding the city with horses and chariots. And his servant said to him, "Alas, my master! What shall we do?" So he answered, "Do not fear, for those who are with us are more than those who are with them." And Elisha prayed, and said, "LORD, I pray, open his eyes that he may see." Then the LORD opened the eyes of the young man, and he saw. And behold, the mountain was full of horses and chariots of fire all around Elisha.
—2 Kings 6:8-17

In this account, God is asked to open the young man's eyes. His physical eyes were opened and functioning properly, but the spiritual element of the situation needed to be revealed to the young man. When God intervened, then the young man (spiritually) saw that the battle was God's. Many times, things that are beyond human control happen. But that is when another plane of consciousness must be exercised: spiritual discernment.

From that time Jesus began to show to His disciples that He must go to Jerusalem, and suffer many things from the elders and chief priests and scribes, and be killed, and be raised the third day. Then Peter took Him aside and began to rebuke Him, saying, "Far be it from You, Lord; this shall not happen to You!" But He turned and said to Peter, "Get behind Me, Satan! You are an offense to Me, for you are not mindful of the things of God, but the things of men."
—Matthew 16:21-23

Although Jesus was conversing with Peter, He addressed satan. If Jesus was having a conversation with Peter then why did He address satan? Jesus knew that the source of anything that is contrary to the Will of God came from satan. Although the word or act may come through a human being, the root cause of it is either satanic or Godly, in principle. If humans could understand this, then we would stop fighting with one another. But satan is very deceptive. He knows that since he is a spirit being and invisible to the naked eye, natural people will blame natural elements (people) for his chicanery. Again, I am simply attempting to raise your awareness to the fact that we are not only dealing with elements with which we interact in the natural.

> *Fear not, Daniel, for from the first day that you set your mind and heart to understand and to humble yourself before your God, your words were heard, and I have come as a consequence of (and in response to) your words. But the prince of the kingdom of Persia withstood me for twenty-one days. Then Michael, one of the chief [of the celestial] princes, came to help me, for I remained there with the kings of Persia. Now I have come to make you understand what is to befall your people in the latter days, for the vision is for (many) days yet to come.*
>
> —Daniel 10:12-14

Daniel's answer to prayer was hindered for twenty-one days because of spiritual warfare that occurred somewhere between Heaven and Earth. This further confirms that everything that occurs or exists isn't always the result of human cause. I am reminding you to be mindful of the spirit realm. God, a Spirit being, created this natural world. Why would His spiritual fingerprint not be evident in His creation?

Here is another example of spiritual discernment in the Word of God:

> *He that has ears to hear, let him hear.*
>
> — Mark 7:16

Jesus was referring to a spiritual keenness that tunes to a frequency that everyone else might not be able to sense (similar to a dog's sense of hearing, but spiritually speaking).

1 Samuel 3:1-21 gives us the account of the spiritual discernment of a mentor (Eli) and a child (later to become the Prophet Samuel). Again, this is an example of keenness in the Spirit. Eli discerned that God was speaking to the child, and Eli taught the youngster how to listen to God speak and how to commune with Him. This is actually a great lesson to be learned by all of us: children can know God and fellowship with Him. God created children and He knows how to reach them on their level.

We should stop oversimplifying God to the children and allow them to walk in these Eli/Samuel-type examples. The interesting thing to note is that God called Samuel, pursued him, and the child responded. We shouldn't be so quick to discount some things that children say. Sure children have imaginations and make up things, but not always. Be discerning when it comes to children, because they are very innocent and many times they are very keen spiritually.

Yours in Christ,

Turn the Other Cheek

Dear Friends,

There is another misconception that needs to be addressed. This time it is the idea that Christ is passive and a coward, and that He taught His disciples to behave similarly. The premise for the accusation primarily comes from the following Scripture:

> *Ye have heard that it hath been said, An eye for an eye, and a tooth for a tooth: but I say unto you, That ye <u>resist</u> not evil: but whosoever shall smite thee on thy right cheek, turn to him the other also.*
> —Matthew 5:38-39

People assume these Scriptures are teaching us to be docile and passive. That is not the case. The word "resist" comes from the Greek word "antihistemi" which means to fiercely/violently oppose something, and to be determined to do everything possible within their power to defy it. So verse 39 could be more accurately stated:

> *But I say to you, do not fiercely/violently oppose and be determined to do everything possible within your power to defy the evil man (who injures you); but if anyone strikes you on the right jaw or cheek, turn to him the other one too.*
> —Matthew 5:39

The natural reaction when someone gets hit is retaliation. But Jesus teaches us not to lash out and repay evil for evil, rather to turn the other cheek. Now we have to reconcile this and get the context of the account, because to take physical abuse is one thing, but to ask for more abuse sounds very passive on the surface. What was Jesus really teaching us?

He was really teaching His disciples how to keep their composure, to be mentally strong, and how to overcome the opposition without resorting to violence. What are the main responses to opposition?

1. Retaliation.
2. Pacifism.
3. Non-Violent Resistance.

Human nature will typically take one of the first two responses without thinking about it. But the third is the one to which Jesus was referring. But we have a King James translation anomaly that makes the Scripture a bit unclear. From King James' standpoint, he wouldn't want to encourage his seventeenth-century subjects to get the idea to fiercely/violently oppose and be determined to do everything possible within their power to defy him. The ruler/subject relationship would be damaged and the king's authority would be severely compromised if he was violently opposed as the original Greek states. So, King James had the words "resist not" inserted during the translation process in order to quell any potential uprising or hostility that could occur.

So Jesus taught us that if someone hits you on the right cheek, don't retaliate, but turn the left cheek to him, as well. But why did He specifically call out the right cheek? Was this literal or symbolic? How does one strike another on the right cheek anyway? It can be done in one of two ways: with the attacker's open left hand, or the backside of the attacker's right hand (since most people are right-handed). Now, to get slapped is a disgrace, but to get a backhanded slap is an absolute insult. This is proven in Jewish Law; the fixed scale of compensation for certain acts of disgrace, i.e., a backhanded slap was double the penalty of a regular openhanded slap.

I believe the slap to which Jesus was referring was a symbolic teaching, rather than a literal one. I believe what Jesus was saying in Matthew 5:39 regarding the slapping and the turning of the cheek was if someone offends or insults you (backslaps your right cheek), don't retaliate and offend or insult him/her in return, but let him/her have the left cheek (let them insult you again), as well.

Why would you let someone insult you?

Answer not a fool according to his folly, lest thou also be like unto him.
—Proverbs 26:4

If an insult is the best attack that your opposition has against you, then you have already won the battle. When you don't respond to childish behavior in a childish manner, you are actually taking the moral high road, and you are showing the opposition that their weapons will not prosper against you. That is a position of strength, maturity, and intelligence.

A fool's wrath is quickly and openly known, but a prudent man ignores an insult.
—Proverbs 12:16

Blessed are ye, when men shall revile you, and persecute you, and shall say all manner of evil against you falsely, for my sake. Rejoice, and be exceeding glad: for great is your reward in Heaven: for so persecuted they the prophets which were before you.
—Matthew 5:11-12

In order to walk in this level of discipline, you have to let go of your pride, and realize that people who have low self-esteem are the ones who pick on people and cast unnecessary insults. It's a challenge to your ego to let someone insult you, and it's also a faith walk to be able to ignore the insults, and respond as the Lord has instructed us. But Christ wouldn't have taught us this lesson if He didn't think we could actually do it. We can do it, but we can't do it without Him.

In my experiences, when I've debated or discussed the Scriptures, history, or politics, many times I engage people who are emotional and not principled. They get off of the topic and begin to get frustrated, sometimes resorting to name calling and making ad hominem attacks against me. That's when I know that I have won the discussion.

Let's stand our ground, defend our position, and ourselves. But let's not let the mindless insults of others take our focus off of what God wants to do through us.

Yours in Christ,

ACTS 2:38

Dear Friends,

Please don't be deceived and allow one Scripture to be the entire truth. We must be students of the Word, and we must use discernment. The following Scripture has been a misguided attempt to create a model for salvation in the Pentecostal, Holiness, Apostolic, and other sects of Christianity.

> *Then Peter said unto them, Repent, and be baptized every one of you in the name of Jesus Christ for the remission of sins, and ye shall receive the gift of the Holy Ghost.*
> —Acts 2:38

I have discussed this subject with people for many years, and the responses are always scripted, programmed, and packaged in the same fallacious manner. It's sad, because I have conversed with many good people who misinterpret this Scripture; and unfortunately, they confuse themselves and other well-meaning saints of God.

But the reality is that Acts 2:38 as the formula for salvation (repentance, water baptism, and the infilling of the Holy Ghost) is not repeated anywhere in Scripture. Moreover, Jesus does not confirm it. If those three steps were necessary for salvation, one would think that those three requirements would be used in every case where salvation was granted. It isn't, and we cannot rely on that lone Scripture for the salvation model.

Many times, misunderstandings, misinterpretations of Scripture, extra Biblical revelations, and the traditions of men will cause some people to invent doctrines, to twist doctrines, and to make certain Scriptures fit into their spiritual comfort zone. This is why the Scripture admonishes us to study the Word of God, and to allow the Holy Spirit to lead us into all truth. There are many well-meaning

Christian folks who are deceived, and they are deceiving many well-meaning Christian folks.

However, we can rely upon the salvation that comes from God through faith in the virgin-born, Son of God, Jesus Christ and His death, burial and resurrection as payment for our sins and eternal redemption. Any human being can become the righteousness of God in Christ Jesus, but it only comes by faith in Christ, and not by works of righteousness which we have done. Don't allow religion to teach you otherwise.

Yours in Christ,

Receiving Eternal Life

Dear Friends,

I have had numerous discussions about "eternal life" over the years. It's a doctrine in which a lot of people have faith. Most Christians can quote "eternal life" Scriptures verbatim. One of the most popular Scriptures is the following:

> *That whosoever believeth in Him should not perish, but have eternal life. For God so loved the world, that He gave His only begotten Son, that whosoever believeth in Him should not perish, but have everlasting life.*
> —John 3:15-16

If you ask most people to explain these Scriptures, they might explain that if a person believes on Jesus Christ, the Son of God, then the believer will ultimately live life with God forever. Most Bible reading folks will probably agree with some variation of that explanation.

But what if the Bible, more specifically Jesus, had another definition for "eternal life?" What would that do to our religious culture paradigm? "Eternal life" sounds like "living forever." But let's see what Jesus said about "eternal life."

Before Jesus' betrayal and arrest at Gethsemane, the Lord spent some time praying for Himself, His disciples, and all believers who would follow. In His prayer, He stated the definition of "eternal life." Jesus said:

> *And this is eternal life, that they may know You, the only true God, and Jesus Christ whom You have sent.*
> —John 17:3

Jesus mentioned nothing about living forever or going to Heaven. He simply stated that "eternal life" is to know (having a relationship with) Jesus Christ and the Heavenly Father. "Eternal life" isn't something that you receive one day in Heaven after you are dead. If you are dead without "eternal life," then you are in big trouble. When you receive Christ as your Lord, you receive "eternal life."

So what does this tell us about a doctrine (such as this) that goes against the way "eternal life" is traditionally taught? I use to believe that "eternal life" meant to live forever with God. But I read the Bible for myself and discovered what Jesus said. So what should we do when our Churches and leaders teach one thing, and the Word of God actually states the polar opposite? I'm sticking with the Word.

Yours in Christ,

You Must be Born Again
(The First Baptism)

Dear Friends,

Our purpose is simple.

Jesus saith unto them, My meat is to do the Will of Him who sent Me, and to finish His work.
—John 4:34

Our purpose is the same purpose that Jesus mentioned: to do His will and to finish His work. Think of it in these terms, if a hammer has a specific purpose on this Earth, then shouldn't you have a specific purpose? If a chair has a specific purpose, shouldn't you have a specific purpose? You do have a specific purpose!

Our first purpose is to reconnect back to the Father through the born again experience. I know that it sounds cliché, but sin separates us from a holy God. But in His infinite mercy and grace, God has made a way for us to return to Him on His terms. That is great news, because we don't have to worry about working hard enough or long enough to please Him. There is nothing that we can do in our strength or ability that can make us acceptable in His sight.

But we are all like an unclean thing, and all our righteousnesses are like filthy rags; we all fade as a leaf, and our iniquities, like the wind, have taken us away.
—Isaiah 64:6

All we can do is be born again.

> *Jesus answered him, I assure you, most solemnly I tell you, that unless a person is born again (anew, from above), he cannot ever see (know, be acquainted with, and experience) the kingdom of God.*
>
> —John 3:3 (Amplified)

This is a spiritual rebirth that happens when God convicts a person's heart, and genuine contrition and repentance follows. I'm not talking about saying a religious "feel good" prayer; even the Pharisees prayed. I'm talking about a sincere commitment to God from the heart.

Think of repentance in terms of directions. If you are living life according to the whims of your own desires, and not according to the Word of God, then you are going south. Repentance would be stopping, turning 180 degrees and walking north. The problem with many Church folks is that they walk south, stop and face north, but they start doing the moonwalk (facing north, but still heading south), and their spiritual problems never get resolved.

God desires true commitment. He invested the time, the energy, and the life of Christ for our sakes. How difficult is it to honor God with our lives and allow Him to make us one with Him and other believers by His Spirit?

> *For by one Spirit we were all baptized into one body—whether Jews or Greeks, whether slaves or free—and have all been made to drink into one Spirit.*
>
> —1 Corinthians 12:13

This is a spiritual baptism or immersion into the spiritual body of believers in Christ. It is also the first of three baptisms that **EVERY BELIEVER** should experience. The three baptisms are: the baptism into the Body of Christ or the spiritually born again experience; water baptism; and the baptism in the Holy Spirit. The last two baptisms can be experienced in any order after the born-again experience.

For the sake of this letter, we will only address being born again. The other two baptisms will be addressed in the next two letters.

Understanding what it means to be a born again believer is simply stated in four points:

1. God has a good purpose for mankind.

2. Humanity has a sin problem inherited from Adam.

3. God created a solution for mankind's sin problem: Jesus Christ (born of a virgin) was sacrificed for the sins of all humanity.

4. When convicted by the Holy Spirit, an individual (with genuine contrition) must repent, and believe in the Lord Jesus Christ and His shed blood to wash away their sins, and His resurrection to secure them eternally.

Whenever a person truly desires to make it to this fourth point, he or she is:

- Born again; John 3:3.

- Spiritually baptized into the Body of Christ and one with Him and His believers; 1 Corinthians 12:13.

- A new creature in Christ Jesus; 2 Corinthians 5:17.

- Spiritually regenerated; Titus 3:5.

- Given the measure of faith; Romans 12:3.

- Accepted in the beloved; Ephesians 1:6.

- Written in the Lamb's Book of Life; Revelation 21:27.

You are now on the right team, and heading in the right direction. But don't stop here, because God is always looking to reveal more to those who hunger and thirst after righteousness.

Yours in Christ,

WATER BAPTISM
(THE SECOND BAPTISM)

Dear Friends,

In the Bible, specifically the book of Acts, water baptism generally accompanied repentance/conversion to Christ. When a person would accept Christ, he/she would be immediately water baptized as a part of the package. But today, our modern-day conveniences, fancy hairstyles, and nice clothes don't fit into the traditional water baptism equation.

Water baptism is a symbolic act (an outward manifestation of the inward conviction and transformation) of a believer in Christ being buried with Christ (totally submerged under water), and rising up out of the water as a testimony to a newness of life.

> *Therefore we were buried with Him through baptism into death, that just as Christ was raised from the dead by the glory of the Father, even so we also should walk in newness of life.*
> —Romans 6:4

The word "baptism" comes from the Greek word "baptizó," which means to dip or to submerge. For some reason, some believers believe in sprinkling instead of submerging, but the Word is clear on the proper way to baptize. Even Jesus was submerged.

> *When He had been baptized, Jesus came up immediately from the water; and behold, the Heavens were opened to Him, and He saw the Spirit of God descending like a dove and alighting upon Him.*
> —Matthew 3:16

The water is not the cleansing agent to wash away the sins. Only the blood of Jesus can spiritually do that, and if the person being baptized is sincere, then that washing away of sin should have already happened when they repented and submitted their life to Christ. The water baptism is a witness to the world that you belong to Christ, and this is why babies shouldn't be baptized and why baptism has nothing to do with being a member of a local church. You are supposed to get baptized because you are a believer in Christ, not to become a believer in Christ.

I know many Churches that have new members come to the front of the church. The preacher shakes everyone's hands, they get baptized, and that makes them members of the local church. This model is found nowhere in Scripture. This type of tradition just creates wet sinners.

Finally, water baptism doesn't confer a status of perfection, special insights, gifts or powers upon the new believer. It's just an act of obedience that brings a blessing in following Christ, His example, and His teachings.

Yours in Christ,

Being Filled with the Spirit
(The Third Baptism)

Dear Friends,

The third baptism in the New Testament is the baptism in the Holy Spirit or Holy Ghost. You might see it also referred to as the infilling of the Holy Spirit or Holy Ghost, or being filled with the Holy Spirit or Holy Ghost. However it is referenced, it is generally associated with speaking in tongues; unfortunately, it is a lost doctrine among 21st Century believers.

Is Speaking in Tongues for Today?

> *For the promise (of the Holy Spirit) is to you and to your children, and to **ALL** who are afar off, as many as the Lord our God will call.*
> —Acts 2:39

If you are called of the Lord (meaning that you are a born again believer in Christ), then this gift is for you. Every believer can have the gifts of tongues.

> *And these signs will follow those who believe: In My name they will cast out demons; they will speak with new tongues.*
> —Mark 16:17

Who will speak in tongues? Those who believe that the Bible promises them this gift will speak in tongues. Allow me to make this point clearly, if you never speak in tongues, but you have genuinely confessed Christ as your Lord, you are still a born again believer in Christ Jesus. I know some denominational people get confused about salvation and tongues. But I do want to let you know that this gift is available for **ALL WHO BELIEVE**. This teaching is really very simple. But the enemy has done a masterful job of confusing people with twisted interpretations.

Which Tongues?

There are actually two different gifts of tongues taught in the New Testament. There is a ministry gift of tongues to edify the body of believers.

But the manifestation of the Spirit is given to each one for the profit of all: for to one is given the word of wisdom through the Spirit, to another the word of knowledge through the same Spirit, to another faith by the same Spirit, to another gifts of healings by the same Spirit, to another the working of miracles, to another prophecy, to another discerning of spirits, to another different kinds of tongues, to another the interpretation of tongues. But one and the same Spirit works all these things, distributing to each one individually as He wills.

—1 Corinthians 12:7-11

This type of tongues **IS NOT** for every believer. Verse 11 says that the Spirit of God gives these gifts as He wills. This type of tongues is spoken by one person before the body of believers, and an interpretation is always given by the speaker or another person in the known language of the hearers.

There is also a personal prayer language of tongues. This gift **IS FOR EVERY BELIEVER**, and it is prayer in an unknown language to the speaker, but it is a known language to the omniscient God.

For he who speaks in a tongue does not speak to men but to God, for no one understands him; however, in the spirit he speaks mysteries.

—1 Corinthians 14:2

Why Tongues?

The corporate ministry gift of tongues with interpretation is a means to edify the body of believers according to 1 Corinthians 14:5. This gift is also a sign to unbelievers of the reality of God 1 Corinthians 14:22.

The personal prayer language gift of tongues edifies the praying believer.

He who speaks in a tongue edifies himself.
—1 Corinthians 14:4

But you, beloved, building yourselves up on your most holy faith, praying in the Holy Spirit.
—Jude 20

This gift allows the Holy Spirit to pray the perfect will of God through believers concerning our own lives or the lives of other members of the Body of Christ.

Likewise the Spirit also helps in our weaknesses. For we do not know what we should pray for as we ought, but the Spirit Himself makes intercession for us with groanings which cannot be uttered. Now He who searches the hearts knows what the mind of the Spirit is, because He makes intercession for the saints according to the will of God.
—Romans 8:26-27

All of that Tongues Stuff isn't Necessary

Well, Jesus thought it was necessary. If this experience wasn't necessary, then why didn't Jesus allow the disciples to carry out the Great Commission without it?

> *Behold, I send the Promise of My Father upon you; but tarry in the city of Jerusalem until you are endued with power from on high."*
>
> —Luke 24:49

We don't have to tarry or wait to receive the Holy Spirit any longer. The promise of the outpouring of God's Spirit (Joel 2:28) has come and every believer can freely receive God's gift, today. This gift is the anointing that God left for the saints to empower us for service. As He empowered Jesus, He has empowered us, too.

> *How God anointed Jesus of Nazareth with the Holy Spirit and with power, who went about doing good and healing all who were oppressed by the devil, for God was with Him.*
>
> —Acts 10:38

Can Christians be Filled with the Holy Spirit and Not Speak in Tongues?

Although I phrased it as a question, and many Christians believe it as a statement to be true, the Bible does not confirm that a Christian can be filled with the Holy Ghost and not speak in tongues. Wherever the Book of Acts mentions anyone initially being filled with the Spirit, they are subsequently speaking in tongues and/or prophesying. I truly believe that most people don't understand that there is a huge difference between being born again/indwelt with the Spirit of God, and being infilled/baptized with the Spirit of God. There is only one Spirit of God, but these are two distinct operations of the same Spirit for all believers. Let's see what the Bible says regarding the gift of the Holy Spirit and speaking in tongues:

> *When the Day of Pentecost had fully come, they were all with one accord in one place. And suddenly there came a sound from Heaven, as of a rushing mighty wind, and it filled the whole house where they were sitting. Then there appeared to them divided tongues, as of fire, and one sat upon each of*

them. And they were all filled with the Holy Spirit and began to speak with other tongues, as the Spirit gave them utterance.
—Acts 2:1-4

While Peter was still speaking these words, the Holy Spirit fell upon all those who heard the word. And those of the circumcision who believed were astonished, as many as came with Peter, because the gift of the Holy Spirit had been poured out on the Gentiles also. For they heard them speak with tongues and magnify God. Then Peter answered, "Can anyone forbid water, that these should not be baptized who have received the Holy Spirit just as we have?" And he commanded them to be baptized in the name of the Lord. Then they asked him to stay a few days.
—Acts 10:44-48

And it happened, while Apollos was at Corinth, that Paul, having passed through the upper regions, came to Ephesus. And finding some disciples he said to them, "Did you receive the Holy Spirit when you believed?" So they said to him, "We have not so much as heard whether there is a Holy Spirit." And he said to them, "Into what then were you baptized?" So they said, "Into John's baptism." Then Paul said, "John indeed baptized with a baptism of repentance, saying to the people that they should believe on Him who would come after him, that is, on Christ Jesus." When they heard this, they were baptized in the name of the Lord Jesus. And when Paul had laid hands on them, the Holy Spirit came upon them, and they spoke with tongues and prophesied.
—Acts 19:1-6

Do you want to receive the gift of the Holy Spirit?

1. Review the material again, if necessary. Be in faith and not fear/doubt about this topic. The Holy Spirit won't do anything you won't allow Him to do.

2. Believe that when you ask for it, you will receive exactly what the Bible says that it is. Luke 11:11-13.

3. Start to worship God and thank Him for filling you with the Holy Spirit. Expect to receive exactly what you asked God to give you. If you feel the urge to say a strange word or sound, say it by faith. It's an unknown language to you, but not to God. Speak as the Spirit gives you the utterance. God will not make you speak in tongues, just like He won't make you speak in English.

4. Utilize your prayer language as often as you can. Your words will get clearer the more you use your gift.

5. Be sensitive to the Spirit of God. Through your new gift, God will begin to share more spiritual insights with you as you yield to Him.

Go in peace and in the power of the Holy Spirit.

Yours in Christ,

NEW CONVERT ZEAL VS. WALKING BY FAITH

Dear Friends,

Do you remember when you first received Christ? I do. For me, there was an unquenchable spiritual fire burning in me, and I was on a mission to make sure that everyone was living for God. I was an uncontained, yet moral, explosion of faith. I shared my faith all over the place, even to the point of alienating people away from me. But I didn't care, because I experienced some fulfillment that I had never experienced before, and nothing seemed impossible to me.

That fulfillment is what I call "new convert zeal." The term "new convert zeal" is not a phrase that you will find in the Bible. It's just a phrase that I use to explain what happens to a new believer. The Bible teaches at length about walking by faith, walking in the Word, etc. But until you get to that point of truly walking by faith, God gives a new believer what I call "new convert zeal." The new convert gets a seemingly new burst of spiritual energy, revelation, and spiritual acuteness because the Lord wants to confirm His salvation to the new convert. Since we have natural bodies and live in a sensory realm, most people are not too familiar with the spiritual realm. So the Lord brings the manifestation of the reality of one's spiritual salvation and walk with Him into a reality to which new believers can relate. The best way to explain it is like being on a spiritual high, and nothing seems impossible to you.

It's difficult to explain, but you know it's real. It's kind of like putting a drink on the top tray of the refrigerator. Then when you come back later, the same drink is on the refrigerator door. No one admitted to moving it, but you know you put it on the top tray. It's one of these things that make you ask yourself, "Am I crazy?" Well, if you have a sound mind and are genuinely born again, then you aren't crazy.

You have simply tapped into a (spiritual) realm of living that most people never truly appreciate; even most believers in Christ don't truly appreciate it either. I say that because so many believers never fully commit to tapping into the spiritual things. It's new, and a totally different way of thinking that gets you out of your status quo comfort zone.

If you experience "new convert zeal," then be aware that this is the time when your family will think that you're crazy, a fanatic, overzealous, and/or a kook. When you were running around and living a life of sin prior to giving your life to Christ, no one was worried about your well-being. It's only after you truly commit your life to Christ that folks want to get overly concerned about you. That reaction is either genuine concern masked in fear, the enemy working through folks, or a combination of the two, because the enemy is the author of fear. But don't be discouraged, because natural people can't understand spiritual things.

> *But the natural man receiveth not the things of the Spirit of God: for they are foolishness unto him: neither can he know them, because they are spiritually discerned.*
> —1 Corinthians 2:14

At some point, the new convert will have to transition from "new convert zeal" to walking by faith. "New convert zeal" is more like a tangible confirmation of what you have; while walking by faith means that you must believe the Word no matter what the physical circumstances illustrate. It's a challenge, but if you are truly committed to Christ, He will be with you every step of the way. He has a vested interest in your success, so allow the Holy Spirit to lead you into your new life.

Yours in Christ,

How to Pray Scripturally

Dear Friends,

I'm going to make this letter as simple as possible. How do you pray Scripturally? You pray according to the Scriptures. I will share some examples with you, but the main principle is to find out what God says about a matter, and you should agree with God's Word to be the solution.

Is there a specific way that we need to pray, or is everyone's style of praying correct? Let's go over several Scriptures and find out how to extract the principles of prayer and transpose them over our daily lives in our prayer time.

Allow me to also point out that you can have a sincere heart-to-heart conversation with God without quoting Scriptures as a means of communicating with God. Telling God about your day or telling Him that you don't like something is perfectly fine. But in terms of finding out what God's Will is on a particular situation, you must do so according to His Word.

What does the Word say regarding how we should pray?

> *Ask (demand of something that is due, not asking for permission), and it shall be given you; seek, and ye shall find; knock, and it shall be opened unto you: For every one that asketh receiveth; and he that seeketh findeth; and to him that knocketh it shall be opened. Or what man is there of you, whom if his son ask bread, will he give him a stone? Or if he ask a fish, will he give him a serpent? If ye then, being evil, know how to give good gifts unto your children, how much more shall your Father which is in Heaven give good things to them that ask him?*
>
> —Matthew 7:7-11

> *Now this is the confidence that we have in Him, that if we ask anything according to His will, He hears us. And if we know that He hears us, whatever we ask, we know that we have the petitions that we have asked of Him.*
> —1 John 5:14-15

> *For all the promises of God in Him are yea, and in Him Amen, unto the glory of God by us.*
> —2 Corinthians 1:20

> *If ye abide in me, and My words abide in you, ye shall ask what ye will, and it shall be done unto you.*
> —John 15:7

> *And whatever you ask in My name (authority), that I will do, that the Father may be glorified in the Son. If you ask anything in My name (authority), I will do it.*
> —John 14:13-14

> *You did not choose Me, but I chose you and appointed you that you should go and bear fruit, and that your fruit should remain, that whatever you ask the Father in My name (authority) He may give you.*
> —John 15:16.

All of these Scriptures support the principle that we must go through Jesus to God; we must petition Him according to His Will; and He will manifest Himself to us (through prayer) if we keep His commandments (the Word). It's pretty straightforward.

Here are a couple of simple, Biblical examples of prayers to believe and say verbatim or you can use these as a model for prayer:

For confidence:

> *Greater is He that is in me, than he that is in the world.*
> —1 John 4:4

I can do all things through Christ who strengthens me.
—Philippians 4:13.

In all these things I am more than a conqueror through Him that loves me.
—Romans 8:37.

For Healing:

By Christ's stripes (wounds) I am healed.
—1 Peter 2:24

Christ has redeemed me from the curse of the law, being made a curse for me and sickness is under the curse of the law.
—Galatians 3:13-14

For Protection:

The LORD is my rock, and my fortress, and my deliverer; my God, my strength, in whom I trust; my buckler, and the horn of my salvation, and my high tower. I call upon the LORD, who is worthy to be praised: and I am saved from my enemies.
—Psalms 18:1-3

The angel of the LORD encamps round about me (because I fear Him), and He delivers me.
—Psalms 34:7

To Help Strengthen Your Love Walk:

I forgive people their trespasses (their reckless and willful sins), leaving them, letting them go, and giving up resentment), and my Heavenly Father also forgives me. I seek (aim at and strive after) first of all His kingdom and His righteousness (His way of doing and being right), and then all these (natural, earthly) things taken together will be given me besides.
—Matthew 6:14, 33

I endure long, am patient and kind; I never am envious nor boil over with jealousy, am not boastful or vainglorious, I do not display myself haughtily. I am not conceited (arrogant and inflated with pride); I am not rude (unmannerly) and do not act unbecomingly. I (God's love in me) do not insist on my own rights or own way, for I am not self-seeking; I am not touchy or fretful or resentful; I take no account of the evil done to me (I pay no attention to a suffered wrong). I do not rejoice at injustice and unrighteousness, but I rejoice when right and truth prevail. I bear up under anything and everything that comes, I believe the best of every person, my hopes are fadeless under all circumstances, and I endure everything (without weakening). I never fail (never fade out or become obsolete or come to an end).
—1 Corinthians 13:4-8.

When you need peace:

And the peace of God, which passes all understanding, keeps my heart and mind through Christ Jesus. And whatsoever things are true, whatsoever things are honest, whatsoever things are just, whatsoever things are pure, whatsoever things are lovely, whatsoever things are of good report; if there be any virtue, and if there be any praise, I think on these things.
—Philippians 4:7

These Scriptural prayers are not the be-all and end-all for prayer, because you have to put them and your situation in perspective. For example, if your eyes are hurting because you are sensitive to the UV rays from the Sun, you can't go outside with no protective eyewear on and expect God to heal/protect your eyes. You can pray for God to heal and/or protect your eyes, but then you need to buy some good protective eyewear. Prayer is not an excuse to neglect your natural responsibilities.

Prayer is like starting a car. You put the key in the ignition and you turn it. You don't ask the car if it wants to start. You simply put a demand on the car according to the owner's manual. The Bible is the Owner's Manual of prayer, so remember that we are not asking or begging God to heal us. He already promised us healing. Our job is to make a demand on His promise by declaring what He said regarding healing or any other matter.

These prayers are shown as Scriptures so that you can see what God's Will is regarding the various needs we have in this life. Always remember that the Biblical principle that **MUST** be employed is that God honors prayers that are in faith (believing) and in line with His Will (Word). In other words, you can't ask God to give you John's car. That is covetousness and is against God's Word. So use these insights, experience how simple it is to communicate with God according to His Word, and stand upon that truth. It's a mental paradigm shift, to say the least, but just remember to say what God says, and believe it.

Yours in Christ,

Fine Tune Your Faith by Pursuing God's Word

Dear Friends,

Wisdom is the principal thing.
—Proverbs 4:7

Having the components needed to complete a specific task is one thing, but having the directions to assemble and to use those components is another thing entirely. It's like shooting a bow and arrow north, while the bull's eye is south. For too long, people have been acting on information without sound direction (wisdom).

In (Jesus) whom are hid all the treasures of wisdom and knowledge.
—Colossians 2:3

Direction is what gives clarity to your actions. Moving isn't enough, but moving in the right direction will at least give you a better opportunity to be successful. Your plans can always be fine-tuned. When I was a child, my family had a standard television with an UHF and a VHF channel knob. Each knob had a round fine-tuner attachment pressed against the television. But the fine tuner wouldn't work if the television wasn't turned to the correct channel. The picture would remain snowy no matter how many times the fine tuner was turned. If the show you wanted to watch was on channel five, all of the fine tuning and antenna moving in the world won't get you that program on channel ten.

Pursue the Wisdom

Salvation is an experience with the God when you accept Jesus as your Savior; however, wisdom is revealed in time and you can grow in it, like Jesus did.

And Jesus increased in wisdom and stature, and in favor with God and man.
—Luke 2:52

How do you grow in wisdom and where do you get it?

If any of you lack wisdom, let him ask of God, that giveth to all men liberally, and upbraideth not; and it shall be given him.
—James 1:5

God is the source of all good things (including wisdom); so if you want something that He has, ask Him for it. Growing in wisdom, however, is a bit more time consuming because it is a process. You don't wake up one day and have wisdom; just like you don't wake up one day two feet taller than you were yesterday. Growth in any area takes time, and wisdom is no different. If you truly want to grow in wisdom, then you are going to have to spend time around wisdom, so that you can know and truly understand wisdom. Look at Jesus; whenever He ministered and completed His specific task(s), He went to go spend time with the Father. Jesus didn't just show up ready to perform miracles and teach; He recharged His battery with the Father daily.

The more you give yourself to something and the more you hang around it, the more that it will rub off on you. Just like barnacles on a ship, wisdom will become attached to you.

And ye shall seek me, and find me, when ye shall search for me with all your heart.
—Jeremiah 29:13

I love them that love me; and those that seek me early shall find me.

—Proverbs 8:17

Just like a drug addict has a fervent desire to get that next "fix" is how we should pursue God's wisdom.

O God, thou art my God; early will I seek thee: my soul thirsteth for thee, my flesh longeth for thee in a dry and thirsty land, where no water is.

—Psalms 63:1

Yours in Christ,

WE HAVE THE COMPLETE VICTORY

Dear Friends,

I just wanted to remind you that we serve a great and mighty God. Here is just a reminder of who He is to us and for us.

JEHOVAH-JIREH: God my Provider

This name was revealed in Genesis 22:14 when Abraham was about to offer up Isaac as a sacrifice. The Lord stopped him and provided a substitute lamb for Isaac. This powerful story reveals Jesus and the work of the cross. The name Jehovah-Jireh speaks of the Lord God providing His Son for our redemption and being our provider for all that we need.

JEHOVAH-RAPHA: God my Healer

Exodus 15:22-26, the children of Israel came to Marah in the wilderness and could not drink the water because it was bitter. The Lord made a covenant of healing with His people and said that if they would keep all His commandments, He would be their health and healer continually.

JEHOVAH "NISSI": God my (victory) Banner

This name was made known when Moses lifted up the rod of victory, in prayer, for an entire day as a battle with the Amalekites was fought (Exodus 17:15). The Hebrew word "Nissi" means my banner, or my covering, my protection and, also my victory.

JEHOVAH M'KADESH: God my Sanctifier

The Lord declared He would be the sanctifier of Israel, if they would obey Him (Exodus 31:13). The word "M'kadesh" means our sanctifier and has to do with being set apart for service and belonging wholly to the Lord.

JEHOVAH-SHALOM: God my Peace

In Judges 6:23-24, God revealed Himself to Gideon and comforted him when He told him, "Peace *be* with you; do not fear, you shall not die." Gideon was comforted and made an altar in God's honor. Through this we learn that dependence upon the Lord and reliance upon His name will bring us His peace.

JEHOVAH-TSIDKENU: God my Righteousness

God told the prophet Jeremiah to declare that a "righteous branch" of David would come, and "Judah shall be saved, and Israel shall dwell safely: and this is his name whereby he shall be called, The Lord our Righteousness," (Jeremiah 23:6). In this revelation, we are told that Jesus is our righteousness and that only through Him can we live righteously before the Lord.

JEHOVAH-ROHI: God my Shepherd

In Psalms 23, God is revealed as "Rohi." This was spoken as David declared "The Lord is my Shepherd, I shall not want," Psalm 23:1. The name "Rohi" speaks of both leadership and close intimacy. Once we know the Lord as our Shepherd, our Jehovah-Rohi, all the promises of Psalms 23 will become reality in our daily walk.

JEHOVAH-SHAMMAH: God my Abiding Presence

The book of Ezekiel concludes with these words: "...and the name of the city for that day shall be, The Lord is there."

The Hebrew translation is Jehovah-Shammah speaking of God's abiding presence. The Lord desires that we walk with Him daily. The word "abide" means to stay, not to visit.

Why are these Scriptures and names important? They are important because they reveal the covenant names and character of God; and these Old Testament covenant names were all manifest in the New Testament person of Jesus Christ.

Christ is:

- our Provider. Philippians 4:19.
- our Healer. 1 Peter 2:24.
- our Banner of Victory. 1 Corinthians 15:57.
- our Sanctifier. Hebrews 2:11.
- our Peace. John 14:27.
- our Righteousness. 1 Corinthians 1:30.
- our Shepherd. John 10:11.
- the One who will never leave us nor forsake us. Matthew 28:20.

Why would anyone go anywhere else to find all of the things that Jesus is for us?

Yours in Christ,

How the Mind Works

Dear Friends,

In the battle for the allegiance of humanity, we are in a three-fold battle: spirit, soul, and body. The soul/mind is the second level, but I believe that it is the portion that the enemy attacks most to make Christians ineffective against God's kingdom. The spirit is the life of the body, and the mind/soul is the characteristics of the spirit. So if we can get a better understanding of how to get our minds molded to think the right way, then I believe we can walk in higher levels of success.

> *Do not be conformed to this world (this age), (fashioned after and adapted to its external, superficial customs), but be transformed (changed) by the (entire) renewal of your mind (by its new ideals and its new attitude), so that you may prove (for yourselves) what is the good and acceptable and perfect will of God, even the thing which is good and acceptable and perfect (in His sight for you).*
> —Romans 12:2 (Amplified)

We can learn a lot from parables: spiritual truths via natural illustrations. So, if the human spirit is like the engine and structural components of the car, then the mind/soul is analogous to the driver. If God owns the car, the enemy can still control the driver and go where he wants to go. So it is important, not only to let God be the owner of the car, but also to let Him or one of His faithful disciples drive it, as well.

This will help you to be a more complete and consistent person. Again, humans are three-part beings and it would make life so much easier if there is harmony and agreement throughout the entire being: a surrendered heart to God, a renewed mind to the Word of God, and a yielded body.

How can human thinking be in harmony with the human spirit/heart?

First, you have to realize that it is God's Will for you to have a sound mind that is renewed to truth. If you don't know that it is God's Will, then you can't have faith to believe that you can have it. A renewed mind takes time to develop. So if your faith isn't fixed on God's Word and the process, you will fail.

> *For God has not given us a spirit of fear, but of power and of love and of a sound mind.*
> —2 Timothy 1:7

Second, you have to see that it is Christ's mind that you need. Christ is the Word (John 1:1-3) and He always does that which pleases the Father (John 8:29). Christ's thinking encouraged His actions, so you should imitate His thinking, so that your thinking can encourage your actions in line with His Word. Whoever or whatever controls your thinking will ultimately control your life. Whether it is fear, a job, pleasing people, money, etc. will control you if it occupies your mind.

> *For who has known the mind of the LORD that he may instruct Him? But we have the mind of Christ.*
> —1 Corinthians 2:16

Third, you must meditate on the right things. Meditate means to concentrate on and to mutter aloud to yourself. You have to consciously put His Words on your mind and hide them in your heart so that you will know how to walk in His ways.

> *...whatever things are true, whatever things are noble, whatever things are just, whatever things are pure, whatever things are lovely, whatever things are of good report, if there is any virtue and if there is anything praiseworthy—meditate on these things. The things which you learned and received and heard and saw in me, these do, and the God of peace will be with you.*
> —Philippians 4:8-9

The Television and the Radio

We all have our favorite shows, sports programming or news stations, but the television/radio is a very sophisticated piece of technology. It is a tool like anything else that can be used for good or evil. But don't be alarmed. The television/radio can't harm you, per se; but certain programming is used to target your brain with subliminal messages that you might not want to receive.

Scientists, advertisers, and marketing experts have found a way to feed you information so inconspicuously that you don't even realize it. How? Well, the brain is an amazing creation; it is actually the prototype for modern-day computers. You can input information, the brain processes the information, and either stores it or computes it. When you want to retrieve the information you go into your memory bank and recall it. These are the basic mechanics of the brain and a computer.

The brain is the housing for your mind. The eyes are stalks that grow out of the brain during embryonic development. You may have heard the phrase that the eyes are the "windows of the soul." Well, the mind is your soul, and that is where your will, your intellect, your emotions and your distinctive characteristics are located. We have to understand how the mind/brain works, so that we can make sure that we are putting the right things into it, and not allowing the wrong things into it.

Have you had a commercial jingle that you couldn't get out of your head? It became a recording in your mind. Have you ever seen a horror movie that caused you to have nightmares? Those images go directly into your mind, where they are stored and ready to be played back at some point in the future. The music and the sound effects just hype it all up to make it more of a reality to bypass your conscious mind. If you ever watch a horror movie with no sound, the movie won't be as scary, because the enhancement is gone.

But once that movie or song recording is downloaded inside of you, your mind doesn't differentiate between reality, a dream, or TV. That is why you can dream about an all-expense paid trip to Hawaii and wake up in a good mood, because in your mind that was a reality. Ultimately, the point is to guard your ears and your eyes. We use technology for a good purpose, but many times, these tools can create adverse conditions for us. What you sow into your mind will eventually produce a harvest. So it would be in your best interest to not watch/listen to some of these popular television programs, movies, and radio stations.

Protect yourself!

Yours in Christ,

LISTEN TO AND FOLLOW YOUR HEART

Dear Friends,

God desires to have fellowship with humans, and that's one reason why He made us. We have numerous examples in the Old Testament where God communed with and talked to people directly: God gave Noah explicit instructions on how to build the ark (Genesis 6); God called Abraham (Genesis 12) and made a covenant with him (Genesis 15); God spoke to Moses and commissioned him to deliver the children of Israel (Exodus 3); and God gave Solomon wisdom to build the Temple (1 Kings 5-8). These are just a few Old Testament examples of God speaking expressly to His people, and there are many more examples. But we live in the New Testament of Jesus Christ.

Jesus is the mediator of a better covenant, which was established upon better promises.
—Hebrews 8:6

So how much more clearly and distinctly should we be able to access the counsel of God in our hearts if we have a better covenant and promises?

For as many as are led by the Spirit of God, they are the sons of God.
—Romans 8:14.

God communicates with us, and He leads us by His Spirit. In the 21st Century, we are a society that is enamored with our body, our appearance, our scent, our food, and other natural things. This is fine, but God is not as concerned about the outward, as much as He is the inward.

> *Whose adorning let it not be that outward adorning of plaiting the hair, and of wearing of gold, or of putting on of apparel; But let it be the hidden man of the heart, in that which is not corruptible, even the ornament of a meek and quiet spirit, which is in the sight of God of great price.*
> —1 Peter 3:3-4

A lot of people miss the intent here and use this Scripture to justify that wearing make-up is a sin. That is pure fiction! Peter was merely repeating what Jesus said about the piety of the Pharisee's outward appearance versus their sinful, inward condition.

Jesus said:

> *Woe to you, scribes and Pharisees, hypocrites! For you pay tithe of mint and anise and cummin, and have neglected the weightier matters of the law: justice and mercy and faith. These you ought to have done, without leaving the others undone. Blind guides, who strain out a gnat and swallow a camel. Woe to you, scribes and Pharisees, hypocrites! For you cleanse the outside of the cup and dish, but inside they are full of extortion and self-indulgence. Blind Pharisee, first cleanse the inside of the cup and dish, that the outside of them may be clean also. Woe to you, scribes and Pharisees, hypocrites! For you are like whitewashed tombs which indeed appear beautiful outwardly, but inside are full of dead men's bones and all uncleanness. Even so you also outwardly appear righteous to men, but inside you are full of hypocrisy and lawlessness.*
> —Matthew 23:23-28

Again, there's nothing wrong with a nice outward appearance, but God is more concerned about your spirit and spiritual condition.

Discerning God's Voice

Sometimes, people get confused when they begin to walk with God because they don't know how to differentiate between their own voice in their heads, God's voice, and the enemy's voice. That is understandable, but here are a couple of easy things that you can do in order to spiritually discern and distinguish God's voice from your own mind, and from the enemy's subtle suggestions.

First, be open to receiving messages through your spirit, because that is where the Holy Spirit resides.

> ...according to His mercy He saved us, through the washing of regeneration and renewing of the Holy Spirit.
> —Titus 3:5

The Holy Spirit now resides in every born again believer's heart (spirit). Be conscious of the Holy Spirit's presence in your life, even if it doesn't feel like He's there. Things are constantly moving and changing in your life, like the minute hand or the hour hand on a clock. Sometimes, simply recognizing that there is another path of communication available to you is enough to make an easier transition to commune with God.

Second, it is an absolute necessity for you to be an avid hearer of the Word of God on CD, DVD, or reader of the Word aloud to yourself.

> *Faith comes by hearing the Word of God.*
> —Romans 10:17

This has a dual purpose: increasing your faith, and making your spirit more sensitive to the voice of God. I liken this principle to the frequency on the radio. Radio signals are traveling through the air at all times, but we (humans) don't hear them because we can't hear on that frequency level. So we need a receiver to get the signal. Once the receiver gets the signal, we can enjoy the message being transmitted. The human spirit works the same way. You have to train your spirit to hear on God's frequency level; and that level is the Word of God. The more you hear it, the more you will be able to distinguish His voice.

Additionally, what's interesting is that God speaks in line with His Word, but He may or may not necessarily be quoting a Scripture to you. He might tell you to take an extra sandwich for lunch. It might not make sense, but there might be a co-worker who might need a meal. The more you train yourself to hear and know God's voice, and the more you yield to Him, the easier it will be for God to speak to you and to use you.

Here are a few helpful tips:

- While you're training your spirit, begin to obey the voice you hear even in the smallest instructions. I have phone conversations with people whom I have never met in person. But we have had so many conversations with one another, that we can instantly recognize one another's voices.

- Build up your spirit through prayer; Jude 20.

- Build up a spiritual sensitivity to God through fasting. There are no New Testament instructions for fasting; Jesus only said, "When you do fast." In other words, no one should dictate to you when you should fast, that's between God and you. Jesus fasted, and He is the example, so let Him guide you on fasting. But there are many Old Testament examples of fasting in Esther, Ezra, 2 Samuel and other incidents where the people of God consecrated themselves to God's purpose through fasting.

- Spend quiet time, alone with God. You can pray and talk to Him, but give God an opportunity to speak to you. Wait and listen to His voice. Don't just go into prayer and walk away. Listen, and give God a chance to respond when you're quiet and listening.

- Don't talk to unbelievers and unbelieving Christians about spiritual matters like: hearing God's voice, prayer, fasting, consecration, holiness and other things. Carnal Christians and secular people may mock what you are doing and try to discourage you from pursuing God's Will for your life. This isn't to say that you have to alienate yourself from people, because Jesus fraternized with sinners.

- Surround yourself with strong Christians who will support you and help to build you and your faith.

- Invest in sound materials that will enhance your growth and walk with the Lord.

- If you hear a voice and you still aren't sure if it is God or not, judge the voice by asking yourself if the voice is asking you to do something immoral, illegal, or strange. The enemy definitely won't encourage you to tell someone about salvation in Christ. However, the enemy may tell you to go preach the Gospel in the middle of the highway. So, by using common sense, you can know that isn't God. God saved your spirit, but he didn't remove your common sense. Remember that!

Follow these steps and give yourself sometime to grow in them. You won't master this overnight, but with practice you will become more sensitive to God and become more aware of His presence.

Yours in Christ,

SECTION THREE: THE LETTERS OF SOCIAL ISSUES

Temptation and Sin

Dear Friends,

I am going to address a very sensitive topic, and my desire is that each of you grasps the true intent of what I am writing. I do believe that the Holy Spirit (through my transparency) can help to set people free of a serious matter that is getting a lot of attention nowadays.

Some people have argued that homosexuality is a genetic gift that God gives to certain people. In other words, they believe that homosexuals are born that way. The opposing argument believes that homosexuality is a sinful lifestyle that a person chooses. Regardless of whether the behavior is that of a sexual nature, or not, many people are looking for the right answers to questions in society.

My response is if God has spoken clearly about the matter, then why would He create someone in a way that is diametrically opposed to His Word? God wouldn't create someone in a way that is contrary to His Word, because that is confusion, which is also contrary to His character/nature. God is a God of abundance, love, wholeness, truth, holiness, honor, goodness, joy, peace, etc. Anything opposed to that is not of God; and although the opposite of God's nature does exist in the world and in the lives of some people, God is **NOT** the author of calamity, sickness, homosexuality, lying, stealing, cheating, murder, etc. God loves homosexuals, liars, thieves, and all other people who partake in lifestyles that contradict His Word; but we have to say what God says about matters.

Recently, we saw the "coming out" of NBA player, Jason Collins, and the media fell all over themselves covering this story. Personally, it wasn't really news to me, because the man made a personal decision, and that's all it was. A very small percentage of the nation is homosexual, but the way the media reports it and schools are indoctrinating children to accept it as a normal alternative, you would think that half of the nation was homosexual.

The Homosexuality Trap

Allow me to explain how the enemy uses the homosexuality trap, and how it was used against me. When I was a child, I used to spend a lot of time at my paternal and maternal grandmother's houses with and without my parents (my grandfathers were deceased). For my paternal grandmother, I was the grandchild who lived closest to her, so I was able to see her often; and for my maternal grandmother, I was the first grandchild for many years. So I had a very close relationship with both women from a very young age.

At my grandmother's houses, I would be a curious kid and play around in their bedrooms. They were women, so obviously they had female things, such as: perfume, jewelry, shoes, earrings, make-up, hats, etc. I would joke around and play with these things, look in the mirror, and laugh. What I didn't realize (and I didn't realize this until much later) was that I was opening a spiritual door. I was an innocent child, but ignorance is no excuse when it comes to spiritual things.

I was, am, and always will be one hundred percent heterosexual, and I have never in my life been attracted to males; I've never desired a male, nor have I ever had any sexual contact with a male in my entire life. I always acted like a boy and I always liked females. I was raised to believe that relationships were to be between one man and one woman, and that is what God's Word teaches. In short, I am one hundred percent against the homosexual lifestyle and there isn't a man dead or alive who can honestly say otherwise.

Over a period of years spending time with my grandmothers, I started to get some strange thoughts/feelings. I wondered what it would feel like to be a woman. I couldn't explain it, but a curiosity just came over me. Again, I had no interest in males, but the thought popped into my head. So, as an inquisitive child, I asked my Dad about it. We were outside doing some yard work one day and I was thinking of some way to tell him about my feelings. I didn't know how to say it any other way than to just say it plainly, "Dad, sometimes I feel like a woman." He stopped working immediately and yelled, "What?! Do you mean that you want to be around women?" His exclamation let me know that whatever thought I was having was definitely on the wrong path, so I quickly agreed with his question. I told him that I wanted to be around women, so that I could quell this sudden eruption that I just caused. That satisfied my Dad, and those feelings never bothered me again.

Decades later, the Lord showed me what happened to me when I was younger and how homosexuality entraps some people.

First, we have to realize that everyone gets tempted in some form or another.

Therefore let him who thinks he stands take heed lest he fall. No temptation has overtaken you except such as is common to man; but God is faithful, who will not allow you to be tempted beyond what you are able, but with the temptation will also make the way of escape, that you may be able to bear it.
—1 Corinthians 10:12-13

Temptations come to us because the enemy wishes to separate God's creation (humans) away from Him and His way of doing things. What we must do is recognize these bad thoughts as temptations, and not view them as "the real me." That is another lie that people choose to believe. You can't get your identity from your feelings; you get your identity from your Creator. When people don't resist these temptations, they accept lies as truth, and a snowball effect occurs and it spreads like a cancer in society.

Professing themselves to be wise, they became fools.
—Romans 1:22

Second, we have to realize that being tempted is not a sin. But giving into the sin is the sin.

Blessed is the man who endures temptation; for when he has been approved, he will receive the crown of life which the Lord has promised to those who love Him. Let no one say when he is tempted, "I am tempted by God;" for God cannot be tempted by evil, nor does He Himself tempt anyone. But each one is tempted when he is drawn away by his own desires and enticed. Then, when desire has conceived, it gives birth to sin; and sin, when it is full-grown, brings forth death. Do not be deceived, my beloved brethren. Every good gift and every perfect gift is from above, and comes down from the

> *Father of lights, with whom there is no variation or shadow of turning. Of His own will He brought us forth by the word of truth, that we might be a kind of first fruits of His creatures.*
> —James 1:12-18

What I learned about my situation was that I was presented with an option in the form of a feeling/thought. The door that was used to peak my curiosity was my grandmother's apparel. I could have pursued the feelings/thoughts and explained it as "I was born with these feelings, and I shouldn't suppress them; I'll just be who I am." Well, the problem with that type of thinking is that God would be a hypocrite and confused to say that homosexuality is wrong, and then create people as homosexuals.

> *Thou shalt not lie with mankind, as with womankind: it is abomination.*
> —Leviticus 18:22

> *Do you not know that the unrighteous and the wrongdoers will not inherit or have any share in the kingdom of God? Do not be deceived (misled): neither the impure and immoral, nor idolaters, nor adulterers, nor those who participate in homosexuality, nor cheats (swindlers and thieves), nor greedy graspers, nor drunkards, nor foulmouthed revilers and slanderers, nor extortioners and robbers will inherit or have any share in the kingdom of God.*
> —1 Corinthians 6:9-10 (Amplified)

Notice that homosexuality isn't the only act listed as a sin. Heterosexual fornication also falls in the impure, immoral and adultery categories, so this isn't a "pile on the homosexuals" message.

It's a Choice

I would like to make it extremely clear that homosexuality is a choice, just like being lazy or being a thief is a choice. Look at many of the men in Church who are a part of the music ministry. Some of the men who exude a more effeminate disposition had some sort of experience with too much femininity or not enough positive masculinity in their lives. There might have been some sexual abuse, sexual experimentation, or whatever, but the commonality is that these men were challenged with a thought or a feeling.

Here is the subtlety of the enemy: he presents the most innocent of things or thoughts to a person. The infinite battle of good vs. evil goes on in that person's mind. Meanwhile, the rationalization of sin and one's feelings will eventually come to a fork in the road (a decision to make) vs. reconciling the homosexual thoughts and feelings to God's Word, one's conscience, or the natural order of things. Only one of the decisions can be the correct decision. So the decision is made (right or wrong); and if the initial decision was the wrong decision, then every subsequent decision (associated with that initially wrong decision) will be wrong unless the first decision is corrected. This is how people get trapped. Little boys who play with dolls, and some guys who fix women's hair, or hang out with the girls like they are one of the girls seems so innocent, but it also can open up a door to something else. The trap doesn't always manifest itself as an identity crisis, but the seeds are planted for an agenda other than what God desires. Remember this, God has a plan for us, and the enemy has a plan for us. You must decide which plan you wish to follow.

The enemy is not going to present you with destruction. He is going to present you with things that are pleasant to the senses. Sin is attractive; it feels good; it smells good; it tastes good; and it is pleasurable.

For we ourselves also were sometimes foolish, disobedient, deceived, serving divers lusts and pleasures, living in malice and envy, hateful, and hating one another.
—Titus 3:3

Sin is bait to get you to see the sin all the way through until the end (destruction). That's why fisherman put worms on hooks, because worms are more attractive to fish than hooks. Similarly, the pleasures of sin are more appealing than their consequences.

I have one final comment about homosexuality being a choice. I get so irritated and I find it extremely offensive that homosexuals continue to make comparisons of the homosexual movement with that of blacks and civil rights. That is like comparing apples and oranges, because being black isn't a choice, and civil rights are for all people, not a select few; and the Bible doesn't say that being black is an abomination.

I thank God that my Dad defused that bomb before it detonated in my life. All it takes is an open door and the enemy will slide in and plant a reasonable sounding argument to legitimize sin. But we can't explain sin away; nor can we make sin fit into our culture just so that we don't hurt people's feelings, or our own egos. Sin is what it is, and we have to see homosexuality and other behaviors that God has clearly defined, as such.

Don't be deceived about temptations and succumbing to the lust of the flesh, the lust of the eye, or the pride of life. The enemy desires to separate us from God through his suggestions and reasoning. But as long as your heart is open to truth, and you aren't governed by your emotions and feelings, then you will find the way to escape any trap the enemy sets for you.

I hope that this letter helped to put some things into perspective regarding how the enemy works, because he sure is deceiving a lot of people.

Yours in Christ,

Right with God, Wrong on the Issues of the Day

Dear Friends,

The title of this letter explains the state of many believers in Christ. Their hearts are right, but their thinking is wrong, whether by ignorance or by indoctrination. It's unfortunate and frustrating, because many times we find ourselves fighting our fellow (spiritual) brothers and sisters in the Lord. It's the emotional element of these arguments and issues that seem to muddy up the waters of debate. I have been in discussions with Christians who have sided with atheists against my Biblical positions, because they were engaged in the *emotional* aspect of the discussion, rather than the *historical and Biblical* perspective; and these are very difficult conversations to have.

Remember the Pharisees? They believed they were doing God's Will by confronting and challenging Jesus. They called Him crazy, a drunken sinner, and they eventually played a part in His arrest, trial, and execution. These were the "Church folks" in Jesus' day. Do you think they were on the right or the wrong side of that issue? They were on the wrong side, but it all worked out in regards to the Will of God being done. But would you want history to show your name included among those who betrayed the Lord Jesus? I wouldn't want that, and if they were walking as spiritual men, they wouldn't have wanted that either.

But we speak the wisdom of God in a mystery, even the hidden wisdom, which God ordained before the world unto our glory: which none of the princes of this world knew: for had they known it, they would not have crucified the Lord of glory.
—1 Corinthians 2:7-8

The religious folks didn't discern Jesus; they simply had mental assent about God and His Law. Jesus told the religious people of His day:

> *Then the Pharisees and scribes asked Him, "Why do Your disciples not walk according to the tradition of the elders, but eat bread with unwashed hands?" He answered and said to them, "Well did Isaiah prophesy of you hypocrites, as it is written: "This people honor Me with their lips, but their heart is far from Me. And in vain they worship Me, teaching as doctrines the commandments of men. For laying aside the commandment of God, you hold the tradition of men— the washing of pitchers and cups, and many other such things you do." He said to them, "All too well you reject the commandment of God, that you may keep your tradition.*
> —Mark 7:5, 9

Jesus basically told the religious folks that they looked good on the outside (keeping the Law), but they were bad on the inside (not having a heart towards a relationship with God). This is what we are seeing among many believers today.

The Spirit of Truth

Jesus told His disciples that after His ascension to the Father, He would send the Spirit of Truth who would guide us into all truth.

> *However, when He, the Spirit of truth, has come, He will guide you into all truth; for He will not speak on His own authority, but whatever He hears He will speak; and He will tell you things to come.*
> —John 16:13

I make this point because whether you are dealing with a spiritual truth, a financial truth, a mathematical truth, a historical truth, a scientific truth, a political truth, a health-related truth, etc., God's Spirit will lead you into **ALL TRUTH** if you ask Him to show you truth. It seems as though many Church folks fail to make the connection between the Spirit of Truth and truth. There is absolutely no excuse for

Christians who have the Spirit of God residing in their spirit to be on the wrong side of issues. I can excuse ignorance, because ignorance is the result of a lack of information. We are all ignorant of something, because no one knows everything. But to be adamant about a position, or to be downright recalcitrant to truth, is totally opposite to our spiritual nature in Christ.

Although there isn't a Scripture that addresses every specific issue we face, the Spirit of Truth will still reveal the principles/character of God or the truth of our circumstances, so that we will know how to respond in given situations. But our hearts have to be receptive, and we **MUST** be yielded to His Will.

Amateur Believers

The leading of the Spirit of Truth led many heroes to victory, because the Spirit of Truth knows **ALL TRUTH**, and will lead us and guide us in it. The wonderful thing about the Spirit of Truth is that we don't need to be well-educated, of high social status, or privileged by societal standards in order to be successful. All we have to do is be willing and obedient.

> *If ye be willing and obedient, ye shall eat the good of the land: but if ye refuse and rebel, ye shall be devoured with the sword: for the mouth of the Lord hath spoken it.*
> —Isaiah 1:19-20

Harriet Tubman was an amateur. John the Baptist was an amateur. Moses was an amateur. But they discerned and followed their God-given calling. As a result, they made history that impacted many lives for good. It was their obedience to the Spirit of Truth that was the key; not the local seminary, a title, big buildings, or notoriety.

Please brethren, don't be on the wrong side of what God is saying and doing, because the Spirit of Truth is willing to lead us into all truth.

Yours in Christ,

Tattoos and Piercings

Dear Friends,

In this letter, I'd like to address the subject of tattoos and unique piercings. Many people consider tattoos and piercings to be trendy, counter-culture, and cool; but let's look at them from another perspective.

Although there is nothing wrong with adorning yourself with nice clothing and accessories, our main focus shouldn't be on the outward appearance, because God is more interested in your heart (spirit).

> *Do not let your adornment be merely outward—arranging the hair, wearing gold, or putting on fine apparel—rather let it be the hidden person of the heart, with the incorruptible beauty of a gentle and quiet spirit, which is very precious in the sight of God.*
>
> —1 Peter 3:3-4

If you got a tattoo or unique piercing before you accepted Christ, then it is what it is. You can't erase the past. All you can do is move forward. If you got a tattoo or piercing since you have been saved, that isn't a death and Hell sentence either. But I wouldn't recommend getting tattoos or unique piercings going forward. I would be concerned about some of the health risks regarding sterilization, or if the inks contain lead, mercury or other additives, etc.

Additionally, tattoos and unique piercings are not a good witness, and it distracts many people from the message that God might want to bring to people through you. I'm sure that people with tattoos and/or unique piercings would freely accept the ministry or message of another person with tattoos and/or unique piercings. But just be aware that you will be limited in how God can use you. Also, remember, as a believer in Christ, you submitted your will to His Will, and your body (the temple of the Holy Ghost) is now committed for the Master's use.

Be sensitive to how doing certain things can bring unnecessary attention to you, and it can limit the amount and the kinds of opportunities that could be presented to you. Judging people by the outward appearance isn't the right thing to do, but unfortunately, that is the way it is in our society. It's hard to believe that a reputable firm would take a candidate seriously if he or she interviewed with a lip piercing and neck tattoos. That person might have the best skill set and temperament for the job, but many times, perception is reality, and tattoos and unique piercings are not widely accepted by all.

Tattoos and piercings are by no means the unpardonable sin, but we must be sensitive to opportunities that might elude us until society changes. So surrender your desires to God's Will and what He would have you to do, and the tattoos and piercings argument doesn't become a point of contention.

Yours in Christ,

Bro. Jay

Racism in America and in Church Folks

Dear Friends,

I am writing this letter in order to remind people that real racism needs to be identified and eradicated. Racism, discrimination, and hatred are very touchy subjects for many people around the world, and God is one hundred percent against all of these terrible things. All of us have been affected by and/or have experienced some form of the three (directly or indirectly) at some point in our lives. The concept of racism (or any form of hatred) has never made sense to me. Even during my childhood, I always liked or disliked a person based upon how they interacted with me, not based upon their skin color or ethnic characteristics. I know that we all have different mindsets, we view things differently, and as a society, we aren't perfect; but we are better off today, than we were yesterday, and we can be even better tomorrow.

What is Racism?

By definition, racism is the belief that one's race is superior (in any way) to another race. So based upon that definition, one can dislike someone and/or disagree with someone and NOT necessarily be a racist. One can dislike a person and/or their views and not necessarily feel any superiority over that person or a group of people; and even if a racial slur is used (by definition) that does not necessarily constitute racism. Remember, racism entails a sense of superiority of one race over another. In addition, one could argue that the use of a racial slur or some other insult is ignorant, insensitive or hurtful, and I would agree; the person who hurls the insult could be a racist, but their ignorance and saying hurtful things are not necessarily racism.

Racism doesn't make a lot of sense. It's kind of like judging a drink based upon the container in which it was bottled, rather than the contents/quality of the drink. You shouldn't judge a product in that manner or people either. People should be judged based upon their individual merits, not based on their racial characteristics, or the actions of those in their racial group.

The unfortunate reality is that overt and covert racism are still real factors in the 21st century, but we must continue to be better than the low levels where some in our society wish to drag us. I believe that when we illustrate what is and what isn't racism, we can build a case to expose the misconceptions of racism, so that we can get a better grasp of what we are truly facing as a society, and act upon viable solutions to combat the ignorance.

The Race Card and the Media

I have found that it is very difficult to have an intelligent discussion with people who are racists, biased, bigots, prejudiced, etc. Generally, these people have pre-packaged and programmed thoughts; and they can't turn off the filters in their minds long enough to hear reason and truth. There are a small number of people in the media, politics, and in our society whom I consider to be the "race brokers." These (white, black, Hispanic, etc.) people thrive on stirring up racial matters and injecting a person's ethnicity into conversations and debates, even if it doesn't fit. Their audiences tend to be a very gullible and emotional crowd who are usually less interested in facts. But they are always ready to hear of the next injustice, so that the racial case can be made once again.

When the "race card" is carelessly tossed around, we water down the clarion call to combat real racism and hatred. I liken it to one of Aesop's fables, "The Boy Who Cried Wolf." It's the tale of a shepherd boy who repeatedly tricked his neighbors into thinking a wolf was attacking his flock. When a wolf actually did appear one day, the neighbors didn't believe the boy's cries for help, and the flock was destroyed. The moral of the story illustrated how liars cannot be trusted; even when they tell the truth, no one believes them. This is what happens when the "race card" is played ad nauseam; we become numb to it, so when the real threats of racism show up, there is no real motivation to resist it. If we are objective and use the definition of racism as one's feeling of racial superiority over another race, then we will quickly learn that a lot of today's claims of racism are not accurate. But these false claims continue to stir people up.

The Southern Strategy

One of the most popular examples of the cry of racism in American history is the "Southern Strategy" of Richard Nixon and the Republican Party of the 1960's until the 1980's. By the 1980's, the South became a very strong Republican region for presidential races. The claim is that since Nixon and the Republican Party started swaying and eventually winning the Southern Democratic, white racist vote; by default, the Republicans are racists. But a deeper historical look into the infamous Southern Democrat "voting shift" to the Republican Party during the 1960's to the 1980's, paints a much different picture, than the claims of racism suggest. I do believe that racism had a part to play in it, but let's get the full picture.

What happened in the shift of the South? Traditionally, the South was one of the poorest regions in the U.S. As industrialism and manufacturing increased and prospered, the South's anti-union economy, lower taxes, lower wage labor and cheaper land costs became very attractive to many northern businesses and northern Republicans. As businesses began moving to the South to take advantage of these benefits, wages increased and lifestyles improved for many white, racist Democratic Southerners. In politics, the best campaign tool is economics. If people feel as though they are (financially) better off today than they were yesterday, political candidates/parties have a better chance of winning support. As a result of being better off economically, these white Southern racist Democrats eventually started to switch over to the Republican Party for the economic benefit, not because Nixon and the Republicans were racists. Besides, in 1968 (when the "shift" began) the racist Southern voters overwhelmingly supported their racist Democratic candidate George Wallace, not Richard Nixon or Hubert Humphrey. So the claim that "dog whistle" politics was used is inaccurate.

Further, the claim that the Republicans used "dog whistle" politics and political code words to call in the votes in 1968 continued on with the "welfare queen" comment during Reagan's 1976 Presidential campaign, and the 1988 Bush (41) Willie Horton political ad. Neither of these incidents fit the definition of racism. Again, insensitive, exaggerated, insulting, misleading, or even scare tactics might be a reason to debate the matter; but not racism, because neither incident insinuated or stated that whites were superior to blacks.

If They are Trained to be Racists/Dividers; I'm Trained to Combat it

Some of you might be asking yourself, "Why are you defending these hatemongers?" I'm not defending anyone. I just want us to properly label things as they are so that we can locate the real issue and provide some real solutions. Or some of you might be asking, "Are you one of those naïve black folks who believes that we live in a post-racial America?" Absolutely not! But I do know what the true definition of racism is, and I am doing my part to combat it.

> *Unto the pure all things are pure: but unto them that are defiled and unbelieving is nothing pure; but even their mind and conscience is defiled.*
> —Titus 1:15

In other words, to whatever you give your attention is what you will see. Think about it. An accountant is trained to read, to understand and to decipher income statements and balance sheets. By a force of habit, I imagine that many accountants routinely analyze random numerical values and do number crunching when it isn't even required. They can become a victim of their own training. Construction workers will walk through a brand new mall with family and friends, and critique the architecture rather than shop for the products for sale. Why? Accountants, construction workers and others are trained to see things that the average person can't see through casual observation. They can see a bad financial deal, a crooked doorjamb, or an out of square wall, or some other thing that is obviously out of place to them, but not necessarily to the average person. Likewise, people who spend a lot of time cultivating a collectivist mindset and focusing on the past (rather than growing from those experiences and moving forward) can find racism in a bottle of ketchup and a pile of pencil shavings. I have asked myself many times in various situations, "How did he/she conclude that these statements were racist?" It's all about training and/or intellectual honesty. Those who are trained to see goodness and truth, will find goodness and truth all around them. Others might say that is naïve, but I call it a good way to combat ignorance, and to keep your composure in the midst of weak-minded people.

Why be reactive? Why not be proactive and control your own destiny and your emotions? How would you react if someone called you a "nigger," "a white cracker devil," "a spic," "a kraut," "a nip," "a mick," "a ruskie," "a kike," or whichever racial slur was created to be offensive to your race? Would you be ready to fight? Would you retaliate with a racial slur of your own in order to offend that person?

Answer not a fool according to his folly, lest thou also be like unto him.
—Proverbs 26:4

Well, you have to remember that racism is not an intellectual or a reasonable position to have. So, if you are dealing with a racist, you are dealing with an unreasonable person, and you don't want to get into a mindless war of words with an unreasonable person. Think of it as trying to convince a two year old that Elmo isn't real. Yes, Elmo is on TV, and yes, Elmo said he was your friend; but he isn't real. Why engage someone in an unreasonable argument if you can't win the argument or get the other person to focus on reality?

Likewise reckon ye also yourselves to be dead indeed unto sin, but alive unto God through Jesus Christ our Lord.
—Romans 6:11

Personally, I am dead to racism. I am not a "nigger" and I liken that word to be a sharp knife that stabs me. But I can't feel the stab because as far as that word is concerned, I am dead to it. If I am dead to it, then I can't react to the usage of it. I know my name and I know who I am in Christ Jesus. The use of that word will only alert me to the level of maturity, education and/or the spiritual condition of the person using the word. If I chose to retaliate, I am no better than the person using the word, and I have already lost that battle. I want everyone to remember that, because it's how we react to racism (in part) that helps us to defeat racism.

There is also the game of racism, where certain people encourage division, and they benefit as a result of our societal ignorance. Civil rights were and still are a serious issue. People fought and died for the very rights that we enjoy today. We have to continue to fight in that same spirit and tenacity in order to expose the dividers, and to support the defenders of everyone's God-given unalienable rights of life, liberty and the pursuit of happiness.

The only way to identify error (the dividers) is with the truth, whether it is a spiritual truth, the definition of racism, or a historical perspective. You have already been armed with the true definition of racism. So the next time someone is acting like a racist, or you are called a racist, you can inject the true definition into the conversation and conclude whether or not the accuser is fighting to stamp out racism and hatred, or if they are promoting another agenda. Don't let these people make you play defense, and divide us. These same people who casually throw the race card around are actually the ones who are muddying the waters of an intellectual discussion of the issues.

All of our blood is red and it all came from God. So if God doesn't play racial favorites, then we shouldn't either. If you let these people divide us through (a combination of) their calculated agenda and our ignorance, then they will destroy us one by one. If they destroy a person, that will destroy families. Destroyed families will destroy neighborhoods. Destroyed neighborhoods will destroy communities. Destroyed communities will destroy cities. Destroyed cities will destroy counties. Destroyed counties will destroy states. Destroyed states will destroy regions; and lastly, destroyed regions will destroy the nation. But the destruction or the rebuilding starts with individuals. Will you be a part of the destructive force of racism and division, or will you be a rebuilder of people in order to rebuild the nation? Will you educate yourself and speak up to inform others? Will you stand up against racism, and promote unity and humanity? Can you see the divisive attempts to tear us apart? Will you be a part of the solution? Let's ERACISM!

Yours in Christ,

WHERE ARE THE MEN(TORS)?

Dear Friends,

Although I do love all races of people, and I believe that humanity (as a whole) needs to make some adjustments, I am writing this letter to my black brothers and sisters. If some of my brothers and sister of other races can relate to this message, then please feel free to enjoy the content. The black community has been hardest hit regarding many of the social ills that exist; and many of us are at least professing Christians. I attribute a lot of our problems to the absence Godly men. We don't have a shortage of males; we have a shortage of Godly men.

> *"A little less complaint and whining, and a little more dogged work and manly striving, would do us more credit than a thousand civil rights bills."*
> —W.E.B Du Bois

Men, the Familial Head Have Been Cut Off

The Bible teaches us that God created man in His own image and likeness (Genesis 1:26-27), and He also created man to be the head of the wife, as Christ is over the Church (Ephesians 5:23). Now the issue here is familial authority and it is abundantly clear from Scripture that the man is the head of the family under Christ. If you read (Genesis 3:1-7) there is an exchange between the serpent (satan), Adam, and Eve. The authority/dominion that God gave to Adam was what was in question (Genesis 1:26 & 28). The evil deceiver, satan (a spirit being with no tangible body) can't randomly kill people, and wreak havoc on the Earth; even though his purpose is to kill, to steal and to destroy (John 10:10).

Humans have authority to be on the Earth and we have the natural ability (a body) to physically operate in this realm. But satan is not manifest in this material world, because he has no physical body. Let's think of our bodies as Earth suits, and satan doesn't possess an Earth suit. So if he has no authority to operate in a material world, then how does satan fulfill his purpose in killing people, stealing and destroying things? He uses the (bodily) authority of willing vessels that will submit to his purpose. In other words, if someone is willing to kill people, then satan has found a willing vessel (an Earth suit) through which he can work. That person didn't just have a coincidental thought. That thought had an origin, and that origin is the enemy, satan.

Why is this important? It is important because this is precisely why satan is out to destroy the human male species, especially the black male. If satan cuts off the head of the family (the husband/father) then the remaining structure (the family) will be without leadership. Look at some of the males as you walk through the malls. Could you imagine some of these guys as a responsible head of a family? Have you noticed some of the scathing statistics that plague our race? Illegitimate births; drug use; the abortion rate; percent of single mother homes; HIV and AIDS contraction; heart disease; violent deaths; gang related incidents; deadbeat dads; the exploding prison population; increased welfare recipients, and a host of other devastating statistics that have proven to be a disaster for our community. These results have nothing to do with the white man or the Government. However, these statistics have everything to do with (generally speaking) a race of people who have succumbed to a belief system that is counterproductive. Let's not forget that other races have struggles and issues as well, but the black community (as a whole) is doing a poor job of being responsible and setting the next generation on the right path.

We need for our males to become men. But if we don't have our men showing the young males how to become men, then we are rowing upstream without a paddle. There are some instances where the male influence in the home suffered an untimely death, and that is unfortunate. But most cases of a fatherless home are deliberate demonstrations of irresponsible behavior and abandonment.

The head (the man) is the one who provides direction, insight and leadership. Insight connotes vision or thought. These are concepts that are associated with the brain or head. Can your natural body live without a head? No, it cannot; neither can families survive without a head. Some families do make it by the grace of God, but it was not God's Will to have a fatherless home. God made it so that a man and a woman could procreate and raise the child in the nurture and the admonition of the Lord (Ephesians 6:4). But without a head, which is the location of the brain (the housing for the mind); there is no future, vision, or direction. So with men being ever so absent in the lives of our women and children, it is easy to see why the black community is in such shambles.

> *Where there is no vision, the people perish: but he that keepeth the law, happy is he.*
> —Proverbs 29:18

Where are today's children getting their images of males to emulate? Celebrities and other bad influences are the pseudo role models to which many children look, because they are available and relatable figures who are present in place of absent fathers. So the young people choose who looks cool, who is popular, or rich. We have to remember that young people are unskilled in life; hence, they need guidance. All the while, a good family member, a caring schoolteacher, a local doctor, or a respected business owner can be a positive role model in the family or in the community. This situation presents a perpetual dilemma for our posterity.

Women, a Battered Support System

This leaves the women in a very precarious situation, especially if they have to raise a male child alone. Since most households are without a stable father/husband, the pressure is truly on the women if they are going to make it and raise their child(ren) properly. I do applaud the good women who were and are acting as the support post for the family. While that pillar of our community (the man) is down, the good women need to rise up in a big way until the man can get back on track. In his absence, the women have to pull double duty and do whatever they can to be the nurturing, caring mother, and to supplement the absence of the positive male influence.

Unfortunately, I do see many women being a part of the problem when it comes to the behavior of many males, and many of the bad women are ruining it for the good women. The bad women put their stamp of approval on the wrong males who are:

1. Unproductive.
2. Irresponsible.
3. Disrespectful.
4. Dependent.
5. Unkempt.
6. Immoral.
7. Immature.

So now there's a supply and demand market for immature males. What incentive do these males have to improve? What does this say about the low self-esteem of many females these days? Fortunately, women can change the situation in a positive direction very quickly. If there is no market that will settle for immature males, then the supply goes away. These males will either begin acting like men, or they will become homosexuals. Women have to realize that they have a huge influence over male behavior. But if women don't demand better and hold these guys accountable for their actions, then nothing will change for the better.

> *"The black man must step forward, but that doesn't mean that black women have to step back."*
> —Shirley A. Chisholm, U.S. Representative from New York, 1969–1983

Over-Mothering the Male Child

Motherhood is an integral part of raising successful children. Mothers bring unique qualities to childrearing that fathers cannot, and vice versa. But an excess of anything is too much. One mistake many mothers make is that they are afraid to let go, especially of their boys. In many ways, that failure to let go is manifest in many mothers defending their irresponsible children's behavior. There are many mothers who are naïve and believe that their boys can do no wrong. Or they just live in utter denial. You have to know the personality of your child and face the facts if your child has issues. If your son is a crack head, then it is what it is. If he is a gangster, then so be it. If he is a thief, then call him what he is. You pray for him, you love him, but you don't support or defend your child's foolishness. You get the child some help, if they genuinely want help. You can't pretend the world is against them and that everyone is out to get them. At some point, people must exercise some accountability and personal responsibility.

Of course injustice exists. But when mothers don't let sons grow up, or be accountable and face the music of their crimes and actions, then they are delaying the inevitable destruction of that child. Additionally, these boys will never become men. They won't know how to properly relate to a wife, and they won't know how to properly raise children. What does that all mean? It means that a dysfunctional family trend is in motion, and it needs to stop now, because the black community is dying.

Recidivism, an Inner City Merry-Go-Round

America has approximately five percent of the world's population, but it holds approximately twenty-five percent of the world's prisoners. That is an alarming statistic. There are over two million people locked up in American prisons, and nearly one million of those prisoners are black. I am not writing you to make any excuses or to spread any conspiracy theories, but the facts speak for themselves.

I am no advocate of drugs use, but one of the biggest jokes that has ever been sold to our society is the war on drugs. I was just a kid when former First Lady Nancy Reagan started the "Just Say No" to drugs campaign. I agree with the message, but the campaign for harsher drug laws and minimum sentencing is an absolute failure. I believe America has failed in the drug war for many reasons, but mainly because drugs are not a violent criminal offense. Using drugs is a moral and/or mental health issue; but drug users are criminalized under these stiff penalties (in some instances fifteen years to life) for being a drug addict. Again, I am not advocating for drug use, but I would like to see the punishment fit the crime.

> *Excessive bail shall not be required, nor excessive fines imposed, nor cruel and unusual punishments inflicted.*
> —Eighth Amendment to the U.S. Constitution

Most black men get into the system because of drugs, and most of those cases are plea bargains. Think about it...if you fight the charges and are found guilty under these harsher drug laws, you could serve fifteen years to life. Or you could take the plea bargain and serve two years and maybe get out in one year on good behavior. Would you roll the dice with a Public Defender as your attorney?

About fourteen million whites, and two and a half million blacks are drug users, but blacks are sent to prison for drug offenses at ten times the rate of whites. Again, look at the options; when the whites who can afford to fight the charges decide to go to trial, they retain the best defense, whether they are guilty or not. However, inner-city black folks who don't have those types of resources are encouraged to do the time. Many Public Defenders are more interested in minimizing time spent on these same cases and they would rather move people through the system, instead of doing the right thing. It's kind of like the teacher who wants to pass the kids who are failing and who aren't paying attention in class; these teachers won't have to deal with those bothersome students again. People can try to make excuses and say that I am giving Public Defenders and the system an unfair criticism, but I will only refer you to the statistics; and from there, you can analyze the information objectively, and draw your own conclusion.

So, the disproportionate number of black men in jail, prison and on parole plays a tremendous role in the lives of the black family. Either the black men will return home as homosexuals, or they will

be dysfunctional role models. A small percentage of black men do find the right path and stay on it; but that is the exception, and not the rule. The reality is that many of the black men who do time on drug charges, become a product of their environment and become hardened criminals. Prison life teaches them to be tough in order to survive. So when they return home, that is what they know, that is how they act, and that is what they teach the next generation. It's a vicious cycle, because all of these guys eventually get caught. Some people might get away with the dirt longer than others, but eventually, the law catches up with you. So, back on the inner city block, the "oldheads" teach the young guys about life in the legal and the prison systems; and like I said earlier, "Kids emulate what they see."
Look at the statistics:

- One in nine black children has an incarcerated parent.
- One out of six black men have been incarcerated as of 2001.
- Blacks represent over half of the youth admitted to state prisons.

Personally, I believe that a strong, Godly man with vision, a career, goals, drive, common sense, and authority, can eliminate at least ninety percent of these horrible statistics. Many black churches and many black leaders are failing to address the true nature of these problems. The root of the matter is immorality: individual immorality becomes familial immorality. Later, it becomes the "new normal," and it eventually becomes generational immorality; ultimately, it morphs into societal immorality.

For out of the heart proceed evil thoughts, murders, adulteries, fornications, thefts, false witness, and blasphemies.
—Matthew 15:19

If we would focus more on regenerating the heart of man, rather than the actions of man, then the root issue will, by default, resolve the irresponsible actions of man. But as long as a broken system tries to right the wrongs of society, the most vulnerable people (and in this instance it is poor, inner-city black folks) will always be disproportionately victimized. Meanwhile, most Church folks are not being salt and light on this issue. Additionally, I believe that many (not all) of our black politicians are gaining wealth, power, and influence from some of the societal ills that face us. While few in the black community will openly admit this, just look at the number of "activists" in our communities who are well-compensated advocates for justice, equality, and change. Meanwhile, in the aggregate, not much has changed for good in many inner cities across America.

> *There is another class of colored people who make a business of keeping the troubles, the wrongs, and the hardships of the Negro race before the public. Having learned that they are able to make a living out of their troubles, they have grown into the settled habit of advertising their wrongs — partly because they want sympathy and partly because it pays. Some of these people do not want the Negro to lose his grievances, because they do not want to lose their jobs.*
> —Booker T. Washington

We must be more intimately involved with our personal lives, families, neighbors, and friends, and who we elect to govern our communities. Our society is dying right before our eyes.

Yours in Christ,

SUICIDE

Dear Friends,

Recently, I received a letter from a family who needed prayer regarding a very sensitive matter. A husband and wife wrote me about their child who committed suicide. As you can imagine, the family was heartbroken and thankfully they went to the saints of God for encouragement and consolation. Unfortunately, the family felt less encouraged after the counseling sessions with God's people, than they did immediately after the tragic incident.

In the letter, the parents told me a little bit about their son. He was your average, good Christian kid who was raised in a good Christian home, and never gave the family, friends, teachers, or neighbors any trouble. Granted, in some people's minds the term "Christian" is very subjective, because in the twenty-first century so many people and things are considered to be "Christian." But for the sake of argument, he was a born-again believer, but not the strongest of believers.

I believe somewhere along the way, this young man was influenced by American TV culture and his peers. He began to hang out with the wrong crowd, and experimented with the wrong things. When his parents and other good influences in his life confronted him about the matter, he rebelled, and he intensified his use of drugs, alcohol, and other illicit behavior. The young man had a difficult time reconciling his upbringing with his current actions, and he decided to go to a drug rehabilitation program. The facility had Christian ministers and doctors who were trained and willing to work with the patients until they walked out the door "clean" six to nine months later.

The young man vowed to get clean. He struggled, and suffered some horrible side effects, but he was clean for ninety days. Then one day, he decided he didn't want to struggle anymore, and he killed himself.

It's hard to console the family in such a time as this, because you really don't know where their faith level is, and what their true belief system will allow them to believe. After the young man's death, their Church told them about the Ten Commandments and "thou shall not kill." Their method of ministry was to tell the parents that their child went to Hell, because he sinned against God. That was the wrong move! Now, it is true that "thou shall not kill" is one of the Ten Commandments, but that is not a very consoling Scripture in light of the events that transpired.

Let's look at suicide in practical terms. God has given us a built-in mechanism for survival, and for someone to bypass that survival mechanism, they would have to be suffering a severe spiritual and/or mental breakdown. It would have to be a point of such hopelessness, confusion, and despair that they could see no hope for tomorrow. Suicide is not a normal, natural response to a problem, and my point is that Church folks can't assume that every case of suicide equates to a Hell sentence for the victim based upon one or two Scriptures. We agree that murder is wrong, but we also have to look at the heart of the matter, because there are a lot of cause and effect things to consider.

What if someone had a gun to your head and told you to rob a bank or they were going to kill your family or you? Would you do it? The point is that your innate God-given mechanism on the inside of you to survive will activate, and wherever your level of faith is, your level of hope, and ability to believe, that's how you'll act in the hard times. It's easy to be a man or woman of faith in the easy times. But what happens when your faith is challenged at crunch time, especially in a split second, life-or-death situation? How would you react? No one knows until you get there. This young man got there and his reaction was a fatal one. He lost hope and he didn't see a way to recover from his mistake. This doesn't mean that he wasn't born again in spirit. The toxicology report confirmed that he was clean and the chaplain confirmed that he was in the Bible meetings faithfully. It was also documented that he was struggling with his faith, and he had a hard time forgiving himself for what he had become. He was remorseful for letting God and his family down, and he wanted to try and fix it. But he went as far as he could go in his own strength; and he couldn't grasp enough faith and hope at that point. Where do you go when you're at the end of your rope? We should look to God, but everybody's faith isn't there. Some people need more natural and tangible things to help them in their faith, such as: an accountability partner, more structure, more supervision, or something else to help them get through the dilemma.

Again, I'm not excusing murder and taking a life that God created, but these events were definitely outside of the normal progression of life. This young man fell and got back up, but he just got tired of trying to do it on his own. Maybe things would've been different if someone reached him earlier. Who knows? But we as a body of believers have to be more discerning of people's needs.

How can a young man be a candidate for Hell when his heart was right, but his mind wasn't? He felt despair and contrition, but he just wasn't in his normal state of mind to make a sensible decision about his life. Doesn't society excuse people who are mentally handicapped and we give them grace because they lack the capacity to function like the rest of us? Why can't we see some victims of suicide through the same eyes of grace? What about the woman who feared for her life and jumped to her death from the Belle Isle Bridge in Detroit in 1995? She feared for her life, because a three hundred pound man was beating her up. In a split second, she had to choose to take more of the abuse or to jump off of the bridge to escape. She obviously feared for her life, because jumping off of a thirty foot bridge is not a rational thought. What about the many people who jumped out of the upper floor windows of the Twin Towers on 911? Again, these were decisions made by people who were reacting to their fears and sense of hopelessness. It's easy to judge them from the comfort of our homes, but these incidents prove that people have the propensity to act upon their innate survival instincts, even if their decisions don't make much sense.

Again, suicide is wrong, but it is not the unpardonable sin. I communicate with a lot of Christians who lack perspective and insight regarding the grace of God. It's easy to judge folks and assume they are in Hell. But the reality is that no one can truly understand the depth of someone else's suffering, or the reasons that could drive a soul to such desperation. Only God knows what is in a person's heart, and only He knows the extent of pain that might bring a person to the point of suicide.

Obviously, I have never committed suicide, but I did have suicidal thoughts decades ago, so I can empathize with this family's struggle. It's a hard place in which to be. If problems were always easy, then God's help would not be necessary. But something like this requires the deliverance of the Lord, and some people need some extra help in getting to the finish line. You can't give up on folks who haven't given up on themselves. But more people need to be spiritually sensitive in critical moments such as these.

Yours in Christ,

Legislating Morality

Dear Friends,

I wanted to clear up a misconception that has permeated the thinking of many people of faith. We must understand what law is and why we have law. Law is that which defines right and wrong; and Governments are mandated to use their authority to restrain and to punish evildoers. Additionally, the Government's other major function is to protect and to provide justice for the innocent. But the statement, "You can't legislate morality" has caused a lot of confusion, because there is a difference between saving people by law, and having laws regarding morality. Laws are very much concerned with morality, and we **MUST** legislate morality.

Aren't the laws against murder and perjury there for moral reasons? Yes, they are; because murder and lying are immoral. Even our speeding laws are moral laws in a sense, because they are designed to protect life and property.

Sometimes, the problem with people and with laws is that some people desire to change/reform people through the law. The law can't change people's heart. The law can only define right and wrong, and warn people of the consequences for breaking the law. But if you want a heart-felt change in a person, that can only be done by the convicting work of the Holy Spirit, and repentance by a free-will individual.

> *Knowing that a man is not justified by the works of the law, but by the faith of Jesus Christ, even we have believed in Jesus Christ, that we might be justified by the faith of Christ, and not by the works of the law: for by the works of the law shall no flesh be justified.*
> —Galatians 2:16

We can't take a humanistic view and try to make society better without looking at the whole human element: spirit, soul, and body. If society attempts to answer all of our problems through secular eyes, then we will always be provided with a false diagnosis. Some issues are spiritual in nature, and many times, the secular world provides natural solutions for spiritual problems. I liken that to putting a Band-Aid on someone's forehead in order to cure a headache.

These things we also speak, not in words which man's wisdom teaches but which the Holy Spirit teaches, comparing spiritual things with spiritual. But the natural man does not receive the things of the Spirit of God, for they are foolishness to him; nor can he know them, because they are spiritually discerned. But he who is spiritual judges all things, yet he himself is rightly judged by no one. For "who has known the mind of the Lord that he may instruct Him?" But we have the mind of Christ.
—1 Corinthians 2:14-16 NKJV.

We can't legitimize immorality and we can't regenerate evil hearts through the law. But we must legislate morality.

Yours in Christ,

The Causes of Poverty

Dear Friends,

Cause and effect refers to a relationship between actions or events that produce a result. Gravity is the force that causes things to fall to the ground. People sleep because they are tired, and people eat because they are hungry. People want to be healthy, so they exercise. These are simple examples of cause and effect; something caused something else to happen. A catalyst of some sort causes everything; and poverty is no exception.

Most reasonable people would agree that poverty is not a good thing. If it was a good thing, most people wouldn't be fighting to stay away from it or fighting to get out of it. There are people who have been known to voluntarily take vows of poverty and equate poverty to humility, but there is nothing good about lacking the necessities of life. I believe that if we can pinpoint the true causes of poverty, then we can begin to find real solutions to make occurrences of poverty as infrequent as possible. Jesus did instruct us that poverty would always be with us according to John 12:8, so let's see where poverty starts.

First, poverty is a curse.

> *But it shall come to pass, if you do not obey the voice of the Lord your God, to observe carefully all His commandments and His statutes which I command you today, that all these curses will come upon you and overtake you.*
> —Deuteronomy 28:15

Then, the rest of the chapter (for the next fifty plus Scriptures) lists all of the ways that curses of lack, calamity, disease, oppression, etc. will come upon a person and overtake one's life for disobedience. This is the spiritual element of poverty that manifests itself in the natural. It's quite simple; poverty is a curse. If you obey the Lord, you will be blessed; if you don't, you will be cursed. However, that is not the be-all and end-all of poverty, because there are other causes of poverty.

Second, poverty can be caused by laziness.

The soul of a lazy man desires, and has nothing; but the soul of the diligent shall be made rich.
—Proverbs 13:4

Laziness casts one into a deep sleep, and an idle person will suffer hunger.
—Proverbs 19:15

But we command you, brethren, in the name of our Lord Jesus Christ, that you withdraw from every brother who walks disorderly and not according to the tradition which he received from us. For you yourselves know how you ought to follow us, for we were not disorderly among you; nor did we eat anyone's bread free of charge, but worked with labor and toil night and day, that we might not be a burden to any of you, not because we do not have authority, but to make ourselves an example of how you should follow us. For even when we were with you, we commanded you this: If anyone will not work, neither shall he eat. For we hear that there are some who walk among you in a disorderly manner, not working at all, but are busybodies. Now those who are such we command and exhort through our Lord Jesus Christ that they work in quietness and eat their own bread. But as for you, brethren, do not grow weary in doing good. And if anyone does not obey our word in this epistle, note that person and do not keep company with him, that he may be ashamed. Yet do not count him as an enemy, but admonish him as a brother.
—2 Thessalonians 3:6-15

How many people do you know who are able-bodied and can work, but they choose to be lazy and make excuses? Well, the Bible doesn't make excuses and it clearly states that laziness is unacceptable behavior.

Third, poverty can be caused by inequity and fraud.

A false balance is abomination to the LORD: but a just weight is his delight.
—Proverbs 11:1

Often times, people do not realize that there are many variables to consider when dealing with poverty, wealth creation, and the economy. One element that people don't generally tend to address is the currency system. Let's pretend that our U.S. currency is one full glass of milk. If there are four people who want their own full glass of milk, then four glasses of milk need to be poured. The problem is that in today's economic society, our politicians want to bypass the laws of economics. So when they need four glasses of milk, they get one full glass of milk and evenly divide it into four glasses. Then they fill the balance of the glasses with water, and say that they have four glasses of milk. Those are not really four glasses of milk. Those are four weak quarter glasses of milk that are devoid of the full spectrum on nutrition, which is generally contained in a full glass of milk.

You might be wondering why this is so important. Well, this analogy explains the fraud of our monetary system. It illustrates how our politicians use (as the Bible states) a false weight to steal and to use a hidden tax called inflation, to hurt the poor and the middle class. Most people don't understand this part of the economy and that is why so many politicians use this tactic against the masses.

Every time our Government wishes to spend more money, they dilute the value of the currency by injecting more fiat currency into circulation. In the original example, a person would have to drink four glasses of the diluted milk to receive the nutritional benefit of one full glass of milk. Our currency has become much weaker over the past several decades. In 1913, a one-ounce twenty dollar gold coin was of equal value to a twenty dollar bill. In 2013, that same one-ounce twenty dollar gold coin is worth more than fifteen hundred dollars. It's the same one-ounce gold coin. So, why is there such a huge price difference? In 2013, more diluted dollars are needed to equal the value of that same gold coin. Today, each dollar is worth less, so those who provide goods and services require more of those (weakened) dollars.

I remember when a postage stamp cost twenty-five cents; I remember when a gallon of gas cost fifty cents; I remember when milk cost a dollar per gallon. But we have these false weights that our leaders have set against the poor and the middle class, and the Lord says that it is an abomination.

Fourth, poverty can be caused by poor stewardship over one's resources. The story of the prodigal son illustrates this very clearly.

He also that is slothful in his work is brother to him that is a great waster.
—Proverbs 18:9

Fifth, poverty is caused by a lack of resources, such as: the result of a famine, the lack of people, the lack of minerals, etc.

Sixth, poverty can be caused by a lack of or no marketable skills.

I am the LORD thy God which teacheth thee to profit, which leadeth thee by the way that thou shouldest go.
—Isaiah 48:17

Seventh, poverty can be caused by a lack of knowledge, wisdom, or understanding of economics and how the world works.

A prudent man foreseeth the evil, and hideth himself; but the simple pass on, and are punished.
—Proverbs 22:3 and 27:12

And of the children of Issachar, which were men that had understanding of the times, to know what Israel ought to do; the heads of them were two hundred; and all their brethren were at their commandment.
—1 Chronicles 2:32

Eighth, poverty can come from a lack of generosity.

A generous man will himself be blessed, for he shares his food with the poor.
—Proverbs 22:9

But this I say, He which soweth sparingly shall reap also sparingly; and he which soweth bountifully shall reap also bountifully.
—2 Corinthians 9:6

Ninth, poverty can be caused by wrong thinking.

As a man thinketh in His heart, so is He.
—Proverbs 23:7

Tenth, poverty can be caused if money is viewed as a source, rather than a resource.

Whoever trusts in his riches will fall, but the righteous will thrive like a green leaf.
—Proverbs 11:28

If you are poor, I have just listed some possible causes for poverty, and there could be more. But this list is a good place to check to see if anything mentioned speaks to you and your particular situation. But please know that poverty does **NOT** come from God, and for those who act as though poverty is a blessing in disguise, then I firmly disagree. But neither poverty nor wealth should define us.

And he said unto them, Take heed, and beware of covetousness: for a man's life consisteth not in the abundance of the things which he possesseth.
—Luke 12:15

But there is no Biblical proof that God is pleased with poverty. The blessing of the Lord, it maketh rich, and he addeth no sorrow with it.
—Proverbs 10:22

Yours in Christ,

Christian Left (Liberal) vs. Christian Right (Conservative)

Dear Friends,

There are two topics that many people refuse to discuss: religion and politics. Primarily because there are so many opinions and beliefs, and the average person doesn't take the time to learn enough about either or both topics to make a coherent argument one way or the other. I think that is sad because, whether we believe it or not, politics and religion governs/regulates a lot of areas of public and private life.

To some degree our banks, education, insurance, how we spend our money, food production/consumption, taxes, moral conduct, etc. are all affected by our politics and/or religion. In my opinion, if two things could influence our lives in that many ways, then we have a duty and an obligation to ensure that those who have our best interests at heart govern our communities.

> *Righteousness exalts a nation, but sin is a disgrace to any people.*
> —Proverbs 14:34

The People of God, the Conduit of Righteousness

Who is going to be the purveyor of righteousness in the Earth? Who is going to be the conduit through which God will manifest His goodness and truth? Well, Jesus was clear and He said:

> *Ye are the salt of the earth: but if the salt have lost his savor, wherewith shall it be salted? it is thenceforth good for nothing, but to be cast out, and to be trodden under foot of men. Ye are the light of the world. A city that is set on an hill cannot be hid. Neither do men light a candle, and put it under a bushel, but on a candlestick; and it giveth light unto all that are in the*

house. Let your light so shine before men, that they may see your good works, and glorify your Father which is in Heaven.
—Matthew 5:13-16

To whom and about whom was Christ speaking? The answer to both questions is the born-again believers in the Lord Jesus Christ. So, if Christ declared that we are Christ's representatives, how is it that we are so divided in our political and Biblical beliefs? Christianity isn't right-wing or left-wing, the Christian Right vs. the Christian Left. These designations are secular modifiers that the Church has adopted over the years in order to fit God into certain humanistic agendas. But a closer examination into these modifiers will clearly demonstrate that neither designation is how God would actually represent Himself.

The New Testament title "Christ" comes from a Greek word transliterated Christos, which means Anointed One, the Messiah, the Christ. The suffix "ian" means "of" or "pertaining to" the noun or proper noun to which it is connected; hence, a Christian is a person who is "of" or "pertains to" Christ. Unfortunately, society has made a habit of adopting Christ into its agenda, or splitting Christ for the purpose of promoting an agenda. Either way, the motive of compartmentalizing Christ is very divisive and disingenuous, and the idea is not of Christ; and although every politically involved person is not a Christian (a spiritually born-again believer in Jesus Christ), I am writing this letter from the perspective of a Christian to Christians. I'm writing this way because I believe that many people of God have lost their way. We have compromised many Biblical positions for the sake of tolerance and equality, and we have become seeker-friendly rather than standard bearers of the truth.

Division in the Church

If you examine the demographics of many Churches, you will find white Churches, black Churches, and any other racial divide that exists. On the surface, there is nothing wrong with this because we all have a natural desire to gravitate towards people with whom we have a cultural bond. As a sub-division of the cultural divides, you may find some youthful Churches with more contemporary music, and some mature churches with more traditional music; and from there the categories expand into doctrine, dress codes and a whole host of issues that divide the Church.

Christ and His Word taught us that we are salt (preservation agents of the truth) and light (agents that manifest the cause of Christ). He also taught that the Holy Spirit would lead us into all truth. If this is the case, then why are we so divided? For example, Christian Group 1 is standing for principle A, and Christian Group 2 is standing for principle non-A. Both principles can't both be of God, because "A" and "non-A" are polar opposites, and God is not confused. Both can be wrong, or one can be correct and the other can be wrong. But both can't be correct. But the two Christian Groups stand their ground claiming that they are both following God. This is one of the biggest impediments to winning people to Christ: division in the Church.

Now I beseech you, brethren, by the name of our Lord Jesus Christ, that ye all speak the same thing, and that there be no divisions among you; but that ye be perfectly joined together in the same mind and in the same judgment.
—1 Corinthians 1:10

Christ would not be a modern-day liberal, nor would He be a modern-day conservative; and there is no such thing as a Christian left or a Christian right. There is only Christ and His principles. Every Christian needs to understand that. Christ's way is the only correct way; and that is why I believe that if you are going to live a Christian life, then you should find out what God's Word says and just adopt that position. What many people do, however, is they establish a viewpoint and then find some way to justify it by hijacking a piece of God and shoving Him into the agenda. The funny thing about this is that so many people spend their time trying to eliminate the very mention of God from any public discussion; yet socialists, conservatives, liberals and others continually try to convince others that Jesus was a socialist, a conservative, or a liberal. How ridiculous is that?

My main concerns with the Republicans and the Democrats are quite simple. The Democrats concern me because they think they can, or are supposed to impose their utopian will and agenda on people to solve all of this nation's problems through think tanks and bureaucrats with taxpayer's money. The Democrats believe that no cost is too big to rid the world of the social ills that face us, and the taxpayer will be on the hook to fund their agenda, or else. Democrats are also hypocrites, because they espouse tolerance and equal rights, but they routinely oppose any thought (especially Christian thought) that opposes their agenda. The Republicans concern me because they think they can, or are supposed to impose their will and agenda on people to solve this and other nation's problems through big corporations, military might, and big banks. The Republicans pretend to be the Party of Christianity, but most times they are just as phony as the Democrats. Both parties thrive when individuals relinquish their personal responsibility, inherent and unalienable God-given rights of life, liberty and property in exchange for a small, false sense of security. Why? It is because when individuals give up power, the Government, by default, becomes the recipient of that power.

> ...*Governments are instituted among Men, deriving their just powers from the consent of the governed.*
> —From the second paragraph of the Declaration of Independence

The Government has very a limited scope in the founding documents, and it has few viable answers to most of the problems that we face. But if we have the will and the desire, we can put Government back in its proper place; and we (with God's help) can figure out the best ways to resolve our political, social and economic matters as close to home as possible. Unfortunately, I truly believe that a lot of people are afraid of that challenge and commitment. However, I will continue to stand on my principles, in spite of what the American culture and/or political parties accept and do.

How Should We Vote on the Issues

Life of the Pre-born

The Declaration of Independence states: We hold these truths to be self-evident, that all men are created equal, that they are endowed by their Creator with certain unalienable Rights, that among these are Life, Liberty, and the pursuit of Happiness. The pre-born child, whose life begins at fertilization, is a human being created in God's image. God hates murder (Proverbs 6:17), so the duty of the State is to protect life, including the life of the unborn.

The Scope of Government

The closer the Government is to the people, the more responsible, responsive, and accountable it is likely to be. The Constitution, Articles I through VI, lists the limited powers that may be exercised by the federal government. Article I, Section 8 specifies the authority of the Congress. The Tenth Amendment states: "The powers not delegated to the United States by the Constitution, nor prohibited by it to the States, are reserved to the States respectively, or to the people."

Death Penalty

It is the right and the duty of Government to execute criminals convicted of capital crimes (Genesis 9:6) and to require restitution for the victims of criminals (Exodus 22:1-7). Romans 13:4 states that the civil magistrate "bears not the sword in vain." Swords aren't used for spankings or timeouts; they are used for executing people. The governmental structure has this authority from God to punish lawbreakers who deserve this type of punishment.

However, since we have so many inequities in our judicial system, I believe that capital punishment should be less frequently implemented. Too often, poorer minorities who are not able to pay for the best legal defense teams are generally the recipients of unfair capital punishment at a more disproportionate rate.

For this reason, I favor life sentences in prison. Prison should be a hard punishment, not a vacation or an educational re-tooling. I believe that recidivism needs to be addressed. Rehabilitation and redemption are great, but only God has the ability to change people's hearts, not the Government. There is no reason why taxpayers should be burdened with providing state-of the-art facilities and accommodations for criminals. I also believe that more jury trials would be a reasonable deterrent and a good checks-and-balances system to protect against lawyers who are more interested in a high percentage conviction rate, rather than justice.

Military Defense

It is a primary obligation of the federal government to provide for the common defense according to the Preamble to the U.S. Constitution. Threats and potential enemies foreign and domestic should be included as those against whom we need defense. We should not use a financial agenda, or some other ulterior motive or nefarious pretext to spread our defense across the globe.

The Educational System
The Federal government has no authority to control, to regulate, or to fund education. I know a lot of Christians don't like to deal with that, but it is true nonetheless. The Bible assigns the authority and responsibility of educating children to their parents (Proverbs 22:6). Parents should decide if they want to home school, or have some other sort of private schooling for their child. Collecting property taxes to fund a public school where your children are not attendees is not fair or Constitutional. As a father whose child was homeschooled and went to private school, I had to pay tuition to the private school for my daughter, and I was obligated to fund the public school system.

Definition of a Marriage
God defines marriage as the union between one man and one woman, and nature confirms this truth. You can look at the animal kingdom and see how they pair off: male and female; or the males will fight to determine who mates with the female, not each other. Also, God caused one male and one female of all species of animals to enter into Noah's Ark. The marriage covenant is the foundation of the family; families make communities and communities make a stable society.

Foreign Policy
In 2 Chronicles 19:2, Jehu went out to meet King Jehoshaphat to ask him, "Should you help the wicked and love those who hate the Lord?" We should ask ourselves the same thing regarding our global enemies. Should we be helping all of the nations on our foreign policy list? Are we allocating our resources properly? Are we making good investments with taxpayer dollars? I know that we live in a complex world. But as long as the problems remain domestically, we need to be less involved in running the world and start resolving the problems we have at home. There is no reason to have over nine hundred bases in over one hundred countries around the world while people are hurting on U.S. soil.

Declaration of War
Only the Congress has the Constitutional authority to declare war, grant letters of marquee and reprisal, and make rules concerning captures on land and water; to raise and support armies, but no

appropriation of money to that use shall be for a longer term than two years; to provide and maintain a navy; (Article 1 Sec. 8). We are not authorized to give the President the authority to send troops anywhere to enforce U.N. or N.A.T.O. resolutions.

Gun Control

The right to bear arms is a constitutional right that shall not be infringed. It is inherent in the right of self-defense, defense of the family, and defense against tyranny, which is the original intent of the Second Amendment.

Today, we are seeing a political football being thrown around, and it is unfortunate that politicians are using people's personal tragedies for their own personal gain.

Restricting the law-abiding citizens from owning firearms means that the only people who would have guns would be the Government and the criminals. Who is going to defend the average person if we accept gun control? Would America exist, as we know it today, if the Colonists would have accepted gun control?

Healthcare and Government

Healthcare is not a government issue; it is a private matter between patients and doctors. The Government should stay out of this private sector matter and let the free-market determine the best practices. The good healthcare professionals will get the patients and the corrupt doctors will be out of business or in jail if the patients are allowed to handle their own health matters without Government intervention.

Immigration Reform

If we can lock the doors on our homes and put a fence around our property, we should be able to secure our country, as well. People don't walk in and out of our homes without an invitation and/or permission. Why can't we establish and/or re-establish the same kind of respect for our Country's borders?

I will add my solution to this matter. I don't like amnesty, but with ten to twenty million immigrants here illegally, it is unrealistic to believe that they will all just voluntarily go home. I know from personal experience that their absence would hurt a lot of manual labor jobs, namely the construction industry.

My solution:
Those who are living here, working, staying out of trouble, and being productive members of society can stay and become citizens on the following conditions:
1. A fine must be paid for breaking the law of coming here without permission: five thousand or ten thousand dollars (or whatever the amount) can be paid over a period of time.

2. Candidates for citizenship must be able to read, write and comprehend the basics of the English language.

3. Every person who came here illegally will have to go to the back of the immigration line. The people who went through the proper channels to come here legally will become citizens first.

4. They must learn and understand basic American history and know the history of the U.S. Bill of Rights, the Declaration of Independence, the Constitution, individual liberty, personal responsibility, federalism vs. anti-federalism, and the differences between this nation and other nations of the world, i.e., socialism, free-market capitalism, etc.

5. All new applicants who reside in the U.S. must begin paying taxes immediately.

6. All prerequisites of citizenship must be met before any new citizen is eligible to vote.

7. All lawbreakers must leave immediately at the expense of the person's country of birth.

Money and Banking

In Article 1 Section 8 of the Constitution, only the Congress has the authority to coin money, regulate the value thereof, and of foreign coin, and fix the standard of weights and measures. We don't need a private bank, the Federal Reserve, that charges us interest to borrow money. Besides, how can a branch of Government depose themselves of their Constitutional duties and allow an unelected and unaccountable (to the voters) private bank manage our financial system?

Security of Personal and Private Property

The Fourth Amendment affirms the right of the people to be secure in their persons, houses, papers, and effects against unreasonable searches and seizures. We do need to protect our nation, but we can't do so at the expense of the U.S. Bill of Rights via unwarranted electronic surveillance, wiretapping, national computer databases, various laws, and national ID cards. Again, I understand that we live in a complex world, but at some point we have to see that some of the legislation that is being proposed is an egregious affront to liberty and privacy.

> *"They that can give up essential liberty to obtain a little temporary safety, deserve neither liberty nor safety."*
>
> —Ben Franklin

Religious Freedom

Article 1 of the U.S. Bill of Rights states: "Congress shall make no law respecting an establishment of religion, or prohibiting the free exercise thereof." Our Constitution grants no authority to the federal government either to grant or deny religious expression; and Article 10 leaves matters such as this to the States and the people.

According to IRS publication #557 (Tax Exempt Status for Your Organization), it states: "Although a church, its integrated auxiliaries, or a convention or association of churches is not required to file Form 1023 to be exempt from federal income tax or to receive tax deductible contributions, the organization may find it advantageous to obtain recognition of exemption."

> *"A more certain way to attack religion is by favor, by the comforts of life, by the hope of wealth; not by what reminds one of it, but by what makes one forget it; not by what makes one indignant, but by what makes men lukewarm, when other passions act on our souls, and those which religion inspires are silent. In the matter of changing religion, State favors are stronger than penalties."*
>
> —Baron de Montesquieu,
> *The Spirit of the Laws* (1748)

"The federal government has proved a tremendous impediment to the ongoing work of Christians. In all the laws that they have passed against Christian schools, gagging the church, taxation, and all kinds of things that they have done, they have made it harder for the church to exercise its prerogatives and to preach the gospel...There were numbers of things that I knew that I was never able to say from the pulpit because if you advance the cause of one candidate or impede the cause of the other, you can lose your tax exemption. That would have been disastrous not only for the church, but for our school and our seminary, everything. So you are gagged. You cannot do that. The IRS, a branch of our government, has succeeded in gagging Christians."
—Reverend D. James Kennedy.

Corporate and Social Welfare

God, who endows us with life, liberty, property, and the right to pursue happiness, also exhorts individuals, families, and His body of believers to care for the needy, the sick, the homeless, the aged, and those who are otherwise unable to care for themselves (James 2:15-17). There is no mandate or authority given to the Government to care for the poor. In order for us to fully grasp a solution, we must fully understand the problems with the welfare system. This goes beyond Democrats and Republicans. Spiritual laws have been broken, and what we are witnessing is the Government trying to use a bucket to get the water out of the boat while the bottom of the boat has a few large holes in it.

My solutions: cut all corporate welfare immediately. Let the hard work, innovation, good business acumen, and market forces determine winners and losers, not the Government. For social welfare, have a three to five year transition period to end social welfare as we know it. For the next three to five years, all current able-bodied recipient benefits will be tied to a job. If recipients are physically and mentally able to work, then they will be required to work thirty to forty productive hours weekly somewhere (for free to that company). The welfare benefits will be the wages for the hours worked. The company will fill out a document and stamp it in order for the recipient to receive that month's benefits. If the recipient is tardy, lazy, disrespectful, or a bad worker, then the benefits will be reduced for that month.

That is a hard solution. But don't you believe that recipients would appreciate that check more if they actually earned it and didn't make a bunch of excuses regarding why they aren't working? I'm not talking about those who are truly in a bad place with no family, elderly, or handicapped. But there are too many able-bodied people who know how to use and abuse the system at the taxpayer's expense. Besides, these people would quickly learn that the gravy train would end soon. I believe my solution is a good place to start a conversation.

Minimum Wage and Price Control

The Government has no authority to set wages and prices. Let employers and employees decide the wages that each is willing to accept and to pay. It seems like a good thing to raise minimum wage higher in order to help poor people live better lives. But the reality is that those higher wages equate to higher costs to the goods/service provider, which will result in higher prices to the public, and higher prices always hit the poor and the middle class the hardest.

Taxes

The Constitution, in Article I, Section 8, gives Congress the power "to lay and collect Taxes, Duties, Imposts, and Excises, to pay the Debts and provide for the common Defense and general Welfare of the United States." So as long as the Government is using our tax dollars for things that they are authorized by the Constitution and God to do, I'm all for paying taxes. But when the size and the scope of Government deviates from God's Word and the Constitution, that is when it is hard to justify higher taxes. Is the return on investment what we thought it would be or should be? If not, then I believe we need to revisit the size, scope and the amount of money we pay to the Government.

Political parties can be used as vehicles for good or for bad. But ultimately, we must be people who stand on Godly principles. Will you join the cause of truth?

Yours in Christ,

WHAT DOES LIBERTY LOOK LIKE?

Dear Friends,

As I stated earlier, many on the political right and the left (especially in the Church) are on the wrong side of a lot of issues. I don't like to get caught up in a bunch of labels and categories where others like to box you in and control you. But in order to organize ideas and people, we adhere to certain labels.

Many times, the use of semantics clouds the course of intellectual discussion. Some words and meanings have changed over the years for various reasons. However, many times the agenda stays the same. Classical liberalism, in its original form, is the belief in liberalism's root word "liberty."

According to dictionary.com, the word "liberal" means: favorable to, or in accord with concepts of maximum individual freedom possible, especially as guaranteed by law and secured by governmental protection of civil liberties. "Liberty" is defined as freedom from arbitrary or despotic government or control.

Who would be against a person being personally responsible for their actions, individual liberty, private property, free markets, peace, limited government, and the rule of law?

The concept of liberty permeates the Bible, the Declaration of Independence, the Bill of Rights, the U.S. Constitution, and other founding documents for this country.

> *Now the Lord is that Spirit: and where the Spirit of the Lord is, there is liberty.*
> —2 Corinthians 3:17

> *If the Son therefore shall make you free, ye shall be free indeed.*
> —John 8:36

> *We hold these truths to be self-evident, that all men are created equal, that they are endowed by their Creator with certain unalienable Rights, that among these are Life, Liberty and the pursuit of Happiness.*
>
> —Excerpt from the Declaration of Independence

The only legitimate purpose of government is to protect these unalienable rights that we have received from God. There is no authority from God for Governments to provide people with jobs, education, or to regulate where people work, when they work, the wages they earn, what they can buy, what they can sell, the price for which they can sell it, etc.

Liberty is a Biblical concept and the construct of liberty cannot encompass an agenda whose ideas are contrary to Biblical teachings. This is why I previously stated that words and meanings were changed over the years, but the agenda is the same.

> *As free, and not using your liberty for a cloke of maliciousness, but as the servants of God.*
>
> —1 Peter 2:16

So, in the classical sense of the word, I am a liberal. Modern-day liberals are more for state control/regulation of industries, higher taxes, central planning, and more of a managed society to solve all of the world's problems whether people like it or not. That doesn't sound like liberty to me.

As believers, let's choose to support the issues and principles of liberty for all people, and let's shun the political fanfare of party loyalty and popularity contests.

Yours in Christ,

The Emperor has No Clothes

Dear Friends,

 Many of you remember Hans Christian Andersen's story entitled, "The Emperor Has No Clothes." It was a short tale about two crooks, posed as clothiers, who offered to make the emperor the finest clothing. They claimed to possess fabric that was invisible to those who were unfit for their positions, stupid, or incompetent. They were hired, and after some time, the Emperor sent some of his subjects to monitor the progress of the two clothiers. When his subjects couldn't see the invisible fabric, they pretended to see the clothing and comment accordingly because they didn't want to appear unfit, stupid, or incompetent; eventually the Emperor did likewise.

 When it was time for the Emperor to showcase his new clothing in the town procession, the clothiers mimed dressing the naked Emperor. Obviously, no one saw the clothing (not even the Emperor), but everyone played along so that they wouldn't appear to be unfit for their positions, stupid, or incompetent.

 At the town procession, the Emperor's helpers simulated carrying the train of his new robe, while all of the citizens played along and celebrated the Emperor's clothing. Suddenly, a small child said:

   "But he has nothing on!"

 Everyone gasped; even though they knew what the child said was true. Even the child's father quickly and publicly dismissed what he said as silly. But the people whispered what the child said from person to person until everyone in the crowd was shouting that the Emperor was wearing no clothes. The Emperor heard it and felt that they were correct, but held his head high and finished the procession.

That classic, fiction tale was humorous, but in many ways it is so true, even in our society. We have too many people who buy into the lies of the so-called Church leaders, and experts (in this case the clothiers). Our leaders and their faithful constituents are often times complicit when it comes to propping up nonsense. This emotional, fearful, ego-driven sentiment of "going along to get along" is a shameful and unacceptable reason for not speaking the truth. I imagine Jesus Christ, John the Baptist, Paul, and the multitudes of people in Foxe's Book of Martyrs would agree with that statement.

Only knowing the truth and acting on that truth will set people free. I'm not asking people to die; I'm only asking people to join me and to speak out for the truth. It is obvious that the twenty-first century Emperor is naked. Today, the "Emperor" is whatever or whoever is wrong in our society, but the masses accept him/her as normal and their practices as the normal way of doing things. It's nothing more than the status quo. In the Church, in the Government, in the workplace, in our families, etc., we must get to the foundational roots of the matters that are before us, and stop pretending that they don't exist.

I decided long ago to stop being a follower of what people were doing, and I decided to be a person to question what people were doing and why. As many of you know, people will fight for their right to follow their pastor, chief overseeing apostle, evangelist, bishop, reverend, or their favorite politician over the side of a mountain, down the razor blade embankment, and into a witch hazel alcohol lake. These people will defend their religious and political leaders ad nauseam, and any challenge or resistance to these leaders is seen as a personal attack, racism, or some sort of offense. Although I don't agree with this type of homage being paid to an individual, I will always allow them to operate in their free-will to pursue what makes them happy; however, I will exercise my First Amendment right and speak out.

I can understand the secular world and their mindset, but the Christian community is truly in bad shape. We are a divided bunch with factions on both sides of the same issues. At times, I understand Paul's frustration of leaving all of this misery behind and going to a better place, when he said:

For I am in a strait betwixt two, having a desire to depart, and to be with Christ; which is far better: nevertheless to abide in the flesh is more needful for you. And having this confidence, I know that I shall abide and continue with you all for your furtherance and joy of faith; that your rejoicing may be more abundant in Jesus Christ for me by my coming to you again.
—Philippians 1:23-26

But he realized that his voice and presence in the Earth was more important to the mission of the Kingdom, than his own desire to see the end of his salvation. That is where many of us are right now. We see the danger, and the red flags that are posted before us. We see the separation occurring in the body of Christ. We see the lukewarm compromise among the Christian community, as well as the manipulation from the Christian leadership. We see that our secular leaders are not accountable to us, and many of them promote things that are an absolute affront to Heaven.

Will you join this anti-status quo movement? Will you be like the small child in the crowd, and in the midst of the onlookers blurt out that the Emperor has no clothes on? Don't be afraid, because it only takes one voice of conviction and truth to spark the boldness and conviction in others. Your voice must be heard! You never know whom God will touch through you. But if you don't stand up and speak, you will never know.

Yours in Christ,

WHITE RACISTS AND BLACK PACIFISTS IN THE CHURCH

Dear Friends,

I've always been exposed to multi-cultural surroundings. During my early years, I attended schools with mostly white students and other minority groups represented. I went to a historically black university; and in my professional career, the majority of my co-workers are whites and Hispanics. In my experiences and as my parents taught me, good and bad people exist in every race, and people should be judged based upon individual merit. The issue shouldn't be the race of the person, but the heart of the person.

I believe that every human was/is/will be created by God in His image and likeness to be a sovereign, and free-will sentient being.

> *And God said, Let Us make man in Our image, after Our likeness: and let them have dominion over the fish of the sea, and over the fowl of the air, and over the cattle, and over all the Earth, and over every creeping thing that creepeth upon the Earth. So God created man in His own image, in the image of God created He him; male and female created He them.*
> —Genesis 1:26-27

> *And hath made of one blood all nations of men for to dwell on all the face of the Earth, and hath determined the times before appointed, and the bounds of their habitation.*
> —Acts 17:26

> *We hold these truths to be self-evident, that all men are created equal, that they are endowed by their Creator with certain unalienable Rights, that among these are Life, Liberty and the pursuit of Happiness.*
> —U.S. Declaration of Independence

We are all one in humanity, and whether our policies, beliefs, or the avenues by which we desire to facilitate change are the best or the most efficient means to do so, I believe that most reasonable people are working to make society a better place. There are no perfect solutions, and there are no quick fixes; but we do have trade-offs and access to certain variables that we can modify in order to achieve a desired result. We have the ability, and the need to work together, but there are always certain individuals and groups who don't have the will to work together; and for whatever reason, race is always one of the biggest obstacles.

One of the strangest anomalies with the race relations issue is the white guilt (**WG**) faction of the white culture. I have a lot of experience with white folks who suffer from **WG**, and I truly believe that many of them are decent people who feel as though they are doing their part in helping their fellow man. But my assessment of **WG** views it from another perspective. **WG** is a liberal mindset (held by many whites) that superficially stands against hatred, racism, and discrimination. It is a pseudo-compassionate way of thinking that clothes certain segments of minority groups in perpetual victimhood and puts them in dependency mode. **WG** claims to support equality for all; but in reality, it treats certain minorities as an inferior group (the actual definition of racism) by promoting an agenda of low expectation, excuses, and a lack of personal responsibility and accountability.

In my opinion, **WG** has caused tremendous damage to many able-bodied minorities; and while the intended actions might have been well-meaning in trying to level out some of our societal inequities, many of the results of **WG** have been very counterproductive.

WG is a very patronizing and condescending attitude towards people of color, and it is an insult to the intelligence of reasonable and educated people everywhere. I consider it to be offensive that some very visible white media personalities and community leaders get a pass from black and Hispanic leadership for their **WG** and the false sense of care and understanding attached with it. Meanwhile, some **WG** folks and the minority supporters of this **WG** culture will label white non-supporters of the **WG** agenda as racists. The **WG** operatives have become the masters of deception, and now the **WG** promoters of racism are now the accusers of it; and the relevant issues and discussions of the day get lost because of misconception and a lack of intellectual honesty. I am amazed to see how this **WG** agenda continues to prevail and to hurt the cause of racial unity, a strong sense of family/community, and economic empowerment. **WG** is a dividing wedge that must be clearly identified and stopped if we are going to continue to make societal improvements.

The **WG** advocates further claim to empathize and to identify with the plight and the historical misfortune of minorities. As a result, the **WG** crowd embraces and becomes endearing towards the minority community, or turns to self-hate and blames white racism for many problems in the lives of minorities. This leads to the **WG** proponents offering more entitlements to poorer minorities, lowering the societal bar of achievement, and encouraging minorities to be less concerned with personal responsibility and consequences. This introspective guilt (**WG**) acts as a means for **WG** proponents to subconsciously correct the wrongs of the past; and this **WG** agenda seems to be some sort cleansing or purging of their consciences of the racist and oppressive sins of their forefathers.

Additionally, I view **WG** as bait that is used to create the perennial "I'm sorry for what my people did to your people, so please allow me to **GIVE** you something in return" mentality. So the entitlement mentality never goes away, and the minorities who buy into this rhetoric (unbeknownst to them) are continually used and abused. It's a pathetic spectacle and a moral hazard, to say the least. I have forgiven the past, and not only should the **WG** crowd do the same thing, but the minority communities need to stop allowing the status quo system (as well as their respective religious and political leadership) to use them as the poster children for victimization.

We can't live in the past; live in the present, and move on towards the future. We can't legislate all of our problems away. We can't make everyone's economic situation equal. We can't enact policies that force everyone to do the right thing. We can't prevent every bad situation from happening. We will just have to deal with certain things, and work through them the best way we can. But we cannot continue to accept divisive behavior as a solution, and then turn the tables on the people who are speaking out against the divisive content.

What would Dr. M.L. King Jr., Frederick Douglass, or any other freedom fighter think about **WG** in the 21st century? Frederick Douglass did not want revenge, reparations, or any **WG** special treatment. He believed that access to education, and enforcement of the Thirteenth, Fourteenth or Fifteenth Amendments of the U.S.

Constitution were enough for blacks to share the American dream. Dr. King wanted freedom for all, harmony among the races, and for us to judge one another by the content of one's character, not by the color of one's skin.

We don't need any more patronizing, demeaning, and **RACIST LIBERAL WHITE GUILT**! God made white people, so they should be proud of their God-given culture. People of color are beautiful creations of God, as well, and God created all of us to work together. All of our ancestors did some things wrong, but we can't bear their weight and burden, and advance simultaneously. **WG** acts from a guilty conscience perspective; that is defensive, reactive, and it doesn't judge individuals based upon their own merits. We need more sincere and educated actions that come from sound principles, and a genuine heart of love, community and humanity. We need to move forward in spite of the past, not because we are ashamed of it.

The Politics of Racism

The black folks who understand the white guilt trip use the opportunity to pile on the situation by philosophically beating white people up with the "white privilege" rhetoric. It is sad, because these white guilt people are being used and abused, and they don't even realize it. The controllers of the racism game are masters of deception and they play upon the ignorance of the participants, i.e., the white guilt bunch, the white privilege bunch, and the race brokers. I have seen many white people become afraid to engage in an intellectual discussion, because either they were wrongly accused of being a racist, or they were afraid that the "racist" label would be cast freely upon them without justification. I can't begin to tell you how many white people have approached me to convince me that they aren't racist. These white people always play defense, and their voice is always neutralized via the "race card" and white guilt.

Racism is also a very marketable business. Division is very profitable, and instability allows certain people to make a lot of money and/or advance a particular agenda. Think about it in terms of the stock market: Do investors make more money when prices are stable or when there is volatility in the market? I equate price stability to all races of people living together in harmony; it's good for the people. However, more market volatility means more profits, because money is made when prices rise and fall. If more division and racial tension can be stirred up, that equates to more protests, more TV viewers and advertisers, more fear, more uncertainty, more civil rights/hate crime legislation, etc. That is analogous to price instability, and the media and their handlers love it. I know that this sounds crazy or conspiratorial to the average person, but some people will always find a way to make a profit at the expense of others, rather than for the benefit of others.

Peace and love to all people!

Yours in Christ,

Thoughts to Consider

Dear Friends,

I just wanted to jot down some rhetorical thoughts and questions upon which we can all reflect.

- What if politicians admitted that they were corrupt and compromised liars before we elected them? Would we care?
- Would Jesus, John the Baptist and others be received as heroes or heretics today?
- Would the U.S. Bill of Rights pass today's U.S. House or U.S. Senate?
- If God told you to buy a plane ticket to a place halfway around the world in order to save an unknown (you would meet him/her when you got there) person's life, would you do it?
- Do you really believe the Scripture, "Is anything too hard for God?"
- What if Christians actually believed in and applied Biblical principles in their lives, circumstances, families, and communities? What would happen to this nation?
- What is the most important thing (not person) in your life?
- Is God, and time with God and His Word, a priority for you?
- If you had the opportunity to change one event in history, which one would you change?
- What if every profession paid five dollars per hour? Which career would you pursue?

- What if families were as functional and wholesome today as they were in the 1950's?

- Would Dr. King or Frederick Douglass issue today's generation of politicians and religious leaders a rebuke or praise?

- How would a young child prodigy named Wolfgang Amadeus Mozart be received in today's American public schools? Would he be bullied?

- If your spouse decided to stop following God and His Word, would you join him/her in that decision?

- If new knowledge and technology are improving medical procedures and overall health, why are healthcare prices going up?

- Would you ever consider attending a church service in someone's home?

- What would happen if no one watched the news, bought a newspaper, paid for advertising, or subscribed to a news site for six months? Instead, what if people went to city council meetings, state legislature sessions, and engaged our representatives?

> *A pure democracy is a society consisting of a small number of citizens, who assemble and administer the government in person.*
> —James Madison

- If the millions of babies who have been aborted in America could speak to us, what would they say?

- Imagine what America would have become if England enforced harsh gun control laws on the colonies, and the Colonists didn't resist?

- What if Bill Clinton and Mitt Romney had a "road to Damascus" experience with Jesus, and they teamed up as missionaries to preach the uncompromised Word of God to the nations? How would the media and the political world handle that?

- Imagine a world where people didn't judge people based upon the color of their skin.

- What if men and women better understood one another?

- What if people read more meaningful and educational books and watched less TV?

- What if there is a cure to cancer and A.I.D.S.?

- What if people decided not to attend Church services for three months? Do you think the Church leadership would be more interested in the people's well-being or the Church's bottom line?

- What if reality TV was never created?

- What would you do with one hundred million dollars?

- If you can balance your household budget or your business's budget, do you believe that you could balance your city's budget? Would you consider running for some local office?

Sometimes, I just think of random things. But it all makes for good conversation.

Yours in Christ,

The Lesbian Gay, Bi-Sexual, Transgender, Agenda: The Religious/Political Football

Dear Friends,

There are about three or four directions in which I could go with this letter. But for the sake of staying focused on the main point that I wish to discuss, I will not make this a moral argument (I will explain later). The simplicity of this debate has truly been blown so far out of proportion, that the true essence of the real debate has been missed. I never thought that the same-sex marriage debate was a battle between the Church, and the Lesbian, Gay Bi-Sexual and Transgender (**LGBT**) community. But since this debate is being prolonged and becoming more divisive in some instances, I figured I would add my perspective to the discussion.

The Litmus Test for Twenty-First Century Christian Political Activism

Many people in the Church have attacked the **LGBT** community, and they have taken a hard political stance against them. In response to the hard political stance, the **LGBT** folks have retaliated and/or (in some instances) initiated attacks against the Church. From a moral standpoint, I can understand the point of disagreement, but I don't understand why the Church is so political and matter-of-fact about its two signature topics of Christian political activism: abortion and same-sex marriage. I know Christians who will go to the end of the Earth to fight against one or both of these issues, but other issues of importance are nowhere on their radar.

Christians will vote, protest, write their political representatives, donate money, and get involved with rallies and other causes when it comes to abortion and same-sex marriage. Why are these two hot button topics the pot stirrers in the Church? Why is the Church so righteous and conscious about these two issues, and not about other issues that the Church considers "sinful?" I don't see Christians as adamant about banning cigarette smoking, profanity, alcohol consumption, fornication, or any of the other "sins." Why is that? The Church has inadvertently muddied the political water of the actual problem that exists. As a result, there is a misdiagnosis; and a misdiagnosis will always produce the wrong remedy.

The Political Red Herring

I liken the misdiagnosis of the real problem to a particular Three Stooges episode. Moe was standing behind Curly, and unbeknownst to Curly, Moe slapped him on the side of the head. When Curly looked up, Larry was standing in front of him and Curly (assuming that Larry hit him) approached him and asked, "Hey, what's the idea?" Larry pointed behind him to Moe and said, "Mistaken identity." In other words, Larry was pointing to the real culprit, and unfortunately, that is what we have in this same-sex marriage debate, mistaken identity.

Just like Curly in the above-mentioned analogy, when he gets hit (as the **LGBT** community gets attacked), the one in closest proximity to the attack (in this instance, the Church) gets the blame, and deservedly so. The political retaliation is a reflex because the Church has mistakenly made this a moral issue, and in return, the **LGBT** community is striking back. Now each side is attacking the other and nothing is being resolved.

The Church is trying to ban behavior and that never works. The Prohibition Era should be the historical model and precedent for what happens when certain people try to impose their will on other people through legislation. As far as the same-sex marriage issue is concerned, forbidding two people from getting married will not stop them from being together. Besides, the Government was not created to protect us from our own mistakes and devices, or to ban things. Today, we have many laws on the books banning murder and theft, yet these laws do not prevent murders and thefts. So we have to put the rule of law in its proper perspective, if it is going to be a good servant.

There are No Group Rights, Just Individual Rights for All

To be clear, I am a born-again Christian, and I believe and accept the Bible as my final moral authority. I will stand up for my right to practice my faith, but I will never impose my beliefs on others. The Bible teaches us about the free will of humanity, and man's ability and right to choose. That was one of the lessons in the Garden of Eden and the forbidden fruit, as well as one of the lessons of Christ coming as the Savior. No one was forgiven when He came, His free gift of eternal life had to be willfully and freely accepted by individuals. We see many examples in Scripture where Christ and His message were rejected. That was not God's intention for people to reject Christ, but we must always remember that God did not create us to be robots. We are free moral agents and sentient beings with the God-given right to say "yes" or "no." That is the essence of liberty.

In addition, one of America's founding documents, the Declaration of Independence, affirms our individual liberty and God-given unalienable rights of life, liberty and the pursuit of happiness. This means that we don't have to agree with one another, we don't have to like one another, but your individual right to live your life is your gift from God; and no one can take that away from you. As long as no one is forced to accept or to embrace another person's behavior, then live your life the way you see fit. Again, we don't have to agree, but we can't force people to accept our morals if they are harming no one.

The Problem and the Solution

Personally, I blame many followers of Christ for this mess of an argument. In regards to the same-sex marriage debate, the issue isn't if we should be defining or redefining marriage; and the answer isn't to have the Government to create/pass amendments to reaffirm how marriage should be defined. God's original definition of marriage and nature's confirmation of marriage has never changed, regardless of how many protests are held to dispute the matter.

> *And He answered and said unto them, Have ye not read, that He which made them at the beginning made them male and female, and said, For this cause shall a man leave father and mother, and shall cleave to his wife: and they twain shall be one flesh? Wherefore they are no more twain, but one flesh. What therefore God hath joined together, let not man put asunder.*
> —Matthew 19:4-6

The real problem is a business matter. The **LGBT** community is marching, protesting and calling on the Government to protect their group's rights. Well, as an individual, each person already has their God-given unalienable rights, and those rights are being protected by the Government. Which rights does the **LGBT** community want? They are really looking for fairness in the marketplace and society, and the same considerations afforded to heterosexuals. But the **LGBT** community is focusing their efforts in the wrong direction, and (although I don't agree with their lifestyle) I can understand the reason for the argument. **LGBT** folks should be petitioning their insurance companies, hospitals (for right-to-visit privileges), healthcare providers, pension fund holders (to transfer benefits to the designate of their choosing), social security (to transfer benefits to the designate of their choosing), etc. They need to target these entities in order to have their partners included in the business portion of their lives. Many **LGBT** folks want their same-sex partner to be on their insurance policy, but the premium for a same-sex couple is a lot higher than that of a heterosexual couple. That is the issue of contention. It's a business matter, not a moral one, because society can't redefine what God has already defined.

So the argument needs to switch to the business matter, because people are going to be together no matter what people say. Personally, I don't care what two consenting adults do in their homes. But when those consenting adults, or the Government forces people to accept things against their will and beliefs is where the problem arises. I am against homosexuality, drug use, heterosexual fornication, drinking alcohol, smoking cigarettes, lying, stealing, murder, etc., but banning behavior won't stop those acts from occurring. Let people enjoy their God-given right to choose their pursuit of happiness. No one said that people have to agree with their decisions, but their unalienable God-given rights must be respected if they are not infringing upon the rights of others.

In conclusion, we are all accountable to God for our actions. Our decisions in life come pre-packaged with their respective consequences. However, we can't allow our understanding of God's judgment, and holiness to be the catalyst for becoming overlords in society.

Yours in Christ,

GAMBLING

Dear Friends,

Many people stumble over different issues. The key is to not get caught up in the issue, but to just live your life. Some people might not understand what I mean, because that sounds too simple. Does "live your life" mean that anything goes? Of course not! What I mean is that we shouldn't get so preoccupied with what we shouldn't do, that we are afraid to just live our lives. Gambling is one of those issues that trips a lot of people up, and it shouldn't. But for whatever reason, people make things harder than they have to be.

Is gambling a sin? Yes, but not because it is the unpardonable sin. Gambling is simply not God's way of doing things. Here is the issue with gambling: there is no guarantee to win. It is a zero sum game: someone wins and someone loses. Even in a mutually agreed upon secular contractual relationship, the service provider and the customer come to terms for a win-win situation. The customer has money and needs a service provided. The service provider has the skill to provide the service, but he/she needs the money. It's a perfect fit, and everyone gets what the other one wants in the end.

Gambling makes one person a winner and one person a loser. That's not how God's economy works. The casino or the lottery usually wins and generates an exorbitant amount of money, and the gamblers get a very small opportunity to win any significant payday.

In God's economy, not only are the giver and the receiver are blessed, but the giver is blessed more than the receiver.

I have shewed you all things, how that so laboring ye ought to support the weak, and to remember the words of the Lord Jesus, how He said, It is more blessed to give than to receive.
—Acts 20:35

It's about stewardship and overseeing the assets that God has allowed you to manage. Who knows which football team will win the game? Who knows if a particular horse will win? Who knows which numbers will be the Lottery picks? It's all chance and probability. We all want to be blessed by God. If that is the case, then we are going to have to be good stewards over the assets that God has given to us, and do things God's way.

Often times, people take the wrong attitude and see the "gambling is a sin" message as a form of bondage that limits the type of fun one can enjoy. That is a gross mischaracterization of the Word of God. God's Word is a protection. I liken it to parents telling their children not to do something because they might get hurt. If people, especially Christians, viewed God's Word in the same manner, I believe a lot more people would have a more spiritual perspective on a lot more issues.

Peace and God bless!

Yours in Christ,

WHY ARE CHURCHES SO SEGREGATED?

Dear Friends,

Have any of you noticed that Church in the twenty-first century is more of a cultural experience than a spiritual one?

In terms of ethnic culture, we are obviously different; but in the Spirit, we are one in Christ. Our expressions might be different, but we still serve the same God.

This subject, like so many others, needs to be approached with a balance in spiritual insight. It is very possible, and very much expected, to be different physically and still be one in Christ.

The Word of the Lord declares:

> *Now when He (Jesus) had taken the scroll, the four living creatures and the twenty-four elders fell down before the Lamb, each having a harp, and golden bowls full of incense, which are the prayers of the saints. And they sang a new song, saying: "You are worthy to take the scroll, And to open its seals; For You were slain, and have redeemed us to God by Your blood out of **EVERY** tribe and tongue and people and nation, and have made us kings and priests to our God; and we shall reign on the Earth."*
> —Revelation 5:9-10

So we have an illustration of people in Heaven singing unto the Lord out of every tribe, tongue, and nation. Why can't we do the same thing on the Earth?

Unfortunately, many Christians are carnal. "Carnal" means to be more conscious of one's physical relationships and surroundings than one's spiritual relationships and surroundings. If a white man is preaching a sound Word, why can't a black person enjoy it? If a black man is preaching the Word, why can't a Hispanic person enjoy it? If an Asian man is rejoicing before the Lord, why can't an Indian join in and rejoice with him? We serve the same spiritual God, but we are too familiar with the natural.

Shouldn't we look like Heaven? Wouldn't it be great to have Heaven manifested on the Earth? I know that seems too idealistic for many people. But isn't our purpose to expand the Kingdom of God on Earth? Well, we can if we use our spiritual eyes. But we remain segregated, because we view one another on the outside and for physical reasons rather than spiritual ones. But the Bible is clear and teaches us not to view things from a strictly human standpoint.

Consequently, from now on we estimate and regard no one from a (purely) human point of view (in terms of natural standards of value). (No) even though we once did estimate Christ from a human viewpoint and as a man, yet now (we have such knowledge of Him that) we know Him no longer (in terms of the flesh).
—2 Corinthians 5:16 (Amplified)

We don't know Christ (in the natural), because we never met Him face-to-face. But we know Him in the Spirit, by the Spirit, and the Holy Spirit makes us one with Him. What do you think would happen if we knew one another by the Spirit, and in the Spirit? Do you think that the genuine heart-felt love of God would flow? Do you think that racism and hate would disappear? Murder? Lying? Adultery? Fornication? If we all valued one another as Christ values us, then we would actually become the salt and the light that Christ called us to be.

Now I beseech you, brethren, by the name of our Lord Jesus Christ, that ye all speak the same thing, and that there be no divisions among you; but that ye be perfectly joined together in the same mind and in the same judgment.
—1 Corinthians 1:10

We cannot continue to allow these secular stumbling blocks to stop us from becoming one. Remember the Tower of Babel; although their motives were bad, they tapped in to the principle of unity, and God said:

> *And the Lord said, Behold, the people is ONE, and they have all one language; and this they begin to do: and now nothing will be restrained from them, which they have imagined to do.*
> —Genesis 11:6

We can all enjoy our ethnic cultures, but we must be one in Christ. When we become one, and we all speak the same thing (in line with the Word), I truly believe that with God all things will certainly be possible through His body of believers.

Yours in Christ,

WHERE IS JEHOVAH JIREH (GOD OUR PROVIDER)?

Dear Friends,

When the 2012 election cycle began, the Republican Presidential candidates condemned President Barack Obama, his policies, and the direction in which the country was going under his leadership. Of course, the President did inherit a terrible situation; nonetheless, the criticism was issued and the rhetoric intensified. The attacks came from all of the Republican Presidential candidates, as they pointed to the President's record going into the General Election. The Republicans started out with nine candidates and then there were four: former Congressman Ron Paul, former Speaker of the House Newt Gingrich, former U.S. Senator Rick Santorum, and former Governor Mitt Romney.

A firestorm of resentment erupted in Iowa and continued into Florida because of a few comments made by Republican Presidential candidates Rick Santorum and Newt Gingrich. Rick Santorum said, "I don't want to make black people's lives better by giving them somebody else's money." This comment was met with verbal affirmations from the audience. It is understandable why this comment would cause some people to be upset, because of all of the ethnic groups in the United States, only one group was singled out as a dependent group: black folks.

Newt Gingrich's comments attracted even more attention during the campaign in New Hampshire. He stated, "I'm prepared, if the NAACP invites me, I'll go to their convention to talk about why the African-American community should demand pay checks and not be satisfied with food stamps."

Later, during the South Carolina debate with Juan Williams (political analyst for Fox News Channel), Gingrich tried to clarify his comment by saying, "What I tried to say [is that] New York City pays their janitors an absurd amount of money because of the unions. You could hire thirty-some kids to work in the school for the price of one janitor and those thirty kids would be a lot less likely to drop out, they would actually have money in their pocket, they would learn to show up for work, they could do light janitorial duty, they could work in the cafeteria, they could work in the front office, and they could work in the library. They'd be getting money, which is a good thing if you're poor. Only the elites despise earning money…One last thing, I believe every American of every background has been endowed by their Creator with the right to pursue happiness, and if that makes liberals unhappy, I'm going to continue to find ways to help poor people learn how to get a job, learn to get a better job and learn some day to own the job." These comments were received with an extended standing ovation and cheers. Not only did these comments incense many in the black community, they also caused more than forty Catholic leaders and theologians to issue an open letter to the Presidential candidates (both men are Catholics), warning them, "to stop perpetuating ugly racial stereotypes on the campaign trail."

The Food Stamp President and the Chains of the Vice-President

In another instance, Gingrich called President Obama, "The best food stamp President in American history." More outrage resulted, and cries of racism were heard because of these comments. Then, Jesse Jackson defended President Obama as a "food stamp President," and said, "It is an honor to be a food stamp President." So which is it? Is it racism or is it a badge of honor?

Food stamps, the idea of dependency and/or a handout are the common denominators in these quotes, and many in the black community have responded that these comments are ignorant, racist, and/or stereotypical. Others chimed in and stated that Gingrich's comments are wrong because the former Speaker failed to cite that there are more white people on Government assistance than any other race in America. Well, we can argue about this and we will never resolve anything. I imagine that people called the offices of Newt

Gingrich and Rick Santorum in protest, and everyone who did call, legally exercised their First Amendment right. However, it was also each candidate's First Amendment right to make his comments, as well.

An argument could be made that some of these remarks were insensitive or the presentation of some of the points were inaccurate; but to make some sort of nexus between these (in context) comments and racism is a stretch to say the least. These are not examples of racism because none of these statements has even the slightest inference that one race was racially superior to another race; that is the actual definition of racism. Again, this is partly the reason why the race debate is a joke, because too many people casually throw the "racism" claim around to the point that people are tired of addressing the false alarm of racism.

Mitt Romney and the Republicans criticized Vice-President Joe Biden for comments he made in Virginia. The full context of the quote was: "Look at what they (Republicans) value, and look at their budget. And look what they're proposing. (Romney) said in the first one hundred days, he's going to let the big banks write their own rules—unchain Wall Street...they're going to put y'all back in chains." Personally, I didn't have a problem with his comment, in context. The media and the Republicans were just looking for a dragon to slay in this instance. The race issue is being played to the point that people are looking for racism and division. It's sad, because the old racial division wounds never heal, and the people who continually get sucked into these racially-charged highs and lows, don't even realize that the media is controlling them with racially charged buzzwords in order to produce an emotional response.

The Statistics

The total U.S. population is approximately three hundred and ten million people. Caucasians/Whites are about sixty-eight percent of the population (approximately two hundred million people) and African Americans/Blacks are about thirteen percent (approximately forty-one million people). A Department of Agriculture report on the general characteristics of the SNAP (food stamps) program's beneficiaries says that in the fiscal year that ended September 30, 2010: thirty-six percent were white and twenty-two percent were black; and out of the roughly forty million people who received benefits nearly fifteen million people were white and nearly nine million people were black. That equates to around seven percent of the white population who received food stamps and around twenty-one percent of the black population who received food stamps. That is bad news (in the black community), and these types of statistics are among some of the reasons why Newt Gingrich and Rick Santorum made their comments.

These statistics are very disturbing; and it is easy to get emotional and call the Republican Party a bunch of racists, but doing so won't change the statistics. Anyone can review this information and verify the findings at the USDA website. I am not defending their statements, nor am I condemning them. The comments are what they are, and the statistics are what they are. They are not racist comments; further, the comments do not infer that either of the Republican candidates or the Republican Party (in part or as a whole) is racist. Are any of them racists? I don't know, and I really don't care, because I can't control people's beliefs. All I can do is control how I live. For their sakes, I hope they are not racist, prejudice, or bigots. But these comments are no more racist than saying that black licorice tastes bad; and these statistics are black licorice for those of you who don't like its taste.

What We Can Do

There are three examples that I would like to illustrate as a part of my solution to this situation. In John Singleton's 1989 movie, "Boyz N the Hood," there was a powerful scene with Lawrence Fishburne (Jason "Furious" Styles) having a very informative discussion about gentrification on a Compton street corner with some young men. He told them that young black men senselessly kill each other every day, and one of the young men asked Furious what he expected him to do if someone tried to kill him. The young man answered his own question and said that he'd kill the other person before the other person could kill him. Furious told the young man, "That's what they want you to do. You have to use your brains, young brother." In 1978, there was a prison documentary entitled, "Scared Straight" that was filmed in

Rahway, New Jersey's Rahway Prison. It was a documentary about teenaged repeat offenders who agreed to have a three-hour session with actual convicts in lieu of jail time and/or probation/public service. One of the convicts, Convict #54936, told the teenagers, "A gun is not going to tear that thirty foot tall (prison) wall down, a pipe isn't going to tear it down, but an education just might tear it down." There was also "Redtails," a 2012 movie inspired by the Tuskegee Airmen, a group of African American United States Army Air Force (USAAF) servicemen during World War II. There was a scene where Colonel A.J. Bullard (Terrence Howard) told the hot-headed pilot, Joe 'Lightning' Little, "You want to fight them (white people)? Fight them with your brains."

That's what has to happen in the black community. Sure, there is racism, and everything isn't perfect, but we have advanced as a society. Ignorance will always be here, but we just have to be smarter in our dealings; we have to make better decisions; we have to stop making excuses; and we have to stop giving the enemy the ammunition to kill us. When people see those USDA statistics, they make comments that reflect those statistics. They have mental pictures of lazy and dependent (black) people. Whether it's fair or not, that's the way it is. Responding to the comments isn't a bad thing, but we have to make sense of the information presented, and make every attempt to make things better. We can do better. Granted, there are some people who really need help. But how many of us know at least one person who "plays the (system's) game" just to get over? Most of us know someone or multiple people who are cheating the system; and although it isn't all black people who are involved, this type of nonsense is a reflection upon all of us. That is why I say that we can all do better. We can reach out into the community in order to make things better. We can all become more informed on the issues that matter and affect us. We can work towards being more self-sufficient. We can get more of the right education. We can take care of our personal responsibilities. We can work harder. We can work smarter. We can work longer, if necessary. I believe that if a person sows the seeds of taking the initiative to better himself/herself, God will show that person the next step in the process of success. These are some simple examples of being proactive and taking your future into your own hands.

We don't need any more excuses, because we are a people who overcame so much adversity, such as: the Trans-Atlantic slave trade and slavery, Jim Crow laws, the Civil Rights Movement, and so much more. If anyone will be denied victory, it will be because of the person that is in the mirror. Life is a challenge, but no one can stop you if you set the principles of victory in motion. No one can stop you, and no politician is going to save you.

Research the "Black Wall Street," i.e., Greenwood, Tulsa, Oklahoma, the area of northeast Oklahoma around Tulsa, home to several prominent black businessmen; Jackson Ward, a thriving African-American business community in Richmond, Virginia; Parrish Street, in Durham, North Carolina, an area of successful black-owned businesses that were patronized by black consumers, and were employers of black people for many years. We have come a long way in America. Barack Obama was elected and re-elected as the forty-fourth President of the United States. Rosalind Brewer was named the President of Walmart South. Ursala Burns was named the CEO of Xerox. Kenneth I. Chenault was named the Chairman and CEO of American Express. Ronald A. Williams was named the Chairman and CEO of Aetna, Inc. Kenneth C. Frazier was named the President, CEO and Director of Merck & Co., Inc. These are the results that silence the critics. Black people are achieving success every day, and there is always room for more people. But we have to change the way we think about certain matters, and then act accordingly. If you don't like what Newt Gingrich and Rick Santorum said, then let's change the statistics that put us in a bad light! Let's beat these statistics with our brains!

Yours in Christ,

DRINKING AND SMOKING FOR CHRISTIANS

Dear Friends,

I am going to deal with a subject matter that has many people bound: alcohol consumption and smoking cigarettes.

Alcohol

The harm from the alcohol in wine is dose related; that means higher amounts cause more damage, but light and moderate amounts also have risks.

The International Agency for Research on Cancer (IARC) is an intergovernmental agency forming part of the World Health Organization of the United Nations. It categorizes alcohol as a Group 1: carcinogenic (an agent directly involved in causing cancer) to humans.

Even in smaller amounts, alcohol can put some brain cells out of order, altering mood, mental function, and motor performance, as well as increase the risk of stroke, depression, anxiety, high blood pressure, and it is also dangerous to developing babies in the womb. That does **NOT** sound like a blessing. Besides, medical literature encourages the public to avoid alcohol for almost every health problem, and as a way to prevent health problems. Why fight the proven science of alcohol consumption, and why accept the lobbyist propaganda of the alcohol industry whose sole purpose is to sell more alcohol and make more money? You choose!

But then there are those who try to justify alcohol consumption by saying things like, "Well, doctors have been known to say that a glass of wine is healthy for you...it comes from grapes." My response is, "Well, then just eat the grapes." Why is it necessary to go through the fermentation process and subject yourself to dehydration, the risk of vitamin and mineral deficiency, among other things, just to be sociable? In the old days, however, people did consume liquor for medicinal purposes. Even Paul taught the body of believers to use alcohol for sicknesses.

> *Drink no longer water, but use a little wine for thy stomach's sake and thine often infirmities.*
> —1 Timothy 5:23

But that is a clear case of when it would be appropriate to consume it. Also, consider this viewpoint: you are a witness for Christ. If the world or another Christian might stumble because of the example that you are putting forth by drinking alcohol, then you need to abstain. Besides, is drinking alcohol that important, anyway?

> *Therefore let us pursue the things which make for peace and the things by which one may edify another. Do not destroy the work of God for the sake of food. All things indeed are pure, but it is evil for the man who eats with offense. It is good neither to eat meat nor drink wine nor do anything by which your brother stumbles or is offended or is made weak.*
> —Romans 14:19-21

Remember, first and foremost, **EVERY BELIEVER IN CHRIST** is a witness for Jesus Christ, and God wants to use your witness to minister to the audience that God wants you to reach. Maybe it is one person; maybe it is ten people, or maybe even one hundred people. But you relinquished ownership to your life when you accepted Christ and now, your life is hid with God in Christ. You were bought with a price: the precious blood of Jesus Christ. If that is the case, then your decision should be simple.

Is winning people to the side of righteousness at all costs your mission?

Cigarettes

Cigarette smoking is obvious. There are no nutritional health benefits to smoking cigarettes. In fact, there have been different warnings issued on packs and cartons of cigarettes for decades. The verbiage has varied, but the content of the message stays relatively the same. "SURGEON GENERAL'S WARNING: Smoking causes Lung

Cancer, Heart Disease, Emphysema, and may complicate Pregnancy." That message is warning enough for me. Besides, it stains your teeth, makes your breath stink, turns your lips purple, and causes your clothes, hair, home, and your car to smell badly.

Alcohol consumption and cigarette smoking have resulted in the illnesses and deaths of untold millions of Americans. Smoking and drinking alcohol also messes up your witness to believers and non-believers. It also creates an environment of dependency on something other than God, and God wants to be a comfort for all of us.

Blessed be the God and Father of our Lord Jesus Christ, the Father of mercies and God of all comfort, who comforts us in all our tribulation, that we may be able to comfort those who are in any trouble, with the comfort with which we ourselves are comforted by God.
—2 Corinthians 1:3-4

The fortunate thing is that He still can be that place of comfort for all of us if we believe that He can be a comfort to us. We all have struggles, and we can overcome them in Christ one day at a time. Try fasting; meditating on the Scriptures that deal with liberty in Christ and God's power to deliver, occupy your time with some other activity, and resist the temptation. Go to the health food store and get a thorough body cleanser to rid your body of the residue of these toxins. Know that any habit can be broken. If God can create the Heavens and the Earth, then I am sure He can help you kick a habit or two. Do you have the will to win against these habits?

I love you guys, and I will see you soon.

Yours in Christ,

Bro. Jay

Thou Shalt Not Kill

Dear Friends,

A wise man once said:

"The Negro cannot win as long as he is willing to sacrifice the lives of his children for comfort and safety."
—Martin Luther King, Jr.

All life that God creates is so precious; yet many of us have dehumanized life and treat life as if we are playing a video game. If you lose a life, there will always be another one. That is the attitude of many people in this country. If we are created in the image and likeness of God, then why would we allow ourselves to walk so diametrically-opposed to His agenda, especially on the life issue?

I'm partly writing this letter out of frustration, disgust, and disappointment in the following statistics. Since the early 1970's, there have been over fifty-five million abortions in the U.S., and approximately seventeen million of the aborted babies were black.

In 2010, black folks were approximately thirteen percent of the U.S. population, but black women accounted for more than a third of all abortions in 2009. Hispanics are roughly fifteen to sixteen percent of the U.S. population, and Hispanic abortions were one fifth of all abortions performed in this country. Compare those numbers of minorities to whites, who make up over sixty percent of America's population, but only account for a third of all U.S. abortions. Do you folks see a serious problem with these numbers?

Over three thousand babies are aborted every day in this country. But those are just statistics to some. To God, those were innocent and defenseless people who were killed. The disheartening part about these numbers is that there are many people who name the name of Christ who support this agenda of murder, whether by open acknowledgement, or by default via support of political candidates. This is an affront to Heaven.

These six things doth the Lord hate: yea, seven are an abomination unto him: a proud look, a lying tongue, and hands that shed innocent blood, an heart that deviseth wicked imaginations, feet that be swift in running to mischief, a false witness that speaketh lies, and he that soweth discord among brethren.
—Proverbs 6:16-19.

Can you imagine what newscasts would be like if over three thousand people were gunned down every day in America? The cries for gun bans would be deafening with each day that guns were legal. But since abortion is the agenda, it gets swept under the rug. According to these statistics, several hundred Hispanic babies, over a thousand white babies, and over a thousand black babies are voluntarily killed by their parents every day in America. What is wrong with our hearts? Are they so dark and hardened towards God that we don't know or care about what His heart loves? He loves and gives life, and the agenda of many is to eliminate life.

In 2009, more than a quarter million blacks died as a result of various ailments, natural causes, and/or accidents, etc. in the U.S. In the same year, over one million babies were aborted. If one thousand black babies are killed on a daily basis in the U.S., that means more blacks were killed by abortion than all other causes combined. These are staggering numbers, and I am purposefully stressing the statistics of the black community because they are so alarming. When my daughter was born, there was no way I could understand the pro-abortion agenda. It wasn't until I realized the spiritual implications of stealing, killing and destroying, and the financial benefit that I began to see why this agenda is protected.

All people, but especially black people, please wake up! You are being used, abused, and used again. The people who tell you that they love you, are convincing you to kill your seed, which is your posterity. What would happen if people began to destroy more and more apple seeds? If the trend continued long enough, there'd be no more apples. Can you see the parallel?

Yours in Christ,

DO WE SUPPORT THE GIFT OF LIFE?

Dear Friends,

For the past several months, we have been inundated with national television and radio ads regarding gun control, gun control legislation, and the many incidences of violence that surround this clarion call to end violence. I agree that senseless violence needs to be stopped. But to those in the media, and to those who are fighting for gun control, I ask: "Is standing up against murder the proper and moral thing to do?" Now, be careful how you answer that question, because there is another part to the violence equation that isn't quite adding up.

Many people have heard of the D.C. sniper, Virginia Tech, Columbine, and the Aurora and Newtown shootings. Unfortunately, these horrible incidents are some of the most tragic examples of gun violence in American history. But those incidents. But many people haven't heard of Dr. Kermit Gosnell, the Philadelphia abortion doctor who was found guilty of murdering babies that survived abortion procedures. His former workers gave testimony regarding the gruesome details surrounding his barbaric abortion techniques. The entire world knows about the gun control debates we are having in this country, and the tragic details of these senseless murders. But very few people have ever heard of Dr. Kermit Gosnell. What are we to make of this disparity?

My problem with these two types of stories is that, while both types of stories are examples of horrible, tragic, and senseless losses of life, why is the gun control violence and legislation getting so much attention, and why is the horrible doctor and his heinous murder of innocent children getting so little attention? Is the issue really about life? If so, then where is the outrage from the same people who are standing up against gun violence for the sake of "saving the lives" of the innocent? Shouldn't these same gun control advocates who want to save lives be consistent and express the same outrage against Dr. Gosnell? Imagine how the news media and the gun control advocates would have reacted if Dr. Gosnell killed these children with an AR-15. Dr. Gosnell would be a household name and people all over the country would have his face pictured in crosshairs.

Unfortunately, pre-born humans are being sacrificed by an agenda that many in this country call, a choice. God calls it murder! Fortunately, this agenda and the proponents of choice are being exposed as hypocrites, and they are silently wrapping themselves in the "out-of-sight, out-of-mind" adage hoping these unconscionable acts just go away. The murder agenda is getting its day in the court of public opinion and public view. It's easy to support evil and call it "a choice" if you can't see it. But when the evil is brought to light, then you have to deal with it. Abortion advocates don't want to deal with the reality of pre-born murder, i.e., abortion; and in this case, revelations of late-term abortions with some of the babies being reported as screaming before they were brutally murdered. But if we expose it and bring the agenda to light, then more people will ask questions, and God will convict people's hearts. If that happens, then people will begin to hold the promoters of the agenda accountable for these atrocities. At least that is my hope.

It sounds innocuous to call something "a choice." But when you take the politically-correct spin off of it, and you see the testimony of these former workers, then there is no way for a reasonable person not to conclude that this agenda is nothing more than a brutal version of murder for hire. Where are the gun control advocates in defense of life? What are we to make of this disparity?

Yours in Christ,

Race, Hype, and Misguided Allegiance vs. Truth

Dear Friends,

By now, everyone has heard of the terrible incident that occurred in Sanford, Florida, a small town outside of Orlando. On Sunday night, February 26, 2012, seventeen-year-old Trayvon Martin was shot and killed by twenty-eight-year-old George Zimmerman; an act that Zimmerman called self-defense.

The Sanford Police Department was criticized for a lot of things regarding this case, but some of the main points of concern were: not releasing 911 calls; sending a narcotics detective to the scene, instead of a homicide detective; and failing to administer a drug and alcohol test to Zimmerman that night. Another troubling aspect of the case is that Trayvon Martin was black, and George Zimmerman is white and Hispanic, so the speculation for a race-related murder was definitely on the media's radar.

So, that is a little bit about the Trayvon Martin case. But have you ever heard the name Clarence Robinson? If you don't live in the Dallas/Ft. Worth area I doubt that you would have ever heard his name. Clarence Robinson was an eighteen-year-old black man who was killed on December 14, 2011, by Thomas Lester Harper, who is also black. On that afternoon, Clarence Robinson arrived at the scene of a multi-vehicle traffic accident as a good citizen to offer assistance. He noticed two little children who were in the backseat of a totaled SUV. Harper, the father of the two children and the driver of the SUV, was intoxicated and had just caused the collision while trying to get away from another hit-and-run accident. Clarence approached the SUV and moved one of the children to safety. That is when Harper shot and killed him, and was later taken into custody. That was not self-defense; that was cold-blooded murder of an innocent man in broad daylight. Another life lost for nothing.

Lord, Deliver Me From Church Folks

Why am I writing to you about Trayvon Martin and Clarence Robinson? I believe that awareness is key and that taking action is a civic and a moral duty. Additionally, I believe that if we are going to be a credible voice for political action, justice, community, righteousness, family, etc., then our actions must be consistent and honest. However, I believe that we are being very inconsistent with how we respond to these types of matters.

I do remember seeing some Church folks make comments or get involved in these types of cases in the past from the wrong angle or with the wrong motives. Some Church folks were motivated to demand justice, while others protested and used profanity to spread hate against George Zimmerman, whom they originally thought was a white man. This is the kind of nonsense that secular-minded saints bring into the body of believers. I can't tell you how many people mentioned George Zimmerman, his race, and sometimes with a racial slur added. It was even worse before the media revealed that Zimmerman is half-Hispanic, and not fully white. But the media and many in the black community made this a racial issue, even though the FBI, the lead detective, and even President Obama did not regard the Trayvon Martin shooting as "a race issue," contrary to the opinions of Al Sharpton, Jesse Jackson, and the New Black Panthers, among others.

There is one thing that I would like to know: where is the outrage in the black community over the Clarence Robinson murder? Clarence Robinson is just one person, but there are many other people who have been victimized in our communities, and we have never heard of them. Why is that? This question isn't being posed in order to discount Trayvon Martin's death. But could the amount of international and celebrity attention that Trayvon's death is generating possibly trivialize Clarence Robinson's death or the death of others like him? I hope not, but I wanted to ask the question. The extent of the responses that I have heard concerning Clarence's death is "Man, that's terrible." But there have been no angry responses, no frustration, and no sense of urgency to do anything.

What should be done, if anything? I don't know, but I would ask why Jesse Jackson didn't speak out about Clarence's death? I don't remember one Church in the DFW area that had a ceremony for Clarence. If there was a Church that did have a ceremony, it wasn't highly publicized. Was a ceremony needed for Clarence? Was all of this attention needed for Trayvon Martin? If so, then why wasn't there attention for Clarence, too? The Dallas Mavericks didn't show support for Clarence like the Miami Heat did for Trayvon? Why didn't Al Sharpton coordinate a march in Texas? Was it because Clarence's killer was brought to justice and the family got the closure that they needed? Where was the Facebook support to organize rallies, protests, school walkouts and ceremonies to light candles in Clarence's honor?

The social media outlets were inundated with outcries of support and demands for justice to be served for Trayvon and his family. People wore hoodies and bought Skittles and tea as a sign of unity with Trayvon and his family, even before all of the details of the case were released. We knew exactly what happened to Clarence Robinson and all of the details of his terrible death, but there was no citywide, statewide or nationwide outcry. Why is that? Again, was it just because Clarence's killer was brought to justice?

Which incidents are worthy of national attention and galvanized support, and why? I would have loved to see another campaign to stop the violence or something for Clarence Robinson. I would have also loved to see some widespread support for the eighty-nine-year-old black woman who was raped, strangled and burglarized in 2012 by Secore Joffee King, a twenty-four-year-old black man in Illinois. Clarence's death was horrible, but the eighty-nine-year-old woman's incident was unconscionable. A young man brutally raped a very elderly woman who probably had been celibate for many years. He threatened her life, strangled her, and stole four frozen dinners and seven dollars from the woman's home. Some might argue that this case was different than Trayvon's, because the criminal didn't murder the elderly woman, and he was prosecuted.

So my question is: What is the purpose of all the tremendous attention for Trayvon? Is this about showing support for the victims? Or is this about making sure that the criminals don't go unpunished? Or what? If the answer is both, then where is the attention due to Clarence and other victims? If it is about something else, then what is it?

Media Hype

The reality is that every human life is of equal importance in God's eyes. So I must ask: Why does the media spend so much time covering inter-racial crimes? It is a legitimate question because by comparison, intra-racial crimes are not given the same amount of media attention. And why does the black community, and black Church folks in particular, seem to get more vocal, unified, emotional and politically active when a particular crime is a non-black-on-black crime? This isn't a conspiracy theory; these are serious thoughts to consider and questions that deserve answers.

Black leaders and residents were irate about the beatings and/or killings of: Amadou Diallo in the Bronx, NY 1999; Michael Griffith in Bed-Stuy, NY 1986; James Byrd in Jasper, TX 1998; Yusef Hawkins in Bensonhurst, NY 1989; Rodney King in Los Angeles, CA 1991; Willie Turks in Brooklyn, NY 1982, and rightly so. But what did all of these cases have in common? They were all heinous crimes perpetrated by whites against blacks, and some of these aggressors were set free. But again, the media coverage and public outrage was different for Clarence Robinson. By comparison, there really was none.

I am not a racist, nor do I discriminate against anyone. But it seems as though the media selectively picks stories that stirs people up, and fits their agenda. How many crimes have occurred in America over the past thirty or forty years? I would guess that millions of crimes have occurred; and if you asked the average person if they have ever heard of Trayvon Martin, James Byrd, or Rodney King, they will more than likely answer in the affirmative.

But what about the other people who were killed in America? We don't hear about those murders. Again, why is that? I will also repeat that I believe that if we are going to be a credible voice for political action, justice, community, righteousness, family, etc., then our actions must be consistent and honest.

Here's another example. In New York 1987, the Tawana Brawley case was another hot topic case. It wasn't a murder case, but it was another national news story that fit the profile of media hype, non-black-on-black crime. A young black girl accused six white men of raping her. The media and black leadership hyped it, and the black community and the leadership demanded justice before all of the facts came out. As we all know, the case went nowhere because she lied, and she is now paying defamation damages to one of the men she falsely accused. What about the 2006 false accusation of rape made against three members of the men's lacrosse team of Duke University?

Again, it wasn't a murder case, but it was a very serious accusation that was made. The prosecution, black activists, and the media ran with the story of a black woman who accused three white men of raping her. In the end, all of the charges were dropped, the District Attorney was disbarred, and the lacrosse coach was fired. Why? Lives and reputations were destroyed because emotion (from the constituents) rather than hard evidence to build a case was the motivation for the prosecution. In these cases, were they looking for justice, a story, attention, a settlement, or a crime?

American Tragedies are Political Footballs

Will we continue to allow the media and our politicians to use our family and community tragedies as political footballs to further their agendas? Trayvon's image and the mention of his untimely death have been used as a political prop for gun control legislation. But there has been no mention of Clarence Robinson in the gun control debate. Political opportunists have found a poster child in past American tragedies, such as: the Reagan assassination attempt; the former White House Press Secretary James Brady shooting; the Columbine incident; the D.C. sniper; the Virginia Tech incident; Newtown; Aurora; the Boston Marathon incident, and others. Trayvon Martin is just another name and face that the American media and politicians are using for their own selfish gain.

The other tragedy is how the national media still talks about Caylee Anthony, Jon Benet Ramsey, and Natalie Holloway. Though their deaths were tragic and unjustified, they were all murdered years ago. Whether it is the anniversary of their deaths, or a recent murder that was similar in nature, the media still mentions them from time to time. But not many people have ever heard of Clarence Robinson. Why is that? Am I harping too much on Clarence Robinson? Well, I hope so, because I will continue to stress that this letter is about awareness, consistency and honesty; and Clarence Robinson represents every person who was killed senselessly, but never made the national headlines.

If people still want to claim that justice was served in Clarence Robinson's murder case and that people got involved with the rallies regarding Trayvon Martin's murder because it seemed like justice wasn't going to be served, that is fine. But, if that is the case, then why are so many people making this a racial issue? Why should it matter if this case involved a black man, and a half-white and half-Hispanic man? A human died; that should be the issue with the Trayvon Martin and George Zimmerman ordeal. If George Zimmerman happened to be a black man would the outrage be the same? Were all of the protests and marches strictly about justice? If all of the coverage and rallies, etc. were strictly about justice, then why didn't the black community stand in solidarity with Caylee Anthony, Jon Benet Ramsey, and Natalie Holloway years ago? All life is precious, and we all want justice for all. Right? Again, my point is that I would like for us to be aware, consistent, and honest.

Any ethnic group can and should love its heritage. Most large cities in America have a Chinatown, a Jewish section, a Germantown, etc., so we are all familiar with the cultural groupings that exist. It's natural to embrace people with whom we share a common cultural bond and history; but that isn't the problem. The problem is when there is an intra-racial problem, we handle it and react to it one way, and when there is an inter-racial problem, we handle it and react to it another way. That is the incongruity that I see; and maybe that isn't true for all people, but if you objectively consider what I am saying, you can think of some incidents where my point is valid. Again, I'm talking about awareness, consistency and honesty.

I didn't know Clarence Robinson or Trayvon Martin, but their lives meant something to God, their families, and friends. They were on Earth for a reason, and now they are gone. All of our human brothers and sisters who have died mattered, too; and their families and friends will never forget them. We can all learn something from Clarence Robinson's and Trayvon Martin's death. It's a hard lesson, because they paid the ultimate price. But I think that we can all draw something positive from these experiences. I surely did. What did you learn?

Yours in Christ,

Protection

Dear Friends,

We once again have God's people on both sides of the same issue, and I can't understand this. There is only one answer to two plus two. If someone gives an answer other than four, then they are wrong. Now, we do have issues and situations in which we can compromise and work towards both sides getting a piece of the pie. But that takes diplomacy, reason, tact, an understanding of historical and present-day context, and a willingness to work together.

The issue is gun control, and the message is so polarized and misunderstood that the conversation has become an emotional, political football while segments of our society clamor for someone to make all of this evil go away. For example, let's look at Chicago, Illinois. Chicago's firearm-related crime figures for 2012 were over two thousand shootings and over five hundred homicides. The political and religious leaders in Illinois should be embarrassed and ashamed.

Illinois' political leaders continue to lead from the same platform of more gun control. Meanwhile, Illinois already has some of the most restrictive gun laws in the nation; yet Chicago led the nation in homicides.

In the Word of God

The Word of God is replete with examples of God's people using violence as protection or as a judgment against the heathen, and God was pleased with the end result. So Church folks are going to have to reconcile the following accounts with their anti-second Amendment stance.

Joshua and the Destruction of Jericho

In the account of Joshua and the walls of Jericho, God commanded the children of Israel to kill the heathens who inhabited their land:

And the Lord said unto Joshua, See, I have given into thine hand Jericho, and the king thereof, and the mighty men of valor.
—Joshua 6:2

And they (the Israelites) utterly destroyed all that was in the city, both man and woman, young and old, ox and sheep and donkey, with the edge of the sword.
—Joshua 6:21

So the Lord was with Joshua; and his fame was noised throughout all the country.
—Joshua 6:27

The Lord was with Him because He was pleased that he obeyed and possessed the land. This is the Word of God teaching us about judgment and war. The inhabitants of the land were neither ignorant nor innocent victims of an angry God. They had been committing terrible sin with the full understanding of God's existence, and they continually rejected Him. For this reason, they were judged.

The Story of Samson and Delilah

Do you remember Samson? He was one of God's mighty warriors, who was mocked and blinded by his enemies after the secret of his strength was revealed to them. But in the end, God granted him the strength to kill the Philistines.

Then Samson called to the Lord, saying, "O Lord God, remember me, I pray! Strengthen me, I pray, just this once, O God, that I may with one blow take vengeance on the Philistines for my two eyes!" And Samson took hold of the two middle pillars which supported the temple, and he braced himself against them, one on his right and the other on his left. Then Samson said, "Let me die with the Philistines!" And he pushed with all his might, and the temple fell on the lords and all the people who were in it. So the dead that he killed at his death were more than he had killed in his life.
—Judges 16:28-30

That was seen as redemption for his previous disobedience.

David and Goliath

Do you remember that David killed Goliath? In fact, David invoked the hand of the Lord to help him kill Goliath:

> *Then said David to the Philistine, Thou comest to me with a sword, and with a spear, and with a shield: but I come to thee in the name of the Lord of hosts, the God of the armies of Israel, whom thou hast defied. This day will the Lord deliver thee into mine hand; and I will smite thee, and take thine head from thee; and I will give the carcasses of the host of the Philistines this day unto the fowls of the air, and to the wild beasts of the earth; that all the earth may know that there is a God in Israel.*
>
> —1 Samuel 17:45-46

Jesus and Peter

There are many more judgment and war stories in the Old Testament. But in the New Testament, the people who wish to hijack the Scriptures to fit their agenda have grossly taken Scriptures out of context. Jesus said:

> *And, behold, one of them, which were with Jesus stretched out his hand, and drew his sword, and struck a servant of the high priest's, and smote off his ear. Then said Jesus unto him, Put up again thy sword into his place: for all they that take the sword shall perish with the sword.*
>
> —Matthew 26:51-52

Jesus wasn't rebuking Peter for having a weapon. He always had the weapon with him. The context of the account is that Jesus was finally going to be taken into custody, and His disciples and He were outnumbered. In short, Jesus was telling Peter: "I'm going into custody and the Will of God will be done. We are outnumbered. If you try to defend me with that sword, they will kill you and take me into custody, anyway. So put the sword away and let the Scriptures be fulfilled." For the most part, that is what happened and that is the context and meaning of what Christ said.

Nature

There is no Scripture that teaches to kill someone who enters your home, and wishes to rob you and do you harm. Similarly, there is no Scripture that teaches you to perform the Heimlich Maneuver on a person who is choking. It's a reflex! If someone is trying to harm you, you do what comes natural, you defend yourself. If someone threw a baseball at you, what are you going to do? You are going to try to defend yourself and get out of the way. You're not going to pray and ask God to protect you. You just follow your innate survival reflex. If it is a reflex, then God must have put it there. It's a means of self-defense.

You don't have to teach someone to have a reflex; you just have to show people the best way to use their reflexes. It is unnatural to tell people to **NOT** defend themselves. For a teacher to tell students, "if someone is beating you up, don't fight back, just look for a grown up and get their attention." No, that doesn't even sound logical. If a kid is getting his head bashed in, his first reaction is to get away or to fight back in self-defense. You do what you can to fight back, or you move to safety. Those are reflexes that are inherent in nature. The concept of self-defense is natural. But some people in our society think that they are smarter than God.

History

We can't be ignorant of history. Look at Pharaoh, Hitler, Idi Amin, Pol Pot, Stalin, King George III, etc. These monsters of world history went on a rampage against their subjects because the people were helpless and defenseless. But the colonists took a stand and refused to be another negative statistic in world history. They took up arms and rebelled against the evil British Crown. Is it wrong to thwart evil and to fight for the right to life, liberty and the pursuit of happiness? How successful do you think Pharaoh or Pol Pot would have been if their subjects were well-armed? Was it fair that the leaders were armed and were able to control, to brutalize, and to kill their subjects?

Weapons are an equalizer in the hands of good people, because good people don't use their weaponry to initiate wrongdoing; they use weaponry to stop wrongdoing. Guns, and other legal self-defense weapons and techniques, are the great equalizer when evil is afoot. Take the power out of the hands of bad people by arming yourself with legal self-defense mechanisms.

Yours in Christ,

Excellence and Achievement have Nothing to Do with Color

Dear Friends,

Have you ever heard a black person tell another black person to stop acting white? Or you may have heard a black person make the comment to an articulate black person, "You must hang around a lot of white people." Why would someone say that? How does a white person act? In parts of the black community, there are many things that are hurting our people, such as: crime, poverty, immorality, the status quo, broken families, etc. In addition, ignorance, disunity, and the lack of education promote and accept the misconceptions, which needlessly tear down our neighbors, and contribute to our own demise. Sadly, we don't have to worry about an outside enemy destroying us, because in many regards, we are our own worst enemy; and unfortunately, I have witnessed Church folks in the midst of this type of nonsense. Will we continue to accept and to promote the self-sabotage and self-destruction? Will we break the chains of the wrong thinking and the wrong actions that are keeping our communities in bondage?

Unfortunately, when people speak out of ignorance, most times any possibility of making a positive connection with others or building a bridge is shut down; and any statements or arguments that follow are generally discounted, ignored, and/or given no credibility. Whether it is fair or not can be debated, but I have seen this scenario occur many times. However, the best way to dispel ignorance is to inject the right information.

So what does it mean for a person to "act white?" This misconception and misnomer of "acting white" is usually associated with success, proper etiquette, excelling, accountability, or achievement. For example, some in the black community would consider getting good grades in school, articulating a grammatically-correct sentence, being on-time, exercising, dressing neatly, being responsible, having a professional job or working towards one, eating at a nice restaurant, etc. as "acting white." So if these positive things are considered to be "acting white," then what is considered to be "acting black?" Should we be failing, always late, lazy, wearing our pants below our waist, unkempt, irresponsible, doing immoral things, only working entry-level jobs, and always eating unhealthy foods? It seems as though the segment of the black community who uses the "acting white" label never scolds our people who are behaving unmannerly. Negativity is accepted, given a pass, seen as a badge of honor, or at the very least considered to be "keepin' it real" by that same segment of people. Is being negative or a bad example what "acting black" is really all about to some people?

We have to expand our minds, so that we can see the world more clearly and in a more complete scope. If not, we will always be left behind and we will never be taken seriously. If all you know is your surroundings, then how can you judge the rest of the world? If all you know is Hamburger Helper, then how can you judge Filet Mignon served Oscar style? If you have never read Harriet Beecher Stowe's 1852 book, "Uncle Tom's Cabin," then how do you know if calling someone an "Uncle Tom" is an actual insult or a compliment? Was "Uncle Tom" a good guy or a bad guy? Again, we dispel ignorance with the implementation of the right information.

I am convinced that ignorance is a tool of the enemy to stop people from achieving God's best. The reality is that no one can stop you from achieving God's best. Only you can stop you, because if you begin to believe the negativity, the ignorant lies, and the misconceptions, you will lose. Negative words can only hurt you if you believe them. Don't let ignorance steal your confidence, frustrate and defeat you. Remember, you defeat ignorance with the implementation of the right information. There is nothing "white" about intelligence, cleanliness, responsibility, proper grammar etc. You just have to make the quality decision that you will not be influenced by ignorance, and that you will do the right thing and succeed. The choice is yours.

Yours in Christ,

Is Going to the Movies Sinful?

Dear Friends,

Allow me to take a few moments to tell you what the Lord has put upon my heart for you. As believers, we have been commissioned to shun the world's way and embrace God's way of doing things. But that is not a reason to retreat from life, and to distance ourselves from enjoying normal activities. When we go to unnecessary extremes in the name of "holiness" and avoid fun times like the movies, amusement parks etc., it puts believers into the spiritual bondage of legalism.

I once heard a woman say that Christians shouldn't go to the movies because of a misinterpretation of the following Scripture:

> *Blessed is the man that walketh not in the counsel of the ungodly, nor standeth in the way of sinners, nor sitteth in the seat of the scornful.*
> —Psalm 1:1

The Church folk assumption is that the movie theater is the seat of the scornful. Isn't that ridiculous? This is a clear example of how ignorant many believers are about the Word they profess. This was a totally misinterpreted verse of Scripture. A scornful person is someone who mocks God, His ways and/or His people. Granted, there are some movies that do just that, but to say that the concept of a movie theater has anything to do with Psalm 1 is an absolute joke. Church folks heard someone say that the movie theater is the seat of the scornful, and they found a Scripture with the word "scornful" in it, and viola, a new doctrine.

I wonder if Church folks believed that the movie theater was the seat of the scornful when it showed the "Passion of the Christ," "Courageous," or other Scripturally based movies. Well, it doesn't matter. Church folks can believe whatever they wish to believe, because I don't live my life based upon someone else's interpretation of the Scriptures. I live my life based upon the Scriptures, in context, with balance, and pure motives; and you should too. We are called to be salt and light, to be a witness of His goodness, and to live victorious lives spirit, soul and body. We can do all of that and still enjoy a decent movie.

Sure, we shouldn't support movies that are an affront to Heaven. But you have to judge your own heart when it comes to viewing movies with questionable content. If profanity offends you, then you probably won't want to go to eighty percent of the movies that are available at the movies. But don't impose your will upon others. You just need to act according to the peace that is in your heart, and pray for others if that is what you feel led to do. But don't be the legalism police!

Yours in Christ,

Secular Music

Dear Friends,

I recently received a few emails that grabbed my attention. An excerpt from one read:
"Brother Brian, I can't believe that there are Christians who drive down the street with Jesus bumper stickers on the back of their cars, while they blast R & B music."

An excerpt from another read: "Blessings to you and your family Brother Brian. I just wanted to tell you that your insightful teachings have helped me to see that the Word of God should be the standard for all Christians; and thanks to you, I have thrown away all of my secular devil music. I use to be a fan of Genesis, Johnny Cash, The Eagles, and others, but I will just continue to praise the Lord with His music."

I was encouraged to read these emails. They said a lot more, but those two people really made me think. Secular music and the Church; can the two co-exist?

I took a few moments to write to both of them, and I basically told them the same thing. I will share with you the gist of what I told them so that you can gain understanding, as well.

For thousands of years, people have used music for singing and dancing for a variety of reasons: to praise and worship God, to celebrate, for traditional reasons, to relax, or just because it is liberating and a free expression. Any way you look at it, whoever it is and whenever people are singing, dancing or both, most times it is a time associated with some sort of joyous expression.

Too often, I hear Church folks criticizing secular music. Many Church folks claim that singing and/or dancing to secular music is of the devil. Well, I'm not so sure that we can make a blanket statement like that, and make it a true statement. Just because something is secular, and secular people enjoy it, or if it doesn't overtly acknowledge God, that doesn't necessarily mean that it is evil. To conclude that secular music and dancing are of the devil is like saying that money is of the devil. Music and dancing are neutral; it's the motive of how and why you do something that determines the morality factor; and the same goes for money. Is makeup sinful just because prostitutes wear it? Isn't that a ridiculous thought? But these are the discussions that Church folks are having, and many times, Church folks are on the wrong side of the issues.

Explicit lyrics and scantily clad women who dance provocatively and promote lust in many of today's music videos are evil. But dancing because you are happy, vibrant, and enjoying life is a beautiful thing. Sometimes, we even find ourselves moving to a catchy instrumental sound playing in the grocery store just because it's a nice sound. Where is the harm in that?

Don't throw the baby out with the bath water. A man would enjoy listening to a secular song that expresses love and desire for his woman. How is that a sin? The artist might be secular, but so what. What is the motive of the song? The attraction between a man and a woman is a natural and beautiful thing; and as long as the song isn't promoting fornication, adultery or pornography, if it has a nice melody and harmony, and sincere words, I'll listen to it. Anita Baker is one of my all-time favorites. She has a great voice, lovely lyrics, she's smooth and kind of jazzy. Musiq Soul Child, the Stylistics, New Edition, and the Spinners are some of my favorite artists. Of course, I love Gospel and Praise and Worship music (classic Fred Hammond and Hezekiah Walker), but I enjoy a good musical balance with some Classical music, as well.

Aside from the theme of love, people also sing and write songs about life, political issues or other secular themes. The songs don't mention God, nor do they mention or promote evil. For example, Genesis sang a song in the 1980's called, "Land of Confusion" which was a political song that questioned the wisdom of world leaders during the Cold War when the US and Russia were threatening to use nuclear weapons. There is nothing sinful about that song. John Fogerty sang a song called, "Centerfield." This song was inspired by Fogerty's childhood memories of baseball, and the stories his father told him about the former New York Yankees centerfielder Joe DiMaggio. He also explained that the song was a metaphor about getting yourself motivated, facing challenges, and getting yourself ready for the job. Secular doesn't necessarily equate to evil. Heavy D made a song called "Nike," because that was his favorite sneaker. Run DMC made a song called "My Adidas," and many years ago Kurtis Blow made a song called "Basketball." There is nothing sinful about these secular songs.

Music in Nature

Music is God's creation and it is God's gift to us. The rhythm of music is in the human heartbeat, there's a rhythm in our walk, we clap our hands, the birds chirp, crickets make a melodious sound, the ocean waves crash, the sounds of seagulls, a running brook, and thunder all have a musical and/or subliminal element to them. Even some Radio Astrophysicists claim that stars throughout the universe are emitting harmonious music (in major keys) via radio waves of energy.

Often times, manipulators have taken the wonders of God's creation (the expressions of music and dance), and have either hijacked it or perverted the beauty and the creativity of it. Music is natural and it stirs the emotions. Have you ever heard the saying: "music calms the savage beast?"

David played the harp for King Saul and it calmed him and it drove evil spirits away.

But the Spirit of the Lord departed from Saul, and a distressing spirit from the Lord troubled him. And Saul's servants said to him, "Surely, a distressing spirit from God is troubling you. Let our master now command your servants, who are before you, to seek out a man who is a skillful player on the harp. And it shall be that he will play it with his hand when the distressing spirit from God is upon you, and you shall be well." So Saul said to his servants, "Provide me now a man who can play well, and bring him to me." Then one of the servants answered and said, "Look, I have seen a son of Jesse the Bethlehemite, who is skillful in playing, a mighty man of valor, a man of war, prudent in speech, and a handsome person; and the Lord is with him." Therefore Saul sent messengers to Jesse, and said, "Send me your son David, who is with the sheep." And Jesse took a donkey loaded with bread, a skin of wine, and a young goat, and sent them by his son David to Saul. So David came

to Saul and stood before him. And he loved him greatly, and he became his armor bearer. Then Saul sent to Jesse, saying, "Please let David stand before me, for he has found favor in my sight." And so it was, whenever the spirit from God was upon Saul, that David would take a harp and play it with his hand. Then Saul would become refreshed and well, and the distressing spirit would depart from him.
—1 Samuel 16:14.23

Music is one of God's creations and it was created for us to enjoy. But it's all about the motive behind your music.

Once the Church gets a true understanding of motive, context, and perspective, then we can enjoy God's gifts freely. Until then, the Church (generally-speaking) will always hide behind this phony veil of "holiness" when Christ has already set us free from the bondage towards which many Church folks gravitate. We have a long way to go, but we are making progress.

I hope to see you all soon. Continue to be steadfast, unmovable, and always abounding in the work of the Lord.

Yours in Christ,

Divorce and Re-Marriage to Another

Dear Friends,

Marriage is simply a lifelong covenant between a man, a woman, and God. It is supposed to be a joyous occasion and it is a good thing to be married according to God's plan. But if the covenant isn't based upon love, substantive connection, and the Will of God, then the marriage probably won't last, and it won't be a happy, fulfilling relationship. Unfortunately, this is the case in many marriages; even Christian couples are divorcing at alarming rates.

Although God isn't a covenant breaker, you must employ some common sense and realize that, sometimes, cutting your losses is the best option. If your mate beats you, abuses you, cheats on you, and totally disrespects the relationship, then you don't have a marriage. Why stay where you are not appreciated, accepted or wanted? This isn't a license to just give up and leave, because I do believe that there is something to be said regarding patience, grace, and reconciliation. But I don't want people to be naïve and think that you must remain unhappy and stuck with no options. I'm merely injecting some common sense into a real issue. I know a lot of old school Church folks just stuck it out no matter what happened. I don't agree with that stance, but each person has to follow what they believe is right.

Divorce is not what God wants for us. His Will is that we marry the right person for the right reason(s) for better or for worse, for richer or for poorer, through sickness and in health, and live happily ever after. But, for whatever reason, the husband and/or wife don't always do the right thing; and sometimes decisions are made that result in regrets. Some Church folks try to hold people hostage with the Matthew 19:6 Scripture, where Jesus said, "What God hath joined together, let not man put asunder." The Church folks will use that Scripture to force people to stay unhappily married. But the Scripture is clear; He said, "What God joined together." Sometimes, people join themselves together in marriage, but not at God's direction, nor with His blessings. Should people stay committed to something that God didn't sanction? Many times, people act out of lust, insecurity, or desperation, and they try to force God's blessings onto their marriages. That's a sad reality, but people have to decide if they want to make things right with God. We are all one in the covenant, but we must remember that our covenant is with God. So make things right with Him.

However, divorce is not the unpardonable sin. But many Church folks act as though divorce is so far removed from God's ability to forgive and to restore you, that some folks stay in horrible relationships for fear of being ostracized by the Church folks. That is a shame, because we should be able to find love, understanding, prayer, and support among God's people.

It's easy to put on a façade and a religious face in front of people, and it's the really Churchy thing to say "Oh, praise the Lord, I'm blessed" whenever you see another Christian. But if you live in a bad situation, you feel horrible, and many times, no one really knows your situation and the full scope of details that make you unhappy, and cause you to consider divorce.

As someone who has suffered through a divorce, I say if one or both parties can't or don't want to reconcile, then you should cut your losses. I know people stay together for the kid's sake; meanwhile, the household situation yields no peace, and two people who can't or don't want to get along are stuck under the same roof as enemies with a pleasant public façade. I'm not encouraging anyone to get a divorce, but I believe that it is better to work alone, then to be on a team and work alone. Life goes on and you must continue to live your life (with or without the other person).

Many Church folks want to bash and to condemn people who get divorced and remarried. Divorce should mean, "I've exhausted every option to reconcile and I want to get out of a bad situation before it becomes an unsafe or unhealthy environment," and re-marriage should mean, "I want another chance at God's blessing." Whatever the circumstances that surround your situation, only God, your spouse, and you are the only ones who truly know all of the facts. So, don't let the pressure from Church folks make you feel uncomfortable, because if there is something that requires your repentance before God, then repent before God. You don't need to explain all of the details of your life to people; it's really no one's business. If you wish to confide in someone, then that is your free-will decision to make. I'll see you soon. Stay blessed and encouraged.

Yours in Christ,

Sex, Sex and More Sex

Dear Friends,

I visited a ministry last weekend, and they were having a marriage conference. The minister was preaching to the single and married people, and gave them some information to encourage, to strengthen, and to inform them about their current and future relationships. He addressed love, God, communication, finances, trust, respect, etc. But when he started to talk about sex, a deafening silence came over those in attendance, and many of the women were blushing. I figured that things were going to get a bit interesting, so I decided to listen.

The minister invited a few couples to the front and asked them to address the audience about some of the issues that they confronted in their marriages. The overwhelming majority of the couples were dealing with sexual issues. Either one of the partners was withholding sex or one of the partners wasn't open to effectively communicate about lovemaking/sex. You could tell that the couples that were speaking had a story to tell, because they were so passionate and you could hear liberation in their voices, as if they were reporting the news of a battle won.

The husbands that spoke were very candid about their former pornography addictions and the reasons why they gravitated away from their wives, and gravitated towards pornography and extra-marital situations. In short, the women felt unloved, unwanted and unappreciated by their husbands. They felt as though their lives were without meaningful purpose, and that the marriage was just a show. This lowered their self-esteem, and caused the women to shut down across the board, especially in the bedroom. This "shut down" caused the men to feel disrespected, trapped, and less than a man (to a degree).

Every man wants to conquer his woman (that's just the inherent nature of a man); and if he isn't conquering her, he feels as though he is not fulfilling a portion of his purpose. I know this might sound savage and degrading, because mutual love and respect should be expressed. But just like a woman has emotional needs that need to be fulfilled, so does a man have (ego) needs that must be fulfilled.

I never excuse or make excuses for a person who cheats on their spouse, but I can understand why it happens. The other couples revealed how they were in bondage in their marriages. They were afraid or ashamed to explore and to enjoy different acts of passion and positions with their spouses; because the unwritten "Church rule" was if you have sex with your spouse, don't talk about it. So the body of believers has all of these issues, questions and confusion, but there's no safe place to discuss sensitive matters. Well brothers and sisters, you have a safe place here with those of us who are not in spiritual and mental bondage.

In reality, people are curious and are always looking for answers. It's best to get the right information and wisdom from God and His people. But if that avenue is unavailable, then unfortunately, some people will go to pornography, swingers groups, prostitutes, or some other illicit type of behavior. I'm not condoning this behavior, but this is a real topic that needs to be addressed, and for too long the Church has sat on this egg without hatching it. So the Church folks get skewed secular information about something that God created (sex), and we wonder why there is so much immorality in Christian marriages.

Oral Sex

What can the prostitute or the woman on the porno movie do that your wife can't do? A better question might be: What *will* the prostitute or the woman on the porno movie do that your wife **WON'T** do? The same can be asked of the husbands, because at times, people's hormones go crazy. Folks get curious about different things and God has given us a safe place to express ourselves: marriage. Many times, people don't take advantage of this gift.

One of the audience members raised his hand to ask a question. He asked, "What about oral sex? Is that a sin in marriage?" Well, the audience gasped in disbelief, but these couples didn't hold back and it was refreshing to listen to them. One couple got really free and talked about how they use to have sex like rabbits before they got saved. But once they came to Christ, they were more concerned with being spiritual and putting on the Christian façade. I'm all for being spiritual, and there is a spiritual element to sex, but for the most part it's a mind and body connection. The couple said that they artificially suppressed their strong libidos and they spent more time being intimate with God in the evenings, rather than being intimate with one another.

Their hearts were fixed towards God and they didn't want to seem too worldly. These people were obviously ignorant and in spiritual bondage when they first received Christ. But this was not a unique circumstance, because a lot of Christians are in bondage in this area.

The couple continued on and recited a verse of Scripture.

> *Marriage is honorable in all, and the bed undefiled: but whoremongers and adulterers God will judge.*
> —Hebrews 13:4

Then the wife shouted, "If your spouse and you are in agreement, then go for it." I agreed with her, and that's how I look at oral sex, and sex (in general) with your spouse. The sex acts that are done are between the husband and wife, and they should be done within the marriage covenant. If that is the case, then enjoy yourself. Too often, we have the Church sex police who want to monitor your activity and deem certain things as impure, even when God hasn't named them as sinful. Things like adultery, fornication, incest, homosexuality, bestiality, etc. are clearly defined as sin; but most times, sex with your spouse is a personal choice with freedom to explore new and different things. Also, while oral sex can be very enjoyable, it is not the be-all and end-all of sexual acts, and there are other ways of producing similar pleasure with your spouse.

Frequency

The couple continued and stated that they broke free from the stigma of equating a high libido to being weird among the body of believers. The couple admitted that they reminisced about their past encounters and how they missed the frequency of their intimacy. Prior to Christ, they were a two or three time a day couple. They'd do "nooners" (going home at lunchtime and hit a quickie), and they had no inhibitions. But since they became Christians, they were once a week couple, maybe. They made it clear that they were very frustrated, but they thought that they were being "Godly." But one day, they decided to go back to the way things used to be. They loved each other, so they wanted to express that love and experience that connection more often; and God set them free to express themselves in more than just the missionary position at night with the lights off, under the covers. They were no longer ashamed or embarrassed about the intimacy or the frequency of the intimacy, because God blessed their union. They are daily lovers once again, and they counsel people about relationships from a Biblical perspective.

I don't want to overstress sex in a marriage, but I don't want to diminish its value either; I want to put it in its proper perspective and share with you an analogy about intimacy. In our personal relationships with God, we all spend time with God according to our level of understanding, love and devotion for Him. God knows all of our hearts, and He communes with us accordingly. Someone that is more excited about God will probably spend more time reading the Word, praying, and seeking God. Someone who may not be as zealous about God will spend less time doing those things. That doesn't mean that both people don't love God, but the proof of desire is pursuit. You pursue and get attached to the thing that or the person who has your attention. The type of intimacy and the frequency of the intimacy that you have with God are contingent upon the type of connection that you have with God. If you are a Sunday Christian, then you probably won't spend a lot of intimate time with God, but the more connected you get with God, the more intimacy will manifest as a result.

The same goes for the intimacy in your marriage. If the connection is strong, the intimacy will manifest, unless there are other issues present. Again, I'm not telling anyone how often to have sexual relations. I know that when you were twenty years old, you probably wanted sex multiple times per day or week. Men and women peak (sexually) at different ages, but the fact remains that it is an innate function of the human experience.

The porn stars shouldn't be the only people who enjoy sexual relations. They are "professionals" in regards to the physical acts and how the body works, but they are in sin and they know nothing of the blessings of a Biblical marriage and the right way to enjoy sexual relations. Maybe one day, someone will create a book entitled, "The Joy of Sex" from a Christian perspective, so people can see that you can still serve the Lord and have a tremendous sex life, as well.

Yours in Christ,

Sexless Marriage

Dear Friends,

I know that I wrote you a letter about sex already, but the subject came up again. Since I wrote that letter, various Christians emailed and called me asking what they should do because they don't feel like having sex with their spouses. That's a tough situation, because the Bible teaches us that sex is only to be done within the marriage covenant; and if one person isn't willing to participate, then the other person (if they are faithful) will end up lacking in that area.

People often respond that they've been married for so long that they don't need sex like they did when they were younger. So, many people tend to downplay sex, and take it for granted like it's no big deal. I even received a marriage joke in my email regarding sex. It asked: Which food takes away a woman's sex drive? The answer was "wedding cake." That's sad, but in many instances, it seems to be so true.

Think about what I am saying in these terms: if you were sick, your body would shut down the body's appetite, and you would begin to lose weight. This is a signal that something is wrong, because eating is a normal function of life. Or if you lose the desire to sleep; that is not normal. Likewise, if your appetite for sex is shut down, then this is a signal that something is wrong (chemically, emotionally, physically, etc.). Maybe you don't need it three times a day anymore, but to have sex once a week or once a month is not very frequent. But if your spouse and you are in agreement with the frequency of your intimacy, then continue with the timeframe that is comfortable for you. If your spouse is not in agreement with the frequency of your intimate times, then the matter needs to be addressed (whether the intimate times are too many or too few). If there are medical issues, then you may want to seek professional help and believe God to restore that part of your marriage.

Although sex isn't the most important part of a relationship, it is a necessary and natural part of it. I liken sex to the spark plugs in your car; they are a small part of the car, but the car won't work without them. If you don't have sex with your spouse, then you are missing out on a beautiful way to connect with one another. Sexual intimacy is the one thing that differentiates your spouse from everyone else in the world. You might hug or share fun times with other people in your life, but sexual intimacy is the distinguishing act that should make your relationship with your spouse unique. You share that special bond that makes you both one (physically), and if you don't share that bond, then you are missing a treat.

Folks, I don't consider myself to be a "Dr. Ruth" or anything. I'm just a man who was saddened by so many reports of sexual frustration from precious men and women of God. I would like for all of us to enjoy all of the blessings and the benefits that God has made available for us. God is so good to us, and He brings insight and revelation to us so that we can grow and improve our current situations.

Stay blessed and encouraged.

Yours in Christ,

The Pornography/ Masturbation Question

Dear Friends,

I believe that I need to have a little heart-to-heart with you folks. There is a very sensitive topic that continues to be asked of me, so I need to address it plainly. Recently, a few people asked me my thoughts on masturbation and watching pornography. Is it wrong? Does the Bible address it? Well, the Bible doesn't address it as clearly as it does murder or lying, but there are principles that do cover the subject. A lot of people masturbate, regardless of whether or not they are Christians. Humans have natural desires, but we should know how to handle our desires and put them in their proper perspective. Also, what better way to put sensitive issues into perspective than to do so in a Word-based setting? God created the feelings, so His Word should be used to clearly explain the matter to us.

To some, masturbation or pornography is viewed as a safe alternative to conventional sex because the desired result is achieved (orgasm) without hearing lies, getting diseases, emotional attachments, or heartbreaks. In short, your hand, your toy, or watching your favorite porno star is your best friend. But the masturbation/pornography issue is a little bit more complex than that, because it deals with the dangers of lust and the consequences of manipulating your body outside of the will of God.

> "Shun immorality and all sexual looseness (flee from impurity in thought, word, or deed). Any other sin which a man commits is one outside the body, but he who commits sexual immorality sins against his own body."
>
> —*1 Corinthians 6:18*

The word "masturbation" is thought to have derived from the Latin words *manus* meaning hand or manual and *stuprāre* meaning to defile (oneself). So combining the two words conveys the idea of manually abusing or defiling oneself with the hand. Naturally-speaking, this might not make much sense since masturbation is supposed to produce a pleasurable release; but the abuse is spiritual, yet manifests naturally.

> *"Let no man say when he is tempted, I am tempted of God: for God cannot be tempted with evil, neither tempteth he any man: But every man is tempted, when he is drawn away of his own lust, and enticed. Then when lust hath conceived, it bringeth forth sin: and sin, when it is finished, bringeth forth death."*
>
> —James 1:13-15

Masturbation begins with a lustful thought (fantasy), which leads to arousal and the temporary sexual release. But that "quick fix" always leads to the need for another "quick fix" and more lustful thoughts, and the cycle never ends. In fact, when the "quick fixes" aren't enough anymore, the need can escalate to more pornography, more vile pornography, and/or illicit relationships. It's like building a tolerance against something.

But Jesus explained the root of the matter:

> *"You have heard that it was said to those of old, 'You shall not commit adultery.' But I say to you that whoever looks at a woman to lust for her has already committed adultery with her in his heart."*
>
> —Matthew 5:27-28

So, this is why I originally said that the abuse is spiritual, because we are dealing with a matter of the heart (spirit). Lusting after the person who aroused your senses constitutes the sexual act being committed in your heart, according to Jesus. Your hand or your toy and the manipulation of your body are not the problem; that is only a manifestation of the problem. No one wants to talk about masturbation, but it is a real issue that needs to be addressed. There are many people who are either addicted to it or the masturbation has manifested into other things, like pornography, or other types of illicit behaviors.

I always tell people that if you want to truly be set free from masturbation, you have to first see masturbation through the eyes of the Word of God. You can't look at masturbation, pornography, and using sexual toys through the eyes of disease-free sexual pleasure that doesn't require cheating on a spouse, lying, or fornicating. Remember, this is a spiritual issue that has manifested into masturbation. A lot of secular folks and Church folks struggle with these types of topics because they aren't free to deal with them in a candid manner. I'm free, so I can address it with honesty and transparency. I use to masturbate years ago, and you will be surprised at the number of folks in their teens up into their 70's (men and women) who struggle with this habit. So let's talk about it and get some solutions in place to help people get free.

Well, I'm going to let you all absorb this lesson for a while. I'm sure I will address it again in the near future. But don't feel condemned, just open your heart, and let the Word of God minister to you. Then we can get deeper and move towards deliverance from masturbation/pornography and living a masturbation-free/pornography-free life. We all have issues, not the same issues, but issues, nonetheless. If we didn't, we wouldn't need God's help, wisdom and insight in our lives. I'm glad to be of service, so feel free to continue to send your questions and prayer requests my way. We've got the victory in Jesus!

Yours in Christ,

INTERRACIAL DATING/MARRIAGE

Dear Friends,

Interracial dating/marriage is becoming a popular trend. Personally, I don't have a problem with it; in fact, I look at it as progress. That which was once forbidden is now practiced, accepted and encouraged by many. If Heaven is going to have all races worshiping before the throne of God, then why can't we learn to love one another and co-exist here on the Earth?

Interracial dating is a problem for many people in every race. In the natural, people want to continue on with their own customs, traditions and cultural celebrations with the integrity of their racial heritage intact; and that is understandable. God created the races and gave each one a unique culture.

Cross-culture dating can become a problem if the entire spectrum is not thoroughly scrutinized. Language, food, wearing apparel, customs, history, and many more factors can play a part in the success or failure of an interracial union.

Unfortunately, some believers in Christ have a skewed view of interracial dating/marriage. Some people believe that interracial dating/marriage is not God's Will, while others would rather stay segregated for other reasons. However, the Bible doesn't teach that a man and a woman of two different ethnicities cannot fall in love and marry. The reality of interracial dating (in God's eyes) is that He doesn't want one of His believers to marry someone who doesn't believe in Him. God takes issue with two different faiths coming together, not two different ethnicities.

"When the LORD your God brings you into the land which you go to possess, and has cast out many nations before you, the Hittites and the Girgashites and the Amorites and the Canaanites and the Perizzites and the Hivites and the

Jebusites, seven nations greater and mightier than you, and when the LORD your God delivers them over to you, you shall conquer them and utterly destroy them. You shall make no covenant with them nor show mercy to them. Nor shall you make marriages with them. You shall not give your daughter to their son, nor take their daughter for your son. <u>For they will turn your sons away from following Me, to serve other gods</u>; so the anger of the LORD will be aroused against you and destroy you suddenly. But thus you shall deal with them: you shall destroy their altars, and break down their sacred pillars, and cut down their wooden images, and burn their carved images with fire."

—Deuteronomy 7:1-5

So, (as far as God is concerned) the issue isn't the color of someone's skin, it's the heart and belief system. Other examples include: Boaz, the son of Rahab the harlot, a Canaanite woman from Jericho. Rahab was accepted by God and she allowed her son to marry an Israelite because she accepted the God of Israel (Hebrews 11:31). Boaz was able to marry Ruth (a Moabite) because she accepted the true God of Israel (Ruth 1:16).

Paul also confirms that it's not a racial matter:

Be ye not unequally yoked together with unbelievers: for what fellowship hath righteousness with unrighteousness? And what communion hath light with darkness? And what concord hath Christ with Belial? Or what part hath he that believeth with an infidel? And what agreement hath the temple of God with idols? For ye are the temple of the living God; as God hath said, I will dwell in them, and walk in them; and I will be their God, and they shall be my people. Wherefore come out from among them, and be ye separate, saith the Lord, and touch not the unclean thing; and I will receive you. And will be a Father unto you, and ye shall be my sons and daughters, saith the Lord Almighty.

—2 Corinthians 6:14-18

As Martin Luther King Jr. noted, a person should be judged by his or her character, not by skin color. Personally, I view people who are opposed to interracial dating/marriage as racists. You can have a preference to stay with your own race, and that is fine. But to oppose the concept of interracial marriage is racism. Think about it, we are all humans created by God. We are the species binomial Homo sapiens. Our skin tones are different, but we are all one in humanity. Black, white and brown animals of the same species pair off and mate. Why should it be a big deal if two God-fearing humans wish to fall in love and have a family? It's only a problem to racists, because if the God-fearing couple is happy with one another, but the family is against the interracial aspect of it; then, by default, the family is saying the opposing race isn't good enough for us. In a nutshell, that is racism; and yes, some Church folks who raise their hands, praise the Lord, tithe, quote Scriptures, and tell people about the goodness of the Lord are some of the biggest racists you will ever meet.

So once again, the Church folks have struck out again on social issues. Interracial couples can marry and be happy with God's blessings upon them. As long as Jesus Christ is Lord over the man and the woman's lives, then the race issue is irrelevant. If the couple is self-conscious about the possible difficulties they may experience because of societal stereotypes, then they have to consider that, and make a decision. The kids might be teased, people might look at your family awkwardly, and a host of other things can happen to interracial couples. The couple needs to take these things into consideration and be prepared for them, should they decide to marry.

Ignorance won't go away, but hopefully, it lessens with each generation. I just pray that wherever a man and a woman find love, may Christ be the center of it.

Yours in Christ,

Using Contraception is a Sin

Dear Friends,

This idea that contraception is a sin is absolutely preposterous. The Bible teaches us about creation; and our mandate from God to be fruitful and to multiply.

And God said, Let Us make man in Our image, after Our likeness: and let them have dominion over the fish of the sea, and over the fowl of the air, and over the cattle, and over all the Earth, and over every creeping thing that creepeth upon the Earth. So God created man in His own image, in the image of God created He him; male and female created He them. And God blessed them, and God said unto them, Be fruitful, and multiply, and replenish the Earth, and subdue it: and have dominion over the fish of the sea, and over the fowl of the air, and over every living thing that moveth upon the Earth.
—Genesis 1:26-28

Many believers take this Scripture to mean that we must have a bunch of kids and that contraception is outside of the Will of God. The following Biblical account is generally the foundation of that teaching.

Then Judah took a wife for Er his firstborn, and her name was Tamar. But Er, Judah's firstborn, was wicked in the sight of the Lord, and the Lord killed him. And Judah said to Onan, "Go in to your brother's wife and marry her, and raise up an heir to your brother." But Onan knew that the heir would not be his; and it came to pass, when he went in to his brother's wife, that he emitted on the ground, lest he should give an heir to his brother. And the thing which he did displeased the Lord; therefore He killed him also.
—Genesis 38:6-10

I can't tell you how many people have used this Scripture to obligate themselves to have a lot of children, because they interpreted this Scripture to mean that contraception is a sin. This is another example of Church folks not having proper perspective and context of the Scriptures.

In short, Judah's firstborn son, Er, was to continue the lineage and the covenantal family blessings through his firstborn son. But before he was able to have a child with his wife, Tamar, Er died. So Judah instructed the next son, Onan, to follow the tradition and have a baby with Tamar for Er, and for the sake of the family name. Onan agreed, but later reneged and thought to himself that the child wouldn't be his heir, but his brother's heir. Nonetheless, he had sex with Tamar, but he decided to pull out (not to ejaculate inside of her) and not to impregnate her. This disobedience angered the Lord.

It was Onan's selfishness and ego that led to his decision to not provide the family with an heir for the firstborn son in his absence. That was the sin, not the fact that he pulled out. But people will erroneously use this account to create a doctrine against birth control. Don't fall victim to the false teachings among believers. I know many people who love their children, but some people have admitted that if they thought that contraception was not against the Will of God, then they would have planned their families out a bit differently. Whether that means that they would have spaced their children, or not had as many children we will never know. But the fact remains that many people are making life-long commitments based upon error and not God's liberating truth.

God help us to seek Your Will and heart in everything; and may we be students of Your Word, not the traditions/interpretations of human intellect.

Stay strong and encouraged.

Yours in Christ,

Should Christians Date?

Dear Friends,

Interaction is a natural part of the human experience. We bond with family members, friends of the same sex, and friends of the opposite sex. But, at some point, nature begins to take its course and males and females will begin to pair off. It's an innate instinct that is inherent in all humanity. If humans never learned about dating, and sex was never taught, dating and sex would automatically happen as a natural reflex. It's like when the doctor hits you on the knee with the rubber mallet. If you're normal, your leg will react. You don't have to make it react, because the leg is naturally responding to the impact. I see dating as a natural reaction.

Some Christians have the idea that dating is an evil, secular process. But like I said, it is a natural reflex. These reflexes can manifest themselves as a date, dating, or courtship. A date can be a friendly and platonic outing, or the dating (multiple dates) could lead to the next step, courtship. Courtship means that things are more serious than just dating, and it also infers that love is felt and has been expressed, marriage has been discussed, and could be a serious consideration in the near future.

The problem with dating and courting is (if you are a Christian) there is the secular world's way of doing it, and there is a way that is pleasing to God. For example, you can't fornicate to the glory of God.

> *Flee fornication. Every sin that a man doeth is without the body; but he that committeth fornication sinneth against his own body.*
> —1 Corinthians 6:18

But you can go out on a date and/or court someone with God's blessings upon you. Again, remember the opposite sex pairing off is a natural reflex, and it can be done honorably and with integrity. The participants in the dating/courtship process have to be in agreement with God's Word that they will remain vessels of honor fit for the Master's use.

> *Nevertheless the solid foundation of God stands, having this seal: "The Lord knows those who are His," and, "Let everyone who names the name of Christ depart from iniquity." But in a great house there are not only vessels of gold and silver, but also of wood and clay, some for honor and some for dishonor. Therefore if anyone cleanses himself from the latter, he will be a vessel for honor, sanctified and useful for the Master, prepared for every good work. Flee also youthful lusts; but pursue righteousness, faith, love, peace with those who call on the Lord out of a pure heart.*
> —2 Timothy 2:19-22

Soul Mates

There is a tremendous fixation these days with finding a soul mate. Most people would like to settle down with that special someone one day and live happily ever after; it's a totally normal desire. While I do believe in special connections as far as mates are concerned, I do not believe in soul mates. Humans are three part beings: spirit, soul and body. A soul (connection) mate would only cover a third of your needs. What about the spiritual (connection) mate? What about the natural or body (connection) mate? How about having a spirit, soul and body (connection) mate? That is your complete mate.

That doesn't mean that you will agree with your mate one hundred percent of the time; it simply means that you are more likely to have more of a balanced relationship on all levels and you will have a better chance of relating to one another in a more complete way. No mate will ever be perfect, but if you can find agreement in most of the things that you need in a spouse, then you will have a better chance of having a successful marriage. If you are looking for just a pretty face, sex, money, or a just a warm body, then your chances of having a meaningful and fulfilling relationship will decrease significantly.

Being a Complete Single

The Scriptures teach us:

And you are complete in Him, who is the head of all principality and power.
—Colossians 2:10

Too often, people are looking for someone to make them whole. Some people are looking for their better half. Some men are looking for "their rib" (alluding to how God made Eve from Adam). But the reality is that if you are looking for a person to be your all in all, then your priorities are messed up. Christ must be your Source for the wisdom to choose your spouse. If you are horny or lonely, then you aren't complete in Him. Sure, we have natural desires and emotions, but marriage isn't an emotional decision. Whether or not to eat a Cobb Salad or crab cakes is an example of an emotional decision.

But marriage is a spirit, soul and body decision that needs to be made by your spirit being led by the Holy Spirit.

Are you physically ready for marriage? Marriage is work. It's a lot of denying yourself and sacrificing for the sake of your spouse.

1. Are you willing to endure snoring or some bad habit that might get on your nerves?

2. Are you willing to change from or correct some of your bad habits to please your spouse?

3. If your spouse needs sex, are you going to be available? If your spouse needs to talk, will you be available?

4. Are you looking for someone to take care of you?

5. What strengths do you bring to the marriage?

6. What weaknesses do you bring to the marriage?

7. Are you healthy?

8. Do you have health challenges, issues, or concerns?

9. Do you have financial problems?
10. Do you have busybody family members?
11. Do you have children from a previous relationship?
12. Are your kids well mannered and respectful?
13. Is having more children an option?
14. Is re-location to be with your spouse an option?
15. Is an ex-boyfriend/ex-husband still in the picture?
16. Are you fun and full of life? Or are you a couch potato?
17. Do you keep a messy house?
18. Are you a good steward with money?
19. Are you kempt?
20. Are you spiritually ready for marriage?
21. Do you have a positive working relationship with Jesus?
22. Have you grown spiritually in the last six months?
23. Are your mate and you spiritually compatible?
24. Do you see your mate as your spiritual partner?
25. Do you go to a church that manipulates the members?
26. Are you familiar with the woman of Proverbs 31 or Boaz from the book of Ruth?
27. Would you follow a pastor or a husband blindly?
28. Do you believe in living a holy lifestyle?
29. Are you struggling with any habits, lifestyles, or addictions that need to be addressed?

30. Can you commit to reading the Word and praying together as a couple at a scheduled time?

31. Are you emotionally ready for marriage?

32. Are you needy and clingy?

33. Are you jealous?

34. Are you insecure?

35. How would you react if you saw your spouse talking to someone of the opposite sex?

36. Are you self-conscious?

37. Are you completely over your last relationship?

38. How do your children interact with you?

39. To which types of people were/are you attracted?

40. Why were the people you were with attracted to you? Why were you attracted to them?

41. Why did your last relationship end?

42. How would your parents or impartial friends/family characterize you?

Friends First

Every positive relationship should be a mutual friendship. If not, it won't last. You have to like each other before you can love each other and spend the rest of your lives together. If you can laugh and have a good time with the person, then that is a good sign. It's not the only sign, but it is a good sign.

Establishing a friendship is a mutual respect from which you can build. When the relationship is strictly platonic and free from any sexual interference, it has the chance to grow the right way.

However, the premature kissing, hugging, and sex always messes up the chemistry.

So be friends first, and let things develop naturally and according to God's way.

Yours in Christ,

Conclusion

Dear Friends,

I would like to thank you for taking the time to read what God has placed upon my heart. There are a lot more issues that I could've addressed, but we will save them for another time. I believe that we have enough information in these letters to begin working through many of the situations that we have as a body of believers and a society as a whole.

Hopefully, you see the sense of urgency in these letters and the need to get the conversations started about the topics presented. The Church folks and the enemy have their agenda, and we need the good people of God to be about God's agenda: to set people free by the power of His Word.

I believe that many people will be receptive to this message, and of course, the haters will have something to say, too. But as you and I go forth to proclaim His truth, we must do so with the understanding that this is His show, not ours. We can only be responsible for yielding ourselves for God's use. If things, situations, or people are going to change, then only God can create that change.

But here is the challenge for you: find a topic or two in this book that truly resonates with you. If you agree with the letter, share it with others who might not agree with the content and get the discussion started. You never know what new ideas, convictions, revelations, or insights might come out of a mature, intelligent, and Word-based conversation. If you don't agree with the letter, then ask yourself why you disagree with my letter. Is your disagreement an emotional disagreement, or do you believe that my Scriptural interpretations were false? If your disagreement is emotional and my Scriptural presentation is correct, then you have to make a decision whether or not you will continue on the emotional path or the Scriptural path. If your disagreement with the letter is the Scriptural content, then please prove me wrong with the context of Scripture.

No one has all of the answers to all of life's problems. I'm just one guys who has been through a lot of mess, and I have dealt with Church folks long enough to spot nonsense when I see it and hear it. As you can see from the amount of topics that I addressed, Church folks have been immersed in a sea of false doctrine for a long time. I'm sure I could have added twenty more chapters to this book, but there is enough information to keep you busy until next time.

Challenge your friends, family, neighbors, and anyone else who is tired of the dried up traditions of man. What have you got to lose? Nothing! But you also have so much to gain, because when the false filters of religion come off of your eyes and your minds, you will be so surprised to see what you couldn't see before. The same Bible that you have been reading all along will become clearer, and the Scriptural passages will have new meaning. God's principles and insights will be revealed to you as a result of you drawing closer to God and His Word, and doing His Will. The more you draw closer to God, by default, you will be going further away from the errors, myths, and misconceptions of Church folks.

So encourage people to read the book and talk about it. Tell your pastor, overseer, apostle, prophet, evangelist, teacher, deacon, reverend, bishop, or any other person that I might have overlooked to check out "Lord, Deliver Me From Church Folks." I pray that it is a blessing to all.

Yours in Christ,